BILLION-DOLLAR BALL

ALSO BY GILBERT M. GAUL

• • •

Coasts in Crisis

Free Ride

Giant Steps

BILLION-DOLLAR BALL

A JOURNEY THROUGH THE BIG-MONEY

CULTURE OF COLLEGE FOOTBALL

GILBERT M. GAUL

VIKING

VIKING
An imprint of Penguin Random House LLC
375 Hudson Street
New York, New York 10014
penguin.com

ISBN 978-0-670-01673-0

Printed in the United States of America

1   3   5   7   9   10   8   6   4   2

Set in ITC Giovanni Std

DESIGNED BY ALISSA ROSE THEODOR

For C, always.

CONTENTS

• • •

Preface

• • •

A REAL UNIVERSITY

THE IDEA FOR THIS BOOK originally came to me more than a decade ago when I was thinking about college sports. I had become interested in what I thought was a simple but troubling question: Why were some of America's largest and most prestigious universities spending ten times more on football players than on their smartest, most ambitious students? I wasn't entirely naive. I knew football dominated the cultures at many of these schools. Still, I was taken aback by the size of the disparities. Penn State, for example, gave $2,250 scholarships to the students in its Honors College, a kind of university within the university for students with SATs above 1400 and perfect 4.0 grade point averages. By comparison, a football player on a full scholarship received $25,000 in aid. And that didn't include the cost of tutors, counselors, writing and reading specialists, and an array of other academic advisers required to keep players eligible.

At the time, Penn State was being touted by the media as a model for balancing education and big-time football. Unsurprisingly, school officials embraced this narrative. Penn State even had a slogan, courtesy of its iconic coach, Joe Paterno. It referred to its approach as "The Grand Experiment," as though the idea of balancing studying and playing football were so challenging—or possibly heroic—that it deserved its own motto.

I wondered what I was missing. At $42 million, Penn State's budget for athletics was ten times larger than its budget for the Honors College (a gap, incidentally, that has only widened in the last decade—a football scholarship now costs about $50,000, an Honors College scholarship, $4,500). So I called the professor in charge of the Honors College and asked her if I was misreading the budgets.

No, she told me, I had it right. The university could afford only so much.

It was at this point, I think, that I sputtered: "But what about football?" or words to that effect.

"Football pays for itself," she said. "They get to spend as much as they want."

"You mean football isn't part of the regular budget?"

I could almost hear her laughing, only I wasn't imagining it. She *was* laughing at me.

"I'm sorry," she said after a moment. "Football operates according to its own rules, and the rest of us just go along for the ride."

A few days later I briefly met with Graham Spanier, the president of Penn State, and then shared a longer telephone conversation. Spanier enjoyed a reputation as a savvy guy who rarely passed up a photo op or a chance to boost his school. He was trim, handsome, and engaging. Certainly he was persuasive in explaining to me how much Penn State valued the students in its honors program. Among other advantages, the students had access to the university's best professors and smaller classes, he said. Some of them even qualified for additional aid: A physics major, for instance, might get aid from the physics department.

I asked Spanier if he knew how many honors students got additional aid. It seemed like something he might want to know.

"Penn State has a lot of majors," he replied.

"How about football?" I asked. "How many scholarships does football get?"

Spanier seemed disappointed by my question. "They get eighty-five," he said. "But none of that money comes from the university."

He said this as though it were a good thing—as though all football teams should operate like stand-alone businesses.

Spanier suggested that I call several academic departments to see if they had information on scholarships they awarded to honors students. So I contacted the English department and asked if it had a secret stash of money to help its brightest students. "That would be nice," a professor told me. "We have a lot of good kids who could use the help." The woman who answered the phone at the physics department must have thought she was getting a crank call. She kept asking me which research lab I was with, and when I explained that I was a writer, she abruptly hung up.

•   •   •

All of this occurred in the spring of 2000, nearly a dozen years before the Jerry Sandusky child sex abuse scandal derailed Graham Spanier's career and tarnished the reputation of Penn State. In the intervening decade, college football vaulted ahead in both popularity and wealth and came to occupy a transcendent place in American sports. It was, in nearly every respect, the key component of a vast money culture that dominated college campuses. There were billion-dollar television deals and games on ESPN virtually every night of the week. Billions more flooded in from ticket sales and luxury suites and premium seating in massive Erector-set stadiums. These arenas were draped in corporate logos, and even the players' uniforms were adorned with advertising.

At the University of Oregon, Nike consultants decided which color uniforms—there were scores of possible color combinations, all bearing the company's ubiquitous swoosh—the players wore on a given Saturday. Nike's founder, Phil Knight, an Oregon alumnus, had single-handedly reinvented Oregon football, spending more than $100 million of his own money on lavish training facilities and stadium renovations. It was no wonder some of the students now referred to their school as the University of Nike.

The corporatization of college football was on one level unsurprising. It could even be viewed as inevitable. After all, hadn't universities themselves become giant entertainment businesses that happened to do a little education on the side? Certainly the athletic departments of the largest and richest football schools operated like entertainment divisions, with CEO-style executives and celebrity coaches collecting Wall Street–level salaries. The athletic directors had even invented a new financial model built around monetizing every last detail of their football programs. It was so successful that schools like Texas, Michigan, and Auburn now had profit margins that put the oil companies to shame.

When I asked DeLoss Dodds, the longtime athletic director at Texas, how it was that his football program had made $80 million in profit in 2012, he grinned at me as if to say, *Silly boy.* Dodds once boasted that Texas didn't need to keep up with the Joneses because it *was* the Joneses, implying, among other things, that the normal rules didn't apply. Now he looked at me through dark, pebbly eyes and said: "Football is the train that drives everything and pays for everything. It just is. Everything begins and ends with football."

So there it was: a perfect summary of the new economics of college sports.

Of course, the new financial model was not without irony or problems. The same college presidents who encouraged their athletic directors to turn their departments into businesses now lamented that spending on football was spiraling out of control and smothering the culture and mission of their schools. The hand-wringing was, in a way, even humorous in its predictability. Every few years the presidents would gather to "study the problem" and then issue a report that immediately went up on a shelf with all of the other reports while they hustled off to their luxury suites to watch the game with wealthy donors. "We are our own worst enemies," the president of one football factory told me. "We're all afraid to go first."

Less visibly, the new financial model had inspired a radical shift in the economics of football, with the largest and richest programs pocketing about $2.5 billion from television broadcasts, luxury suite rentals, seat donations, and corporate advertising while all the others scrapped over what few leftovers remained. In effect, the game had devolved into a zero-sum experience, with clear financial winners and then everyone else, mirroring what seemed to be occurring in the larger economy.

The flood of cash—nearly all of it tax free, thanks to the extraordinary generosity of senators and congressmen from football-mad states—had also fundamentally altered the core mission of these schools. Instead of touting their educational offerings, they now promoted their football programs because football, after all, was exciting and attracted media attention. When I tried to ask college presidents about this, many of them ran for cover. The few who did open up were embarrassed. The message was backward, and they knew it. But the world had changed, they insisted, and they ignored the changes at their own peril.

And so, the presidents told anyone willing to listen, it was okay if the first thing people thought of when they thought about their schools was their football team. Football was the new brand, a way to lure both students and alumni to campus. Some of the presidents even took to calling football the "front porch" of their universities, while others rhapsodized about its healing powers and uncommon ability to unite the campus. Others contended that a winning football team attracted more and smarter students. After it won a couple of national championships, the University of Alabama began promoting this narrative, with several major publications repeating it nearly verbatim. I didn't doubt football and championships could boost a university's Q score—albeit temporarily. But what I wondered was how presidents could differentiate all of the other possible explanations for why a school's applicant pool might grow—for example, more and generous scholarships, the ease of filing applications online, or a new, attractive major in nursing or engineering. And more to the point, what happened when a football team struggled? Did the applicant pool shrink? Did the student body become dumber?

Alabama touts its football program as one of the biggest and richest in the land. It has a stadium that seats 101,000 fans; a waiting list for season tickets 26,000 strong; a coach it pays $6.5 million a season, not including bonuses; and a support staff that rivals any in the NFL. Every year Alabama adds another shiny new bauble to its football program. In 2013 it opened a new weight room featuring 37,000 square feet of racks, weights, juice bars, and nutrition stations. Alabama already had one of the largest weight rooms in the country, but apparently it wasn't enough to impress the seventeen- and eighteen-year-old recruits who keep the team humming. So Alabama invested $9 million in this facility and, while it was at it, added a new locker room with hydrotherapy pools and a waterfall. On paper the Alabama athletic department appeared to be piling up debt like a third-world republic, owing bondholders more than $200 million on its athletic facilities alone. I had a sense—and not for the first time—of the *Titanic* steaming blindly into an ice field. But when I asked Bill Battle, Alabama's athletic director, about it, he assured me that everything was under control.

"Do you ever worry all of this might be a bubble?" I asked.

"A bubble? No, I don't think so," Battle replied. "I do worry that we could start losing. But honestly, I don't think that's going to happen. It's just a good time to be around Alabama football, a very, very good time."

And then, I think, he actually winked.

•   •   •

Given the potential riches to be gained, it isn't very surprising that other college presidents would develop football envy. When they see Alabama and Oregon raking in millions or tens of millions, it inspires a kind of magical thinking: Why not us? Why shouldn't we collect millions and be on ESPN's *College GameDay?* Many college presidents simply can't imagine a campus without a football team. And then, once they have a team, they can't imagine its playing in anything but a big, shiny new stadium costing tens (or even hundreds) of millions of dollars. How else can you explain why so many otherwise smart men and women with "PhD" appended to the end of their names would risk economic ruin in hopes of winning the football jackpot?

The data, however, show that the presidents are on the wrong side of a losing bet. The preponderance of the schools that start football programs, or shift from lower levels of competition to higher levels, lose money. And not just a little: millions and millions of dollars that might otherwise be used for building a new lab or lowering tuition. But there is no telling the presidents. Even as they lose huge sums, the presidents tell themselves football is their winning ticket—the quickest and surest path to a competitive advantage. What they don't seem to recognize is that if every school plays football, then it is the same as if no one played football; if everyone has a competitive advantage, then no one has a competitive advantage and, thus, such massively expensive wagers are for naught.

One of those who ardently believed in the transcendent nature of football was Anthony Catanese, president of the Florida Institute of Technology, a private university of six thousand students located in Melbourne, on the central Atlantic coast. On its Web site, Florida Tech cleverly describes itself as an A+ school for B students. In 2013 it ranked 167th among national universities in the *U.S. News & World Report*'s college rankings. Two thirds of its students are from out of state, including several thousand from foreign nations. Like those of many other Florida colleges, the campus appears new and shiny, a cross between a Disney theme park and a summer astronaut camp.

During his first decade at Florida Tech, Catanese started many new programs, expanded the campus, and added a football team. It was not his first experience with football. Prior to arriving in Melbourne, Catanese had spent a dozen years as president of Florida Atlantic University, a larger public university in Boca Raton, where he had also initiated a football program. "As far as we know, Dr. Catanese is the only president to start football teams at two different schools," Florida Tech's spokesman, Wes Sumner, told me. And like me, he seemed to marvel at the audacity of the idea.

I decided I could learn something from Catanese, so I arranged a telephone interview and later visited the campus. The president is seventy years old but looks younger, with feathery white hair and a healthy tan. He has run more than thirty marathons and used to drive a red Corvette. "Actually, my wife hated the way it drove," he said. "We traded it in for another car."

Catanese grew up in New Brunswick, New Jersey, and went to Rutgers for his undergraduate education. He told me he "loved football as a kid" and enjoyed watching Rutgers play. Thus, a football team was an important part of his strategy for raising Florida Atlantic's profile from a commuter school to a regional university. "I don't have to tell you, football is incredibly important in Florida," he said. "I did it primarily because a school that big [25,000 students spread across several campuses] really should have a football program."

Catanese had heard that Howard Schnellenberger was living down the Florida turnpike in Miami and invited him to lunch. The pipe-smoking Schnellenberger was a Florida legend. A decade earlier he'd led the University of Miami to a national championship and then went on to coach at Louisville and the University of Oklahoma. When Catanese laid out his plan to start a Division I football team, Schnellenberger agreed to help him raise money and volunteered to be the coach.

The Florida Atlantic Owls began play in 2001, competing in a lower division, and broke even. But then they moved up to Division I and promptly started losing to bigger and better teams. Between 2005 and 2013 the Owls posted a 0.379 winning percentage, among the worst records in college football. Attendance was dismal, which probably had as much to do with the proximity of the beach as with the team's woeful performance.

Like many struggling programs, Florida Atlantic lost money. The exact amount is unclear, but it was easily in the millions—and probably, tens of millions in the aggregate. With few fans and little revenue, Florida Atlantic needed another way to raise cash. So it agreed to play more powerful, richer teams on their home fields in return for a hefty payment—what athletic directors call a "guarantee." Alabama, Auburn, or some other football powerhouse might pay it up to $1 million, far more than it could ever collect playing a lesser opponent at home in

Boca Raton. For the bigger, richer school, playing a lesser opponent like Florida Atlantic was virtually a guaranteed win—a way to pad its record with a win against a weaker team. Catanese called these "money games." Tellingly, Florida Atlantic collected more from guarantees than it did selling tickets to its games. But the money games took a toll: The Owls went 0-11 against ranked teams and gave up 527 points while scoring just a little over 100.

Even with the payments from larger, more accomplished teams, the economics of football at Florida Atlantic remain problematic. The Owls lose about $4 million a season by my estimate. One of the bigger drains is the school's thirty-thousand-seat stadium, opened in 2007 at a cost of $70 million. The facility was financed with a bank loan taken out at the "worst moment in banking history," the school's athletic director, Patrick Chun, who was hired in 2012, told me. As is often the case, there was a *Field of Dreams* mythology at work: If you build it, they will come. Only the fans didn't come. Florida Atlantic averages about fifteen thousand fans at home games, and it needs twenty thousand to break even. "Normally, schools wait to build new stadiums until after they have established a winning program," Chun said. "We kind of put the icing on the cake before we built the cake."

For years Florida Atlantic lacked a corporate sponsor willing to pay millions to slap its name on the new stadium. Naming rights are usually set before a stadium opens, but Florida Atlantic didn't find a partner until 2013, when a company that operates for-profit prisons offered it $6 million to rename the football complex GEO Group Stadium. School officials were thrilled. But then critics began to question the propriety of a public university's associating with a prison company. Some Florida Atlantic students cheekily referred to the stadium as *Owlcatraz*. Eventually the owners of the prison company withdrew their offer, costing Florida Atlantic the equivalent of $500,000 annually.

"There's only one thing that is going to change the culture at FAU,"

Chun said, "and that's building a consistent winning program. People want to start feeling good about themselves, and the way you do that is winning. Everyone wants to be a winner."

By this point Catanese was long gone from Florida Atlantic. Still, I couldn't help wondering what he thought. Had it been worth all of the money and trouble?

"I think what happens is if you're winning, you get a tremendous turnout. And when you're not winning, it's not so great," Catanese said. "The economics of a stadium also changes things dramatically. They've had some bad years, and now the private money gifts aren't coming in. I think some individuals maybe haven't spent as much time working at it like I did."

Catanese is once again betting that football can help catapult his current school into prominence. In its inaugural season, playing at a lower level, Florida Tech won five games and lost seven. Catanese thinks it is reasonable to expect more—say, even a Division II national championship in five or so years. He told me that students who normally wouldn't consider Florida Tech now enroll because it has a football team. The locals also look more favorably upon the school. "I've had people come up to me and tell me how they now think of us as a real school," Catanese said.

A couple of years back, before Florida Tech football even got under way, a man dressed up as Santa Claus approached Catanese in a Publix supermarket parking lot to thank him for bringing football to Melbourne. "He saw the schedule and knew who we were going to play," Catanese marveled. "This is a Publix parking lot in Florida, and football hasn't even started. I thought: *What has happened to my life?*"

BILLION-DOLLAR BALL

One

• • •

THE GILDED AGE OF COLLEGE FOOTBALL

We eat what we kill.

—UNIVERSITY OF TEXAS PHILOSOPHY OF SPENDING ON ATHLETICS

When you hear presidents and athletic directors talk about character and academics and integrity, none of that really matters. The truth is, nobody has ever been fired for those things. They get fired for losing.

–MACK BROWN, QUOTED IN THE *NEW YORK TIMES*, DECEMBER 30, 2014

WHEN I ARRIVED IN AUSTIN in October 2013, the University of Texas football program was deep into an existential crisis, and the mood in town seemed to be darkening by the hour. I discovered this when I took a wrong turn and wandered into a neighborhood of fading clapboard houses. After looping repeatedly around the same block, I stopped at a convenience store for directions. The parking lot was crowded with vintage muscle cars and rusting lawn chairs. What I took to be a scrum of locals scowled at my appearance.

"Hey, guys," I said, extending my hands palms up in the universal sign of helplessness. "I'm just trying to find the stadium."

To which one of them rasped: "Hell, you're practically close enough you can piss on it."

I quickly surmised I was what passed for entertainment at the end of a long, dull afternoon.

Another of the men pointed toward an elevated highway. "All you got to do is follow it downtown," he said. "You'll see it soon enough."

I thanked him and started back to my rental car but after a moment heard him call to me, "Hey, if you happen to see Mack Brown down there, you tell him for me he needs to quit—and the sooner the damn better." His buddies all cackled loudly. The rooster's tail of venom that now trailed Texas football wasn't necessarily creative, but it was relentless. *Fire the damn head coach. Mack sucks. UT sucks.*

I waved over my shoulder and got into my car. It was an otherwise perfect fall day, seersucker blue and warm but not Texas warm. I imagined leaves burning somewhere in a steel barrel and green apples tumbling to the earth, kids tossing around a football in a backyard. A minute or two later I found the entry ramp at the end of the block, only now I realized it wasn't an entry ramp at all but an exit ramp, no entryway anywhere in sight. I could practically hear in my head the locals' laughter. *Good one, bro. You got that damn Yankee good.*

• • •

Those Texans were not the Texans I knew. My Texans were bighearted, outsized personalities who resented anyone who questioned their unbridled optimism. The locals at the convenience store were impostors, bitter with recriminations real and imagined. Then again, much had changed in the decade since I had last been in Austin. So much of the unbending, take-no-prisoners Texas spirit now felt like a caricature of itself.

There was the dystopian politics of Ted Cruz and his mad hatters, and Governor Rick Perry in his five-hundred-dollar cowboy boots kicking up one controversy after another. But most of all there was Texas football. Texas football had gone to hell in a hurry and now seemed to be sucking the very air out of the state.

At the time of my arrival, the Texas Longhorns were 5-2. In many places that sort of record would be considered cause for celebration. But here in Austin, 5-2 was viewed as abject failure. The corollary of unbridled optimism, after all, is impossible expectations. Texans took as an article of faith that they were exceptional. As such, they believed their Longhorns should go undefeated every year, and they did not submit passively to losing. An acceptable season included one loss, two at most, but you better win the conference and go to a major bowl game. Any more than two losses and you might as well start planting tombstones. These days the smell of panic was in the air: ozone before a thunderous, cloud-splitting storm.

Texas had won nine games in 2012. It wasn't anything to brag about, but it was one more win than they'd had the year before—and four more than they'd had in 2010, when the team had staggered through an unfathomable 5-7 season—no conference, no bowl game, no damn nothing. By the start of the 2013 season the Texas faithful were exhausted from losing and all out of passes to give. "This is it," one season ticket holder practically spit on a talk radio show. "We let Mack have a pass these last couple of years because he won the championship in '05. But he has no excuses anymore."

No less than Mack Brown himself, the southern-gentleman football coach with the $5 million paycheck, had predicted great things for 2013. Texas had a championship-caliber team, he told anyone who'd listen, including nineteen returning starters and greater skill and depth than they'd had in years. He would be surprised if the Longhorns didn't compete for the Big 12 title—and maybe more, wink, wink. "You want to get back to being one of the top football programs in the country," Mack told reporters, "where we deserve to be and our fans deserve to be."

It was unclear if he meant that merely being Texas implied greatness or that Texans by birthright were entitled to a top ranking, if for no other reason than that they spent more money and energy on football than anyone else.

The season had started off well enough, with a 56–7 thrashing of New Mexico State at Darrell K Royal–Texas Memorial Stadium in Austin. By the fourth quarter expectations were once again soaring. What many of the fans dressed in burnt orange seemed to overlook, however, was that it was a victory against New Mexico State. The game was the football equivalent of a set piece. Texas had paid the Aggies $900,000 to fly down from Las Cruces and take a whooping. Indeed, New Mexico State was so bad at football it had to pay its own students to come to the games. And even then they rarely came. In 2012 the Aggies had had a record of 1-11, and most of the scores were so lopsided that it was easy to mistake them for basketball results. Texas's prodigious aspirations aside, this was hardly what you would call a test.

That came the following Saturday when the Longhorns traveled up to Provo, Utah, to play Brigham Young University. The Cougars' running backs sliced through the Longhorns' defense at will, piling up an astonishing 550 rushing yards. The final score was 40–21, but BYU could just as easily have put up 50 or 60 points. With that, all the patience and hope appeared to leak out of the Texas fans. Mack Brown couldn't coach a turnip, they fumed, let alone a five-star recruit. He had grown lazy ever since the trustees had awarded him that $2 million raise in 2009. He didn't recruit well anymore, and his assistants did a poor job of coaching the talent he did manage to bring in, et cetera, et cetera.

Brown did his best to shrug off the carping. He had been around Texas football long enough to know the fans didn't respond well to losing. Despite all of their talk about playing with dignity and class, they were never what you would call good sports. The advent of social media wasn't helping either. Austin was like one big anthill: Everyone had an opinion and was willing to share it, feeding an endless loop of petty grievances and conspiratorial rumors.

Well, at least Mack still had the university president and the board behind him. They were careful to talk up the coach's unquestioned decency and to remind the fans that football was the financial engine behind UT sports. Recent losses aside, Mack had won 85 percent of his games between 2000 and 2009, and what other coach could match that record? Better yet, every one of those games had sold out. Mack was Barnum & Bailey, reliably putting fannies in those 100,000 seats at DKR–Texas Memorial Stadium. The university had even named an endowed chair after him: the Mack Brown Distinguished Chair for Leadership in Global Affairs at the Lyndon B. Johnson School of Public Affairs. The athletic department had kicked in $500,000 for the position and had arranged for Joe Paterno to deliver the keynote speech. So while he may have been on a bit of a losing streak, you didn't just toss a Mack Brown out the door. Give him time; he'd get it turned around. You watch.

The following Saturday the University of Mississippi came to town. By Southeastern Conference (SEC) standards, Mississippi was a small school; it had far less money to spend on football than Alabama, LSU, Florida, or other big, rich football powers. But it was still a member of the all-powerful SEC, and therefore Texas considered the game a must-win. But just as it had the week before, Texas played soft, and the Rebels gutted the Longhorns 44–23. Following the game, some of the Texas players complained that DKR–Texas Memorial Stadium had been so quiet that it was like attending a wake. By now no less than Earl Campbell, the legendary Texas running back and 1977 Heisman Trophy winner, had announced that it was time for Mack to go.

It was at about this point that I became seriously interested in the narrative of Texas football—but not because of the soap opera surrounding the team or the furious calls for Mack Brown's head. Those felt fairly predictable. It was a different question that was nagging me. I was curious what, if any, impact all of this turmoil was having on the financial juggernaut that was Texas football.

In 2012 football generated a remarkable $103 million for the Texas athletic department, with $78 million falling to the bottom line. Note that I didn't say that this windfall went to the university itself. As at many other elite football powers, the Texas athletic department was nominally part of the university but in reality functioned as an autonomous business, free to raise and spend as much as it wanted. Football was by far the largest, richest department on campus—the Department of College Football, if you like. It was overseen by a CEO/coach, Mack Brown, who received millions more than the university president. His nine full-time assistant coaches averaged $555,000, or about four times what a full professor earned.

In the view of most Texans this was acceptable, as opposed to, say, a distortion of the university's primary mission of education. It was perfectly okay that the Texas football budget had grown twenty times faster than inflation over the last three decades. Or that Texas spent $261,728 on each of its football players but just $20,903 on each student. Big was good. Big was what Texas did best. It had the biggest flags, the biggest stadiums, the biggest egos. Texas football was the very definition of big.

True, in 2009 a few of the school's professors had protested Brown's $2 million raise as unseemly, noting that it was "a sum greater than the entire career earnings of a typical university employee." But then, what could you expect from a bunch of pinhead professors? The fans didn't care about them, and University of Texas president Bill Powers Jr. had declared the $2 million raise "a good investment in our financial strength and stability as we go forward."

If expenses and debt kept climbing to improbable levels, the athletic department could always tap its football program for more money. Its vast wealth and lavish spending also attracted attention, and attention was a good thing in the sprawling, media-fed bubble that was big-time college sports. It created buzz on social media and drew the prized recruits and wealthy boosters who kept Texas football churning.

The program's profit margin wildly exceeded those of Apple and ExxonMobil, two of the nation's richest, best-known companies. And Texas football didn't do it for just one year; it did it *every* year, consistently. Moreover, the size of its take was growing—up sevenfold in a decade. Even by Texans' gaudy standards it was an absurd amount of money.

Here some might argue that Texas manipulates its numbers so that football appears more profitable than it really is. What I know is this: After studying scores of financial statements issued by athletic departments large and small, nothing is quite what it seems. Or to put it another way, there are no standard accounting practices. Some schools include the cost of stadium financing in their budgets, while others don't. Some, including Texas, lump the cost of maintaining their facilities into a generic category instead of allocating it by sport, understating spending for some sports.

But if you are trying to examine the financial landscape of college football, you have to use one consistent metric. I decided to use the internal budget reports and detailed financial statements that schools are required to file annually with the National Collegiate Athletic Association. Inexplicably, the NCAA considers these reports secret. I was, however, able to obtain nearly one hundred of them by filing Freedom of Information Act requests with public universities. I had already amassed a trove of financial data on college athletic spending going back to 1999 from another project. I then put all of the numbers onto spreadsheets and analyzed the schools' performance over time. It seemed like a consistent, fair approach—and if the schools complained, well, these were their numbers.

As I mentioned earlier, the pressing question for me was whether the turbulence in Austin was cutting into its profit margin. For example, were fewer fans buying season tickets, or were well-heeled boosters scaling back their donations?

The problem was that no one seemed particularly interested in talking about finances. The writers were too busy chasing ghosts. Was Mack in or out? And if he was out, who would take his place? At one point the blogs blew up with tabloid-wattage threads saying that Texas was trying to lure Nick Saban away from Alabama by offering him $10 million. There were even reports that Saban's wife, Terry, had been spotted looking at Austin real estate—all false, it turned out.

But at a certain point even speculation gets old. What I required was someone with enough history to walk me through the long view of Texas football—someone like the spectacularly named DeLoss Dodds, the veteran athletic director and architect of the Texas miracle otherwise known as Longhorns, Inc.

If the seventy-four-year-old Dodds hadn't exactly invented the new financial model for college football, he had certainly brought it to its most successful expression at Texas, growing what was once a modest business into a hugely profitable, gilded enterprise. During his thirty-three-year tenure as athletic director at Texas, the athletic department budget had swelled from $4.5 million to nearly $170 million; football had grown from about $2 million to $110 million in 2013. No school was bigger, wealthier, or more important.

The trick was getting an interview with him. Dodds was nearing the end of his run and clearly didn't need to burnish his already gold-plated résumé, let alone address all the craziness and noise of the moment. I explained to the media representatives serving as the guardians at the gate that I wasn't interested in the serial drama that was now Texas football. Rather I was interested in how the financial model for college football had changed so radically over the last few decades and how football now dominated the brands of many of our largest and best universities. I emphasized that I could learn a lot from Dodds, but the folks in publicity were still suspicious. They needed time to check me out.

Weeks passed without a word. I sent them periodic e-mails renewing my interest. I told them I liked what I had read about Dodds, which happened to be true. There was an engaging, all-American, up-from-the-bootstraps quality to his story. He had grown up on the Kansas prairie and gone on to greatness. I recited to the publicists his times in the four-hundred-yard dash in high school, when he was a state champion, and they seemed pleasantly surprised. I mentioned that I had thrown the javelin well enough myself to set school records and win a scholarship. I can't say for certain, but I think it was the track connection that finally sealed the deal.

•   •   •

I found Dodds waiting in his seventh-floor office towering above the North End Zone at DKR–Memorial Stadium. He is tall but not Texas tall and has short, wavy brown hair and dark eyes. When he speaks there is a quiet warble behind his words, like birds rustling in the scrub and thistle. Perhaps most impressive of all, he did not take out his cell phone once during the several hours we spent together.

By this point I had visited enough football stadiums that I was starting to notice subtle differences among them. For example, with its sweeping redbrick facade, sunken playing field, and ornate columns, DKR-Memorial appeared to most closely resemble a Roman coliseum. (The "DKR" stands for Darrell K Royal, the beloved football coach at Texas from 1957 to 1976 who delivered 180 wins and three national championships. If you're victorious in that many games in Texas, it pretty much goes without saying that you get a stadium named after you.) A reef of light rimmed the upper decks, slowly working its way down the metal bleachers to the tunnels far below. DKR seats 100,119 fans, making it the sixth-largest college football stadium in the nation and the largest college stadium in Texas. However, its supremacy was about to be challenged. The Longhorns' bitter archrival, Texas A&M, planned a $450 million expansion of Kyle Field in College Station. The Aggies boasted that it would be the largest and most expensive football stadium project in history and, when completed, would increase capacity to 102,000.

"They have to have more seats," Dodds said when I broached the subject. "I don't care. I don't care how big the stadium is. It isn't about that."

At some level, though, it did feel as if it were about size—or, if it wasn't exactly a competition over sheer capacity, then certainly it was a battle for football supremacy in Texas. The rivalry between the schools was epic. If you were an A&M alum, you did *not* go to your brother-in-law's on Thanksgiving if he was a graduate of UT. Nor did you exchange Christmas cards. For decades the schools had played each other on the Friday after Thanksgiving. But in 2012 A&M bolted the Big 12 Conference for the richer SEC. Various explanations were offered for the betrayal: A&M fans blamed Texas for starting its own television network; Texas fans accused A&M of a money grab. In 2013 State Representative Ryan Guillen of Rio Grande City introduced a bill requiring the schools to play each other. It was the kind of thing that could happen only in Texas, but surprisingly it didn't pass.

If nothing else, the antagonism cast a shadow over the fabulously rich investment that was Texas football. Since the early nineties, the Longhorns had underwritten roughly $300 million in DKR-Memorial improvements, adding thousands of premium seats, new locker rooms, and multistory digital scoreboards, always with an eye toward impressing boosters and fans with deep pockets. In this sense, running a high-end football program like Texas is a little like running a Las Vegas casino. There are the fans who buy a season ticket or two, and then there are the high rollers—the trial lawyers, car dealers, and oilmen who write the big checks and get their names on the buildings. While you might not be able to comp them a room with a view, you can make their experience more comfortable with wider, cushioned seats, plasma screens to watch replays, seatside catering, four-star meals, endless drinks, and so on.

Back in 2008 Texas added the sprawling new North End Zone, featuring 2,100 club seats, forty-seven luxury suites, a food court with its own Starbucks, a tutoring center for athletes (Texas has two: one exclusively for football players and one for all of the other athletes), and various administrative offices. The famed car salesman/Texas booster Red McCombs wrote a check covering the upgrades, which Texas officials honored by naming the upper deck "The Red Zone." McCombs is a colorful guy and knows how to give a good quote. A month after my visit he told a reporter for *Sports Illustrated:* "All the money that is not up at the Vatican is at UT." Texas was, in fact, squeezing $170 million out of its athletic department and spending nearly every cent. Other athletic departments paled by comparison. And here was its stadium, so polished and grand, steaming through the middle of campus like a giant cruise liner.

The centerpiece of Dodds's office was a large black wood desk with a matching bookcase behind it. He explained to me that the desk had belonged to the legendary Darrell Royal back when he doubled as the school's athletic director and football coach. For sentimental reasons, Dodds had brought it along when the athletic department moved to the North End Zone. Unlike many athletic departments I had visited, Dodds's office was otherwise largely devoid of mementos. There was, however, a Tiffany lamp squatting on a corner of his desk. It was the shape of a Texas Longhorn. I had never seen a lamp with horns before, let alone stained-glass ones.

Dodds caught me staring and grinned. It was the kind of sly grin I recognized from interviewing farmers—there and gone before it registered. And if you think about it, the job of an athletic director is not all that different from that of a farmer. Each year you throw out seeds and hope you get a crop. Some years you do; other years you don't. The biggest difference is that farmers are selling real products: corn, tomatoes, lettuce, and so forth. Athletic directors are selling what economists call "experience goods," and if those experiences aren't pleasing or lavish enough, a boatload of trouble is bound to follow.

Dodds insisted that we go to lunch before we sat for a formal interview, and moments later we slipped out a secret side door and onto a concrete pad where he kept a golf cart to commute to and from his office. His car, an egret white Escalade, was parked seven stories below. At his age Dodds didn't like the long walk up to his office. Also, he could avoid crowds by traveling this way, a not-insignificant benefit with the team struggling.

Dodds slid behind the wheel and turned the key, and the golf cart spurted ahead at an alarming speed. I braced myself as we flew blindly down a narrow concrete chute used to funnel fans to and from their seats. More than once I was sure we were going to smash head-on into someone racing up the chute in the opposite direction or vault over the ramp. For his part Dodds appeared to be enjoying himself, grinning with the same sly expression I had seen earlier.

·   ·   ·

DeLoss Dodds grew up in the farming community of Riley, Kansas, fifteen miles west of Manhattan, home to Kansas State University. Calling Riley "small" is probably redundant; it numbered seven hundred people, give or take, when Dodds was a boy and decades later still has only nine hundred. The family—which included four sisters, two older and two younger—shared a three-bedroom house with one bathroom, which Dodds jokes that he rarely got to use. His parents were both educators. His mother taught elementary school, and his father was a principal and coach who died when Dodds was eight. Thereafter the family survived on his mother's salary as a teacher.

"I want to say she earned twelve hundred dollars a year," Dodds recalled. "We didn't know we were poor. We thought it was a great life. I'd go swimming in Clay Center, or sometimes we'd go into Manhattan to see a movie. There really wasn't much to do. We'd play football in the fall, basketball in the winter, baseball in the spring."

Dodds now earned $1.1 million a year. We were sitting in a restaurant on the twenty-first floor of the Headliners Club in downtown Austin with a view of an impressive sweep of the nearby Hill Country, where Dodds had a weekend home on fifteen acres. He and his wife, Mary Ann, whom he met when he was six years old, escaped there whenever they could. "I love it up there," Dodds said. "We go up after a game on Saturday and stay through Sunday or Monday morning."

Dodds's graduating class at Riley High School topped out at eleven. "I like to say I made the top half of my class possible," he laughed. He was a multisport star, playing running back on the football team and running track in the spring. He was a better-than-average sprinter and in his senior year won a state championship. It was about then the local paper started calling him the "Riley Flash." Kansas and Kansas State offered him track scholarships, but Dodds accepted a football scholarship to Kansas State instead.

Dodds injured a knee playing freshman football but was able to switch his scholarship over to track, eventually running 46.3 for four hundred yards, an excellent time. After graduation and a six-month stint driving tanks at the Fort Knox Armor School as part of an ROTC obligation, he returned to Manhattan to help coach track and work on a master's degree. A few years later he took over as the head track coach and held that position for fourteen years before switching to athletic administration.

Dodds would have continued coaching, but by now he had a wife and three children to support, and athletic administration paid better. In the midseventies he worked as an assistant commissioner at the Big Eight Conference (now Big 12) in Kansas City, which included Kansas and Kansas State, and in 1978 was hired as athletic director at his alma mater. At the time, college athletics was still more of an avocation than a business. Football teams did occasionally appear on national television, but not like today, when there are games on ESPN nearly every night of the week. The budget for athletics at Kansas State was $2 million, Dodds recalled, "and we were half a million dollars in debt, and the football team had been on [NCAA] suspension for something like ten years. It was a real mess."

As it turned out, Dodds proved to have a talent for finding money. He "cranked up" a fund-raising program and assigned one staffer responsibility for the eastern half of the state and another staffer responsibility for the western half. Dodds not merely managed to erase the department's debt but built a small surplus. In athletic circles he was viewed as something of a miracle worker, and other schools started to take notice. Then, in 1981, something extraordinary happened. The University of Texas called: Would he be interested in coming down to interview for the athletic director's job?

Dodds was flattered by the Texas offer but also cautious, concerned about the politics of the job. The state's governor was known to get involved in hiring the football coach, and Texas boosters weren't shy about sharing their views. "I came down to look around and do an interview," Dodds said, but when he was offered the position he initially turned it down. Dodds was still a Kansas boy at heart and reluctant to leave. "My mom was there. Mary Ann's mom and dad were there. We were happy."

That night a chemistry professor at UT called Dodds. "We talked for two hours about education and kids and he never once mentioned the job." The next morning Dodds awoke riddled with regret. He asked Mary Ann if they were making a mistake. It was Texas, after all, and they might never get another chance. Dodds spoke with a former Texas athletic director who told him he would have only two things to worry about if he took the job: football and basketball. That was all the fans cared about. If those two sports were winning, the rest would take care of itself. Dodds took a deep breath and accepted the position.

On his first day on the job his secretary informed him that there was five hundred dollars in cash in one of his desk drawers, his to use however he wanted. When it ran out, he was to let her know, and she would replenish the stash. Dodds told her, "Let's stop that."

The Texas athletic budget was then $4.6 million, not a small sum of money but hardly an oil gusher. When Dodds needed to hire a new football coach and the preferred candidate asked for $250,000, he didn't have enough to cover the salary.

"How much did you pay the head coach back then?" I asked Dodds.

"It was under a hundred thousand dollars," he replied. "It might have been eighty-five thousand. I think I was getting sixty-five at the time."

The numbers sounded almost quaint by comparison to today's celebrity-level salaries.

The Texas athletic department hadn't been badly managed, Dodds explained, but a lot of things needed fixing. "The facilities were old. Everything about football was old. It was really like high school. The track was still in the stadium. The North End seats were forty yards from the field."

Although he probably didn't realize it at the time, Dodds had arrived at Texas at exactly the right moment. A series of forces, some internal to Texas, others external, were converging in ways that would radically alter the financial model of college football, unleashing historic new streams of wealth while elevating the game in popularity, power, and scale.

"What was changing was the money, especially television and the ability to fund-raise with your seating," Dodds said. "The money was always there, but now it got so big it sort of took over things in the public imagination."

•   •   •

What an interesting and apt way to put it, I thought, listening to Dodds. But while it is true that college football is a vastly different enterprise today from what it was only a few decades ago, bigger and richer by far, it is largely a difference of scale. In some ways football hasn't changed at all. From its inception football has challenged the notion of universities as places of learning and reflection, fostering an awkward if not an inflammatory relationship among coaches, players, and professors, while prompting concerns about commercialism and cheating.

On November 6, 1869, Rutgers defeated Princeton 6–4 in what is widely reported as the first intercollegiate football game. The contest was more like rugby than what we now know as football. The ball was round, there was no forward passing. Fewer than one thousand fans attended the game, according to newspaper accounts. Still, interest in the sport quickly grew. By the early 1900s tens of thousands of alumni and fans routinely watched Penn, Harvard, Yale, and Princeton play. Soon the schools began building large concrete bowls to accommodate their fans and charging modest fees to attend the games, giving birth to the phenomenon of college football as commercial entertainment.

The first postseason bowl game took place on New Year's Day, 1902, when mighty Michigan defeated Stanford 49–0. Neither team made much money. But schools and bowl sponsors quickly figured out ways to monetize games by selling not only tickets but also advertising, later adding corporate naming rights and television fees. Today there are more than forty bowl games, including nearly a dozen created by ESPN to supply the cable network with live content. These contests generate more than $250 million for the schools, with teams in the Rose Bowl alone receiving about $15 million each.

Much as they do today, college presidents saw football as a way to brand their schools and attract publicity. Football was, in effect, another form of advertising. Still, some of the leaders worried about the excesses of the sport. Players were being injured at startling rates, and financial and academic abuses were common.

During one fifteen-year stretch, more than three hundred players died from injuries suffered in college games, foreshadowing by more than a century today's concerns about concussions and brain trauma. In 1905 representatives from Columbia, NYU, and several other colleges met in New York City to debate abolishing football, but they were overruled. That same year President Theodore Roosevelt called for a special White House conference on college football. The meeting resulted in the creation of the National Collegiate Athletic Association as a watchdog over college sports—a role that the now-giant nonprofit, with $700 million in annual revenue, has played ambivalently, even badly, at times.

In theory the NCAA was established to nurture and protect the amateur ethos of college football and other sports. One of its key challenges was to eliminate the influence of money—or at least money that wasn't directly funneled through the nonprofit. But in some ways it was already too late. By the turn of the century, college coaches had been routinely recruiting ringers with promises of money and jobs. And for many of those players classes were viewed as optional.

Ivy League schools were among the worst offenders. In *Unpaid Professionals*, a history of commercialism in college sports, Smith College economist Andrew Zimbalist recounts how Yale University operated a $100,000 slush fund to boost its football team. Meanwhile Lafayette College borrowed a star player from West Virginia University to bolster its chances against then–national power University of Pennsylvania.

Lafayette prevailed 6–4 and then quickly returned the player to Morgantown. Another Ivy League school recruited a star player with the promise of a job at the American Tobacco Company and a ten-day paid vacation to Cuba, according to Rodney K. Smith, a sports historian and law professor.

Harvard University president Charles Eliot worried that colleges were turning amateur games into "commercial spectacles." The university's board of overseers tried—and failed—on three separate occasions to ban football. In 1890 Woodrow Wilson, then president of Princeton University, exclaimed that his school was best known for three things: "football, baseball, and collegiate instruction," in that order.

Despite these concerns college football continued to thrive. Attendance at games climbed steadily—from a million fans in the early 1900s to nearly twenty million fans in 1950. Ticket charges became an important source of revenue for athletic departments, which were then still under the strict control of their universities. Some schools were also beginning to charge fans a premium for season tickets and use booster clubs to raise funds. Though still modest, these groups formed the outlines of what would become the ferociously successful financial model that dominates college football today.

One way to measure the growth of college football is to examine the size and architecture of the stadiums, which have gradually evolved from simple concrete bowls (Princeton, Harvard, Yale, etc.) to hulking, LEGO set–style edifices with multiple stages, opulent luxury suites, and massive digital entertainment screens.

Better yet, look at just one school—Alabama. The Crimson Tide began playing football in 1892 after a law student returned home from New England and introduced the fundamentals of the new game to his classmates. By 1930 Alabama football was so popular the school built a stadium seating 12,000 fans. By the end of World War II, it had increased capacity to

31,000. Nearly every decade thereafter, Alabama added another 10,000 seats. Today Bryant-Denny Stadium holds 101,821 fans and features 159 skyboxes and thousands of club seats. Between the premiums it charges fans to secure season tickets and the actual cost of the tickets themselves, Alabama collects about $50 million annually for its athletic department.

In the 1920s commercial radio stations began to broadcast games, adding to football's popularity and wealth. But it was the arrival of television two decades later that forever altered the arc of college football and its finances. In September 1939 the National Broadcasting Company broadcast the first college game, featuring Waynesboro (Pennsylvania) State and Fordham. According to some estimates, the broadcast reached one thousand television sets.

A year later a local television station in Philadelphia broadcast a game featuring the University of Pennsylvania. The Ivy League school figured prominently in the early days of sports television. In 1950 it sold the rights to its home games at Franklin Field to the American Broadcasting Company for $150,000, then a huge sum. But the NCAA cried foul, concerned that live broadcasts would cut into attendance, and warned that schools playing Penn would be subject to penalties. In the end Penn officials canceled their deal.

In many ways the NCAA-Penn dispute ultimately was a matter of who would control the new, lucrative source of income. Penn wanted to negotiate its own television deals; the NCAA wanted control over all television contracts. The nonprofit put together a plan for a limited number of football broadcasts and sold it to NBC for $1.14 million. Shortly thereafter NBC broadcast its first "national" game, featuring the University of Kansas and Texas Christian University.

The relationship between television and college football was visceral. The camera loved the speed and violence of the game, and broadcasters thrived on the immediacy. It helped that the broadcasts were live, which meant exclusivity and higher advertising rates for the networks, setting the stage for bigger, even more lucrative deals later.

By the 1960s college football was deeply embedded in American cul-ture. In December 1969 President Richard Nixon even took it upon him-self to pick the national champion. The setting was a game featuring two undefeated teams—Texas and Arkansas from the old Southwest Confer-ence. The schools ranked one and two in the national polls. It also hap-pened to be the one hundredth anniversary of college football, and so the media, unsurprisingly, dubbed the contest "the Game of the Century."

The game was broadcast live by ABC and attracted a record audience. Texas prevailed 15–14, and afterward Nixon presented the players with a plaque. Sportswriters back east howled, pointing out that Penn State was also undefeated and had played against stronger opponents. Nixon's pre-mature call foreshadowed a decades-long debate about the need for a true national championship. In 2015 that play-off finally came to pass, albeit in a limited format with only four teams. ESPN purchased the rights to broad-cast the games for $7.3 billion over twelve years—or about $600 million annually.

*   *   *

All of these riches were still years in the future as DeLoss Dodds was packing up to move to Texas. In fact, at that time many football schools, including some of the best-known programs, were *losing* money, which posed an uncomfortable challenge for their presidents. How could they justify using dollars that might be directed toward teaching and research to subsidize their struggling football teams?

The short answer was they couldn't, as that would simply be too em-barrassing. What they needed was a different financial model, one that would separate football from the rest of the university and give it its own budget, so they could at least pretend that football wasn't dragging their schools down. And so the presidents came up with what seemed like a brilliant idea: They decided to turn their athletic departments into separate businesses and leave their athletic directors to fend for themselves. In the future their athletic departments—and football teams—would have to pay their own way.

There was an appealing logic to the presidents' approach. They could focus on what truly mattered—education and research—while boxing up their athletic departments in some dark corner of their campuses. They could then inform their faculty and students that football wouldn't draw a penny from university coffers. From now on there would be a bright line between education and athletics.

It was never exactly true, of course. Lots of smaller, less wealthy athletic departments still required millions in subsidies, usually funded by tuition or student fees. Even large, rich athletic departments like Texas needed the university's backing to issue tax-exempt bonds to build and expand stadiums. Still, the idea sounded plausible and provided the presidents cover, even as some critics were loudly calling for them to become more deeply engaged in policing their athletic programs, not less involved.

What the presidents didn't seem to understand was that by establishing their athletic departments as stand-alone businesses outside the normal constraints of the university budget, they were setting the stage for an unprecedented surge in spending and even more dramatic shifts in the commercial nature of college sports. Part of the reason was that there was no one left to say no. Athletic directors like Dodds were now free to raise as much money as they could. And strange as it may sound, it turned out that not only were many athletic directors good at business, but they were also gifted at finding new and creative ways of adding to their growing piles of money.

Over time, athletic departments at the largest football schools morphed into huge, complex entertainment divisions with hundreds of

employees, in-house radio, television, and marketing divisions, and elaborate back-office operations geared toward monetizing every aspect of their
sports programs, but especially their football programs.

One of their lesser-known but more lucrative inventions was charging
their most loyal, deep-pocketed fans thousands of dollars in fees to secure
premium seating. Initially these fees were limited to the best seats—say,
along the forty- or fifty-yard line. But as the popularity of college football
grew and demand for premium seating increased, schools expanded their
programs to cover ever more seats.

At Texas Dodds created the nonprofit Longhorn Foundation in 1986
to handle these payments. "We never moved anybody if they didn't want
to move," he said. "But when they died, then any empty seats became
foundation seats," meaning Texas was free to attach a mandatory payment
to them. The price of the tickets themselves was separate.

Dodds and other athletic directors came up with a beguiling name for
these payments, calling them "voluntary seat donations," even though there
was never anything voluntary about them. The high demand and limited
supply allowed athletic departments to bid up the required donation levels.

"Today, four seats on the fifty-yard line, you pay about twenty thousand
dollars to get those seats," Dodds told me in a tone that suggested even he
was surprised by the amount. It helped to explain how the Longhorn Foundation now generated $37 million annually for the athletic department—
about $30 million of that from football fans eager to secure good seats.

Television also played an increasingly important role in the finances
of Texas and other major college football teams. In the late 1970s the
IRS decided that college football powers shouldn't have to pay taxes on
the broadcast fees they got from the networks. The service's logic was
that watching a game on television was comparable to the actual experience of watching a game in person. And given that the IRS didn't tax
the games themselves, why would it tax the broadcasts?

At the time of the ruling, the network fees were relatively modest, a few hundred thousand dollars here and there. Also, the NCAA strictly limited the number of times a school could appear on television. But in 1984 the Supreme Court decided that the NCAA limits violated antitrust provisions, freeing the major football conferences to start negotiating with the television networks on behalf of their member schools. Over time broadcast fees surged as the networks and cable companies bid up the price of live content to spectacular new levels, now totaling in the billions for the five largest football conferences (SEC, Big Ten, Big 12, Pac-12, and ACC).

In 2013 the Big 12 passed along $21 million to Texas, with most of that coming from television fees. Separately Texas collected $15 million from its Longhorn Network, which it launched in 2011 with ESPN as a Texas-centric channel that broadcasts several football games a season that aren't part of the Big 12's national contract. "It used to be maybe only a game or two would be on television," Dodds marveled. "Now they're all on. If it's not part of a national deal, it's picked up by the Longhorn Network, and we are grateful for that."

Dodds and the other athletic directors found even more ways to monetize their football programs. Nike, for example, agreed to pay the schools cash bonuses and provide teams with uniforms and shoes emblazoned with the company's famous swoosh logo. A former Nike employee told me he would fly around the country each week with a bag of cash to sign up schools. He wasn't literally a bagman; everything he did was legal. But there was no mistaking Nike's intent: The company was in it for the exposure, pure and simple. Every time a Nike swoosh appeared on TV, it was like found money. The football powers, meanwhile, collected millions of dollars from these arrangements.

Texas and other football powers also collected millions in royalties and licensing fees whenever their logos were printed on T-shirts, fleece pullovers, and coffee mugs, among scores of other merchandise items. Millions

more poured in from corporate advertising. Rich boosters like Red Mc-
Combs contributed tens of millions to slap their names on new buildings.

Suddenly, money was the new metric for success in college sports. And
it all came back to football, the centerpiece of the new financial model. At
Texas football accounts for nearly two thirds of the athletic budget. At
Auburn it accounts for almost three quarters. At Georgia, Penn State, and
LSU, eight of every ten dollars the athletic department generates come from
football. And so it goes. Among the college-football elite, the money always
runs downhill, always follows its own logic, and always seems to grow.

Without such extraordinary riches there would be no track and field,
no women's rowing or soccer, Dodds and other athletic directors say. Football is the cash cow. The challenge is to make as much as you possibly can
from football, which, in turn, means doing whatever it takes to keep football healthy. If that includes paying the head coach $5 million or $6 million a season, so be it. You swallow that particular madness and move on.

"That's pretty much the train," Dodds explained to me at our lunch.
"Football is the train. You ride it for all it's worth."

•   •   •

It is impossible to exaggerate how football dependent many of the largest,
best-known universities have become. If a school wins a national championship, applications go up. Lose, and the school risks being relegated to
mediocrity—to being, say, Eastern Michigan or New Mexico State or Akron.
The big football schools don't boast, "Here is our world-renowned physics
professor." They crow, "Here is our top-ranked football team. Look at us!
ESPN is coming to campus this Saturday. Isn't that wonderful?" Of course,
what they are really saying is "Isn't all of the attention and money great?"

At some point it occurred to me that what Dodds and the athletic
directors had discovered was the blockbuster model of economics. They
were mimicking what the movie studios do by betting the house on one

big movie or franchise—a Harry Potter, say—and hoping that fans show up. It was, in some respects, a smart plan. There seemed to be an endless appetite for college football, so why not take advantage of that and maximize your income? Still, there had to be risks in relying on a single sport to pay all of your bills. What would happen if football suddenly stumbled, as it had at Texas, or became overexposed? For that matter, what if younger fans decided it was easier to watch the game in their man caves or the students just lost interest in going to the games? As strange as that sounds, it seemed like a real risk.

"Are you kidding?" the athletic director of one of the nation's richest football schools nearly shouted at me when I raised such possibilities. "Everything we do would stop. We would have to cut everything and find a new model."

The athletic directors believed in the numbers, however, and the numbers told them football was still growing. There had never been anything like it in the history of college sports. Consider the television contracts the Pac-12 had signed in 2011, which awarded it $3 billion, with the possibility of hundreds of millions more. Or consider the Big Ten, with its hugely successful Big Ten Network (BTN) pumping millions of dollars to its schools. The networks and cable companies couldn't seem to throw enough money at the elite football powers. And if the students stopped coming to the games, well, they would figure out a way to charge them for watching on their smartphones.

A little later I pulled out my spreadsheets. They showed that football revenues at the top programs had grown by staggering levels in the last decade—doubling and tripling at the richest schools. Back in 1999, when I had started collecting data, the ten largest football programs had reported $229 million in revenue. By 2012 revenues for those same ten schools had swelled to $762 million. Meanwhile, profit margins had ballooned to hedge-fund levels.

THE STARTLING GROWTH OF COLLEGE FOOTBALL

SCHOOL	REVENUE 1999	REVENUE 2012	% CHANGE
Texas	$18,712,250	$103,813,684	455%
Michigan	$21,691,978	$85,209,247	293%
Auburn	$22,946,979	$77,170,242	236%
Alabama	$28,248,408	$76,801,800	172%
Georgia	$22,530,118	$74,989,418	233%
Florida	$29,669,188	$72,807,236	145%
Penn State	$25,422,289	$72,747,734	186%
Notre Dame	$27,857,388	$68,986,659	148%
LSU	$17,791,048	$68,804,309	287%
Arkansas	$14,270,879	$61,131,707	328%
Total	$229,140,525	$762,462,036	233%

Source: NCAA annual financial reports obtained from schools; author's analysis.
Adjusted for inflation, revenue grew by 141 percent.

MOST PROFITABLE COLLEGE FOOTBALL PROGRAMS

SCHOOL	PROFIT 1999	PROFIT 2012	% CHANGE
Texas	$10,393,333	$77,917,481	650%
Michigan	$12,157,130	$61,559,910	406%
Auburn	$14,139,705	$43,835,647	210%
Alabama	$21,751,852	$45,221,741	108%
Georgia	$17,249,074	$54,279,278	215%
Florida	$18,724,507	$46,543,697	149%
Penn State	$15,587,997	$53,227,946	241%
Notre Dame	$18,108,207	$43,228,691	139%
LSU	$12,236,173	$44,755,027	266%
Arkansas	$8,330,323	$37,072,514	345%
Total	$148,678,301	$505,641,932	240%

Source: NCAA annual financial reports, the most complete data available; author's analysis.
Adjusted for inflation, profits increased by 146 percent.

Staring at the numbers I couldn't help wondering once more: What was I missing? How was it possible for just ten schools to make half a billion dollars in profit from their football teams? And what did it say about the schools that such exquisite financial madness *was* not just considered acceptable but admired? Clearly I *was* missing something.

So I asked Dodds to break it down for me.

At Texas football revenues grew from about $19 million in 1999 to about $104 million in 2012. The most dramatic part of that surge occurred in the last decade, when Texas added thousands of seats and increased the price of tickets. Mandatory payments for premium seats alone more than doubled, to $30 million. Television fees also doubled, while royalties, licensing fees, and advertising revenue soared nearly fivefold, to $26 million.

"In your wildest dreams did you ever imagine all of this?" I asked.

"Never," Dodds quietly answered. "I absolutely didn't. If somebody told me we'd be at $170 million in our budget, we would have checked them in somewhere."

Dodds explained that Texas now generates $28 million annually "off of the things we built," including but not limited to the North End Zone expansion. "That includes the luxury suites at DKR-Memorial. We charge sixty thousand to ninety thousand dollars to lease those. We got one hundred and thirteen." Here his eyes widened and he began to chuckle. "They say you can never build enough, and you never charge enough."

I was surprised that some people thought Dodds was arrogant. Perhaps it was because he had once boasted that it was Texas, the richest of the rich, that set the bar for spending, and everyone else was left to try to keep up. "We are the Joneses" were his actual words.

Dodds frowned when I mentioned the quote. "That's one I wished I hadn't said," he told me. "It was kind of a smart-alecky thing to do."

Nonetheless, it is true: Texas *does* set the bar, and other schools large and small are left to keep up. Most can't, because they become trapped in an arms race: spending and spending but never actually getting ahead because the other guy is also spending and spending, resulting in a draw. The new financial model for college football isn't much help for these schools, which are too small and will never generate enough cash to be competitive. Their boosters are fewer in number and poorer in comparison. In this way the windfall from the new financial model goes disproportionately to the richest schools, the sixty or so universities belonging to the five superconferences that rule college football. Those conferences benefit from the lucrative television packages and control the biggest and wealthiest postseason bowl games, passing along the dividends to their members. In any given year the checks add up to more than $1 billion after the conferences' take. The conferences do other things, of course, occasionally even disciplining a school, but their primary role is to act as a transfer agent for their members, a kind of giant ATM, if you will, and they serve that function extraordinarily well.

The way the new financial model has evolved, Texas and the other big schools are the college football version of the 1 percent. By some estimates they have netted 90 percent of all the new money that flowed into college football in the last decade or two. The small and midsized schools—the Florida Atlantics and New Mexico States of college football—saw only modest gains, if any. In fact, most lost millions on football, charging it off to their students, but that is another story for later—the story of the haves and the have-nots.

●   ●   ●

In the meantime I wondered where the windfall actually went. Was it really possible to spend tens of millions of dollars on a few football, soccer, and lacrosse teams? And how did the schools know if they were allocating the money effectively? Was Texas, with its $170 million budget, for example, a model of efficiency? Texas boasted that it ran "the nation's premier broad-based intercollegiate athletics program," but what did that mean? I wondered if Texas was equating spending more money with excellence—because, on some level, it was starting to feel that way.

Dodds wasn't embarrassed by the buckets of money that Texas spent and in fact seemed proud that the school spent more than everyone else. "As a university, Texas offers world-class opportunities for its athletes," he said, "and fully funds each team." That included offering the maximum number of athletic scholarships allowed by the NCAA for those teams. "We don't apologize for trying to be the best," Dodds said.

In 2007 reporter Eric Dexheimer of the *Austin American-Statesman* obtained detailed spending records from the Texas athletic department as part of a Freedom of Information Act request. He discovered that the school spent $450,000 on tutoring and advising football players ($3,800 per player) to help them remain academically eligible to continue playing. The team took chartered flights to away games and used a bus to ride the few blocks to practice, at a cost of $300 per trip. Following the team's 2006 Rose Bowl win, the athletic department spent $200,000 to renovate the players' lounge, adding six flat-screen TVs, four Xboxes, and three PlayStations. Several new recliners costing $15,020 each were also purchased for the players' comfort.

The athletic department's chief financial officer told Dexheimer: "We eat what we kill," an unusually blunt summation of the Texas philosophy. It meant, simply, that Texas spends every penny it takes in from football and other sports. If that means spending $200,000 or more on each of its football players to keep them happy and fit, so be it.

In retrospect, the chief financial officer probably should have chosen his words a little more carefully, Dodds told me, and then offered the standard defense for the dramatic increase in the budget. "The way it is set up at Texas, athletics pays its own way," he said. "We don't get anything from the university. The university used to fund women's athletics, but over time we took that over. We cover all of that fully, and the way we do it is with the money we make off of football."

What he was describing, of course, was the financial model at the elite football schools. Football was the summer blockbuster that paid for everything, including all of the so-called nonrevenue sports—what I had now come to think of as the "poor sports" because they had no money of their own and no visible way of making any, short of lucking into a rich benefactor. These were the sports living from paycheck to paycheck—track and field, field hockey, women's rowing, the programs that athletic directors often refer to as the "Olympic sports" because you only see them on television once every four years.

What Dodds told me was true, as far as it went: In one way or another, football was an insurance policy for the other sports. But football was also by far the most expensive sport at Texas, costing as much as all of the other non-revenue-generating sports combined. The financial model was as much about growing and enriching football as it was about underwriting these other programs. Even after accounting for the costs of football and the other sports it supported, Texas's athletic department was left with nearly $100 million to spend each year. That was a fantastic sum of money. And it wasn't being used to pay for scholarships, meals, or books.

I went back to the financial reports. What I saw was that Texas spent $30 million a year just to cover its administrative overhead—the cost of salaries and benefits for back-office workers, printer paper, paper clips, utilities, and the hundreds of other things large and small required to keep its $170 million sports business afloat. While health insurance companies are often criticized for spending 10 percent to 15 percent of their premiums on back-office operations, Texas was spending 20 percent. It could be argued that it takes a village to run a modern athletic department, but the Texas athletic department wasn't a village; it was a small city with more than four hundred employees. Media Relations alone had three divisions and a staff of twenty-six, including a director for new media, a senior Web manager and two other Web managers, three video specialists, a Web video coordinator, three media relations directors for football, and a director for creative services for football. A separate video services branch included three film specialists and two other employees.

The business office listed thirteen employees. The facilities and events staff, forty-four. The Longhorn Foundation reported twenty-five fundraisers and other employees, including a major gift officer for luxury suites. The strength and conditioning staff numbered fourteen. The academic support staff had twenty-three employees, including five counselors just for football. The head count did not include two hundred part-time tutors that Texas employed to keep those football players and other athletes on track.

For its part the football office listed sixteen employees in the staff directory, including a director of player personnel and a recruiting coordinator. There were also the usual executive assistants and administrative assistants, not to mention the nine assistant coaches for offense and defense. More and more, Texas and other big-time football programs were modeling their operations after the NFL.

Even during a period in which the team was struggling, salaries kept going up. In 2005 Mack Brown and his assistants were paid a total of $4.9 million. In 2012 they collected $11.2 million, or double the 2005 figure, after adjusting for inflation. Overall Texas spent more on athletic coaches' salaries in 2012 than any other school in the nation: $24.4 million— again, nearly double what it had spent a decade earlier. I recalled the locals at the convenience store. Their bristling anger was starting to make more sense.

The last item that caught my eye was the breathtaking level of debt at Texas. In 2005 the athletic department owed $64.4 million on its stadiums, arenas, and practice facilities. By 2013 that figure had nearly quadrupled to $243 million, with the annual mortgage payment alone having increased from $7 million to more than $18 million.

The Texas approach to spending could be described as a revenue theory of costs: Each month you empty out the checking account and spend whatever you take in—revenues equal costs, two overlapping lines on a graph. "At Texas and other elite schools there's no end to spending," Penn State economist John J. Cheslock told me. "They will never say they need to spend less, because the assumption is the money will keep coming." The perception at these schools "is that spending more gives you a competitive and strategic advantage," Cheslock added. "That's probably true up to a point, but I don't know that it's true one hundred percent of the time."

•   •   •

All of which brought me full circle to the question of efficiency. For months now I had been thinking about the relationship between money and opportunities. The size of the budget at Texas and the other elite football schools seemed to highlight a very basic question about the purpose of sports: Was it to offer students a chance to play on a varsity team, or was it to win championships, make money, and polish the university's brand? It was such a simple question, I felt foolish asking it: Why do we play?

For example, you might think that, with $170 million to spend each year, Texas would offer more varsity sports and have more athletes than any other school. The school in fact sponsored twenty varsity teams, including football, and had 549 athletes. But by comparison Princeton sponsored thirty-six teams and had 962 athletes. Harvard: forty-two teams and 1,016 athletes. Even tiny Haverford College, with a total undergraduate enrollment of 1,205, had more varsity teams than Texas. These smaller schools were, to one degree or another, well funded enough to afford to pay for a large number teams. But Texas was as well, so money couldn't be the only factor. Something else was involved—a fundamental difference in philosophy at the football powers that favored championships and television over giving as many students as possible a chance to play on a varsity team and hone their skills.

I decided to visit Haverford in suburban Philadelphia to learn more. Its president, Dan Weiss, told me the school's athletic budget was so modest he didn't even know what it was. "I don't really pay that much attention to it," he said. "I don't have to. It's not really that big of a deal here."

"But you know what it is," I said.

"It might be a million or two," he replied. "I know it's not much more than that."

Weiss is short and trim with wavy brown hair and a sharp expression. He served as president of Lafayette College for seven years but left in 2012 to take over Haverford, a smaller school. While he was at Lafayette, which is a member of the Patriot League, he resisted efforts to introduce athletic scholarships, which he believed were a bad idea for several reasons. One was the simple fact that Lafayette was the smallest program in NCAA's Division I, in which it had to compete with larger, richer schools. On a more basic level, Weiss worried that awarding athletic scholarships would change the character of his school. Recruiting would ramp up, pressure to win would increase, and academics would inevitably suffer.

Weiss embraced the idea of holding back the tide of professionalism that had been overtaking even smaller schools, but not everyone agreed with him. There was a heated push by some members of the school and community to boost Lafayette football, and Weiss was criticized by the local paper for his policy. "I was spending enormous amounts of time dealing with social and athletic issues," he said. "It wasn't what I wanted or thought was best for the school." So, after Lafayette voted to add football scholarships, he decided to leave.

Haverford has the reputation of being a serious place. Freshmen average over 1400 on their SATs, and 60 percent go on to graduate school. "The students embrace their image as nerds," Weiss said, which is not to say that they don't like sports. Remarkably, one of every three Haverford students is a member of a varsity team, and its cross-country and track programs are superb. Under longtime coach Tom Donnelly, Haverford has won numerous Division III championships. Several of Donnelly's distance runners have broken the magical four-minute barrier in the mile, a fairly remarkable feat.

"It's not that we don't want to compete successfully," Weiss explained. "Tom Donnelly is a good example of that as a coach. But he also recognizes that the athletes on his team are students first. They are going to become doctors and lawyers. That is the big difference between what we do and the way it works at the big football schools."

•   •   •

Shortly after visiting Haverford I made a trip to Princeton to meet with its athletic director, Gary Walters. Walters played point guard with Bill Bradley (who later played professionally for the Knicks and became a U.S. senator) on the 1965 Princeton basketball team that advanced to the NCAA Final Four. He worked in finance for more than a decade before returning to his alma mater in 1994 as athletic director, a position he held for twenty years until he retired in 2014.

Walters admitted that, all things being equal, he probably shouldn't have been admitted to Princeton as an undergraduate. He was a good student in high school but didn't take his studies seriously. He viewed himself as a basketball player first and wondered if he could keep up academically.

Then something interesting happened. He realized while playing point guard for Princeton that he had a unique talent that first surfaced in the psychology classes he was taking. "My sense of worthiness increased. I began to see I was a leader. Other students looked up to me because I could analyze problems and process the information quickly. My sense of cognitive bandwidth expanded dramatically at that time."

Walters was in his small office on the second floor of Jadwin Gymnasium when I arrived. Every inch of the floor was covered with boxes of athletic shoes and jerseys, documents, posters, and pictures. It was as if I had walked in on Walters in the middle of moving. No, he laughed, this was fairly normal. He wasn't the neatest person, but if you gave him a minute or two he could usually find what he needed.

As we spoke, I noticed Walters's foot nervously tapping the floor. He couldn't sit still for more than a minute at a time and kept jumping up in the middle of sentences to point out another picture of Pete Carril, the legendary Princeton basketball coach and one of his mentors. At one point he practically sprinted down a hallway to show me the head football coach's office—a tiny concrete bunker tucked under a stairwell. "I guarantee you that Mack Brown has a far nicer office at Texas," he chuckled. "It's just a different approach here. It's not about the money or bells and whistles."

At the time of my visit, Princeton had 962 varsity athletes and thirty-six varsity teams, which meant that one of every five undergraduates played a varsity sport. While not quite as impressive as Haverford's number, it was still dramatically higher than those of Texas and the other football powers.

"That's our philosophy. It's the philosophy throughout the Ivy League. If you think you can play a varsity sport, we want to give you that opportunity," Walters explained. He pointed to a sign beside his desk that read EDUCATION THROUGH ATHLETICS. "We actually believe that," he said. "It's the

old Greek ideal of a sound mind and a sound body. We believe that playing a sport should at its core be educational."

It was a good principle, but I still didn't understand how Princeton
could have more varsity athletes than Texas. Princeton had 5,160 undergraduates and an athletic budget of $20 million. Texas had 38,437 under-
graduates and spent $170 million on athletics. Yet Princeton had 413
more varsity athletes than Texas's 549.

"Many of the large Division I schools operate under a different financial model. It is what I would call a deregulated model in which those
people have all the assets they can go out and raise," Walters explained.
"What is that famous quote from Matthew? 'Where your treasure lies so
shall your heart be.' The money has gotten so big for those schools and
their conferences, their focus has become totally self-serving. There is no
relationship between what is taking place and the issue of education.
These are business entities pure and simple."

When I asked DeLoss Dodds about the Princeton numbers, he became
defensive for the first time. "In terms of numbers of sports we're at twenty,
not thirty or thirty-five," he acknowledged. "But every sport we fully take
care of everything within the NCAA and university rules. We have twenty
sports, and we do absolutely everything to do the very best we can to
support them."

So it came down to a difference in philosophy: Texas limited the number of its teams by choice and then spent lavishly on those teams in an
attempt to win championships, which made the alumni happy and helped
to polish the university's brand. Still, with all of that money, it seemed
counterintuitive that Texas wouldn't do more for its students.

"The opportunities are here, just at a different level," Dodds said. "We
got a program in recreation sports that has all of the other sports. I don't
know how many. But if you name a sport, we've got it—club sports."

A DIFFERENCE IN PHILOSOPHY

FOOTBALL SCHOOLS

SCHOOL	VARSITY SPORTS	VARSITY ATHLETES	% UNDERGRADUATES
Texas	20	549	0.02%
Michigan	26	863	0.03%
Alabama	15	478	0.03%
Auburn	15	548	0.02%
Georgia	18	534	0.02%
Florida	17	514	0.02%
Notre Dame	21	716	0.05%
Ohio State	38	873	0.02%
Oregon	18	462	0.02%
LSU	16	481	0.02%
Stanford	35	874	12.4%

Source: Federal records for 2012; author's analysis and interviews.

SMALLER SCHOOLS

SCHOOL	VARSITY SPORTS	VARSITY ATHLETES	% UNDERGRADUATES
Princeton	36	962	19%
Harvard	42	1,016	15%
Yale	33	837	16%
Dartmouth	34	861	21%
Columbia	29	699	10%
Williams	30	745	37%
Amherst	23	566	31%
Haverford	22	415	34%
Johns Hopkins	20	726	12%
MIT	28	747	17%

Source: Federal records for 2012; author's analysis.

•   •   •

For a few weeks after I left Austin, the Longhorns seemed to right themselves, defeating Kansas and West Virginia on back-to-back weekends.
Once again there was talk about winning the Big 12 title and going to a
major bowl. But then Oklahoma State came to town and pummeled
Texas 38–13. After the game some fans suggested Texas should just hire
Oklahoma State's coach, Mike Gundy, and be done with it. Dodds told
me he would be "a fool to fire Mack. If you know anything about football, you know Mack Brown is a good coach."

Texas finished its regular season at Baylor, an hour and a half's drive
up I-35 in Waco. It was the last game Baylor would ever play at its sixty-
four-year-old Floyd Casey Stadium, and the athletic department planned
a nightlong celebration. The following September Baylor would move to
a $250 million architectural marvel it was building along the Brazos
River. The new stadium featured bridges and waterfalls and, of course,
the obligatory luxury suites.

"We view it as our bridge to the future, from the old Baylor to the new
Baylor," the Bears' athletic director, Ian McCaw, told me. Baylor was rising. Its president, Ken Starr (yes, that Ken Starr), was using football to
reshape the school's brand. Baylor wanted to be the Baptists' version of
Notre Dame, which is to say omnipotent. Its head coach, Art Briles, was
considered a football visionary. His name frequently came up when one
of the football powers needed a new coach. It had already been floated at
Texas. But then McCaw put an end to the speculation in November 2013
by signing Briles to a new long-term contract worth $4.2 million a year.

The game was being televised, so I decided to watch. But for all of the
attending drama and hype, it was surprisingly boring. Eventually Baylor
got its offense going and put up 30 points. Meanwhile, the Texas offense
struggled again, managing only 10 points. Texas was now 8-4 and des-

tined for a second-tier bowl game. The caterwaul could be heard all the way to New Jersey, and within minutes of the loss the blogs began to light up with anger and speculation. Once more, Nick Saban's wife was reported to be back in town (untrue). Mack was out. No, Mack was definitely still in. Opinion fishtailed all night.

One of the bloggers was Texas president Bill Powers. The day after the Baylor loss he wrote, "Put succinctly, Mack Brown is and will remain the Longhorns' head football coach." Powers titled his post "Mack Brown Has My Full Support."

There is nothing, I thought as I read this, quite as devastating as when a college president feels the need to endorse a struggling coach. It is as good as a kiss of death.

For his part, Mack Brown appeared remarkably calm. At one point he decamped on a recruiting trip to Florida for a player he had no chance of landing. Then he attended the annual football banquet, at which he cautioned reporters, "Everybody just needs to slow down." It wasn't bad advice, but by this point no one was listening.

The day after the banquet Wescott Eberts, a twenty-nine-year-old writer for a Web site called Burnt Orange Nation, filed the most incredible report. "Somehow, some way," he wrote, "Texas Longhorns head coach Mack Brown survived his imminent demise and is now holding the Texas football program hostage because of his ego, his stubbornness, his spitefulness, his pettiness, his vindictiveness, and because he's too delusional to have any conception of what's best for the program."

Eberts is a Texas grad. He was hired in 2012 by SB Nation, a new media company with more than three hundred Web sites covering college and professional sports. He is a clever writer who once quoted T. S. Eliot in describing a particularly soulless Texas loss. When I asked Texas officials about his blog, they claimed to have never heard of Eberts, which seemed implausible given the ferocity of his attacks.

Less than two hours after Eberts's post, Texas leaked that Brown would not be returning, as had been promised by President Powers. Instead, his last game would be the Alamo Bowl in two weeks' time, when the Longhorns played Oregon.

The following day Eberts filed a mea culpa on Burnt Orange Nation, apologizing for his earlier rant as "poorly timed" and "unnecessarily emotional and vitriolic." It seemed like as good a time as any to ask if he thought his original post had played any role in Mack's decision to quit.

"No, I don't think it had any impact," Eberts told me. "I think it had already been decided."

Why had he specifically unloaded on Brown? I asked.

"I was just ready for Mack to be gone," he said. "I was really fed up with them in general. I am normally not so bombastic. Normally I am a pretty analytical writer. I was just very frustrated with the whole thing. It was a circus."

•   •   •

At his going-away press conference, Brown acknowledged that his beloved Longhorns had not met the exceedingly high expectation of Texans. "We have to get it back to the top five in the country and we weren't doing that," he said. "We set a standard at this place—you better win all of them. I understand that. I'm a big boy. We didn't live up to that standard."

And then he was gone—or almost gone, anyway. One Texas fan purchased a billboard in Austin and put up a picture of Brown with the words "Class Act." Brown landed a severance deal valued at $3.25 million that included serving one year as a special assistant to the university president. A little later he signed on with ESPN as a college football analyst. Eberts calculated that Brown had made $21.16 million over his last four years at Texas, which worked out to more than $700,000 for each of the team's wins.

Texas would endure, Dodds assured me; it always did. He too was stepping down. Dodds said that he had been working in college athletics for sixty-two years, "and that's long enough." It felt sad to me on some level, but at least he would now have more time for his weekend house in the Hill Country.

On December 30 the Longhorns fell 30–7 to Oregon in the Alamodome in San Antonio. It wasn't ever really a fight.

Shortly thereafter Texas announced that Charlie Strong, the head coach at Louisville and one of the few African American coaches to lead an elite college team, would be the next Texas football coach. Although Strong is widely respected by his peers, in Austin the name wasn't deemed quite big enough, and the carping started up again. During a radio show Red McCombs called the hiring a "kick in the face." "I don't have any doubt that Charlie is a fine coach. I think he would make a great position coach, maybe a coordinator," McCombs said.

It was a damaging comment on many levels, and McCombs quickly apologized, telling the San Antonio paper that Strong had his "total support." He explained his comments by saying his only interest was to make sure Texas got "one of the three best coaches in the United States." It deserved no less.

The following January Texas released its latest financials. Despite the turmoil there had been no downturn. Football continued to take in more money than ever and find new ways to spend it. The athletic budget might not grow quite as rapidly as it had in the past, Dodds had told me. "But it will continue to grow—probably two to three percent a year." That didn't sound like much until I did the math; 3 percent of $170 million was another $5 million a year, year after year. The financial model was doing exactly what it had been designed to do: churn out cash like a Texas oil well.

Two

• • •

THE UNLIKELY CHARITY KNOWN
AS COLLEGE FOOTBALL

IN THE FALL OF 2010 I received an unlikely phone call from my mother-in-law, a smart, normally unflappable woman who grew up in the coal-fields of western Pennsylvania during the Great Depression and graduated from Pennsylvania State University. That morning she had received a package from her alma mater offering her "a limited, one-time opportunity to show [her] pride in [her] school." My mother-in-law is nothing if not proud of Penn State. Her home in Allentown is a shrine of blue and white pennants, blankets, and throw pillows. An autographed photo of Joe Paterno occupies a key position on the wall of her den, much like pictures of Jack Kennedy and the pope in Catholic homes. She has also responded generously to her school's pleas for financial assistance over the years.

But this package was not the usual fund-raising pitch. It contained several single-spaced sheets of paper with boldfaced warnings about looming deadlines and the need to act soon, or else. Perplexed, she asked if I would take a look.

"What is it about?" I asked, assuming it was one of those annoying offers for affinity credit cards that universities are always pushing on their graduates.

"Well, I can't say exactly," she said. "It has something to do with my foot-ball tickets. They want to charge me a lot of money to trade them in."

"Why would they do that?" I asked, knowing that my in-laws had been season ticket holders at Penn State for four decades.

"I don't know. They're calling it a donation. And they say I can deduct it from my taxes."

"Huh," I murmured. "Send it down, and I'll take a look."

•   •   •

The package arrived a few days later, and I saw immediately why my mother-in-law had been confused. There wasn't just one offer involved, but two. The first was something Penn State called a Seat Transfer Plan, in which fans were given a small window of time to transfer their season tickets to their children or other family members. In return for this privilege, Penn State intended to charge them up to two thousand dollars per ticket. And, yes, there in the fine print was a line declaring they could deduct the payment from their taxes as a charitable gift.

The second offer involved what Penn State was calling its Seat Equity Plan. Years earlier the largest and richest football schools had realized they could charge a premium for their best seats by adding a fee that was separate from the actual cost of the ticket. Over time they had extended these surcharges to more and more seats, so that now, at many large stadiums, 50 percent or more of the seats included them. Athletic depart-ments called these fees "seat donations," as if they were gifts, not pay-ments required to secure a seat.

For years Penn State had charged one hundred dollars per ticket for these "donations," which was at the low end of the scale. (Some schools levied fees of thousands or even tens of thousands, but more about that in a moment.) But now Penn State officials planned to jack up these fees because they needed more money for their ever-expanding athletic operation. Here too fans were advised in the fine print that they could claim a tax deduction on their payments.

I liked to think I knew a little about the laws of charity, but this left me wondering: How could you charge someone hundreds or thousands of dollars to secure a seat at a football game and then call it a charitable gift? Wasn't a gift by definition voluntary and made without any expectation of receiving something in return? Likewise, how could you tax someone for giving up her tickets and call *that* a gift?

Clearly I didn't know nearly as much as I thought, so I spent the next few days on the telephone talking with ticket managers and athletic directors at some of the nation's elite college football powers. To summarize, this is what they told me: Football was an important part of their educational missions, and as such it was considered a charitable activity, protected from paying taxes.

"For the record," I asked one assistant athletic director, "what part of watching Georgia play Florida is educational?"

"Eighty percent of it," he replied, "according to the IRS."

"That's what fans get to deduct?"

"It's what the law allows," he confirmed.

To be fair, the IRS tried to tax the football seat donations in the mid-1980s but was blocked by Congress, which passed legislation in 1988 allowing college football fans to deduct 80 percent of the cost of their "donations." That works out to about $250 million annually in lost taxes, or $2.5 billion over ten years, according to Treasury Department estimates.

Occasionally someone in one of the athletic departments would call the deductions what they truly are: a giant tax break for college football, not unlike the tax breaks legislators lavish upon oil companies, hedge funds, and insurance companies. But then they would quickly turn defensive, pointing out how state legislatures have defunded public universities, forcing athletic directors to adopt a financial model that enables football to maximize every potential stream of revenue.

"The reality is that football pays for everything (the non-moneymaking sports), and seat donations are a big part of the mix," the head of the seating program at the University of Georgia, Jay Lowe, told me. "We are lucky at Georgia to be well supported."

In 2012 Georgia fans paid $22 million to secure premium seats at Sanford Stadium—again, that amount is above and beyond what they paid for the tickets themselves. Nearly two thirds of the 92,000 seats at Sanford require a donation. The minimum fees are set annually by the athletic department. The less desirable seats include a $250 "donation," but coveted premium seats often require much higher fees, depending on availability and location. And just finding an available seat can be a challenge. At Georgia there is very little turnover from year to year, especially for the best, most expensive seats. Fans bid against one another for those limited seats, with the fees sometimes reaching startling levels. For example, in 2008, when Georgia had a particularly strong team, the "donation" required to get one of the limited premium seats soared to $10,651.

"It's supply and demand," Lowe said. "There were so few seats available that year, it caused the minimum donation to go through the roof."

Supply and demand. That sounded like a market at work, not charity— at least, not any charity I knew.

"We're not in the business of curing cancer," Lowe explained, "but we *are* a charitable organization."

Yes, the unlikely charity known as college football.

•   •   •

I wasn't looking for a story when my mother-in-law called me but, as often happens, one found me. Initially I was interested in why Penn State wanted to charge her to give her tickets to someone else and then call this tax—which is what it felt like to me, a kind of death tax on older, graying fans—a charitable donation. But over time this one question gave way to several larger concerns, including the utopian way we tax—or don't tax—the multibillion-dollar business of college football itself.

Seat donations at the largest and richest football programs now generate more than $500 million annually, according to several estimates. Like nearly everything involving college football, the numbers are growing. The reason Penn State was charging its fans to transfer their tickets was simple: It needed more money, and this was as good a way as any to get it. And the reason the University of Texas could charge a fan twenty thousand dollars for a seat on the fifty-yard line also was simple: because it could.

If you live inside the bubble of college football, writing a large check to lock down a seat at your favorite college stadium, and then getting to deduct 80 percent of the amount from your taxes, feels normal. But if you happen to reside outside that zip code, the seat donation scheme probably feels strange, even wrong.

The issue isn't the lost taxes. I am fairly confident that university accountants would find creative new ways to avoid being taxed if the seat payments were declared a quid pro quo instead of a gift. It is, rather, how calling college football a charity effectively turns the very idea of charity upside down, confusing its power and purpose. Paying a bounty to watch a football game simply isn't the same as writing a check to the Salvation Army or to a homeless shelter. The deduction is legal, because our football-obsessed Congress says so (just as Congress considers the parent organization of the NFL a nonprofit). But that doesn't make it right, let alone effective tax policy.

At its core, paying a premium to secure a seat with a view is a transaction between a buyer and a seller, with the amount set based on the quality of the view and other amenities, including but not limited to whether there is seatside service. The more you give, the better the seat, service, and view. The elite football schools all have color-coded maps on their Web sites indicating how much you are required to "donate" by section: one hundred dollars for red; five hundred dollars for blue; one thousand dollars for yellow, and so forth. It is very much like picking a seat on a cross-country flight: So much for business class; so much for an aisle seat; so much for a window view. Only you get to deduct most of the fee from your taxes.

Of course, if you happen to work in the athletic department of one of the large college football programs, you are likely to have a very different take on all of this. You might even think: *What genius. We get to charge fans thousands of dollars to watch football games, pretend it is educational, and pay no taxes on the millions of dollars we take in. Better still, our fans get to write off 80 percent of the cost.* That is what the folks in business call a win-win.

How big a win? I came across a spreadsheet from the University of Florida listing ticket-related contributions for the last two decades. In 1990 Florida collected less than $5 million from its football seat-donation program. By 2013 that figure had increased fivefold to more than $30 million. Florida is unique in that its entire athletic department is incorporated as a stand-alone charity. In addition it has a separate booster club, Gator Boosters, Inc., also a charity. Gator Boosters manages the nearly ninety thousand seats at Ben Hill Griffin Stadium, including all of the season tickets and seats requiring mandatory donations.

In recent years a Florida fan hoping to buy a season ticket had to write Gator Boosters, Inc. a check for $1,800. But as at other SEC schools, such tickets were few and far between. Therefore, Gator Boosters strongly recommended that fans increase their contributions to have a better chance of getting a seat.

Florida officials declined to speak with me about their contribution schemes, though in the past they had told me it was all for a good cause. Like other SEC schools, Florida offers a limited number of sports but funds them lavishly. Its football and basketball coaches are paid more than $3 million a year, and the athletic department even has its own airplanes and pilots to ferry athletes around.

Florida uses a point system to determine who gets its best seats, as well as to allocate the limited tickets available for away games and postseason bowl games. Think of this as something like frequent-flyer miles or, if you are older, S&H Green Stamps. Donors accumulate bonus points based on the size of their contributions, the length of time they have been season ticket holders, and any checks they have written to endow individual scholarships. (It is now possible to endow a linebacker or quarterback the same way you might endow a chair for a Nobel Prize–winning economist or a Pulitzer Prize winner, and these checks are also tax deductible.) The higher your point total, the more bonuses you receive: in this case, more and better seats; better parking; seatside drinks; skybox access; tickets to bowl games; and so on.

These days seat donations play an increasingly important role in the college football financial model. Consider the University of Michigan, which has the largest football stadium in the country, seating nearly 110,000 fans. In 2005 Michigan introduced a preferred-seating plan for the most desirable seats at Michigan Stadium, which is affectionately called the Big House. It later expanded the program to include all seats, with mandatory donations ranging from seventy-five dollars to six hundred dollars per seat. Recently Michigan also announced its own seat-transfer plan, which allowed fans to give up their seats to family or friends in return for a tax-deductible fee of five hundred dollars per seat.

Donations now bring in more than $20 million a season at Michigan. More than half of that comes from luxury suites and club seats, the highest category of seating. Such donations go a long way toward covering an athletic budget that has grown from $85 million to $123 million in just six years.

Michigan officials point to the high cost of funding 335 athletic scholarships as one reason they turned to seat payments. It costs $22,000 to cover tuition for an in-state athlete and $43,000 for an out-of-state one. With about 70 percent of its athletes coming from outside Michigan, the costs add up. Of course, here you might reasonably ask: Why doesn't Michigan recruit more in-state athletes? After all, it is the University of *Michigan;* shouldn't the opportunities go to its residents first? If it were forced to do that, Michigan wouldn't be as competitive in football—and, like other football powers, Michigan doesn't just play sports; it wants to win championships and use its football team to polish its brand.

In any case, athletic scholarships aren't the real problem, as most of the top football schools spend 10 percent or less of their athletic budgets on them. Far more is allocated to salaries, debt, and administrative overhead. The head football coach alone often earns more than all of the football scholarships combined.

I hoped to ask Michigan officials about all of this, but a spokesman for the athletic department told me they were too busy to talk with me. If by now you've gotten the impression that many football powers are uncomfortable discussing the money and the public subsidies that help to enrich their programs, it's because they are—probably with good reason. How do you tell someone that paying a surcharge to secure a seat in the Big House is, for tax purposes, the same thing as writing a check to the local soup kitchen?

·   ·   ·

Still, I kept reaching out and occasionally did come across a brave soul who was willing to speak. One of them was Chris Besanceney, who oversees the season-ticket plan at the University of Alabama. You would probably not be wrong if you guessed that Besanceney has the toughest job in Alabama's sprawling athletic department. Because the school has won three national championships in the last eight years, the demand for football tickets is preposterously high. And with almost no one ever willing to give up a seat, Besanceney has only a few new tickets in any given season to dole out.

I talked with Besanceney in 2013. That season just forty football tickets turned over at Alabama, usually after someone died or moved away. Forty works out to 0.0004 percent of all the seats in 101,000-seat Bryant-Denny Stadium. "To put it in perspective," Besanceney explained, "we have a waiting list of 26,000. Those are the fans waiting to get a season ticket at Bryant-Denny."

There are only sixteen towns and cities in Alabama with a population of 26,000 or higher. Tuscaloosa, with a population of 90,000, is one of the largest. It is as if every third person living there were waiting in line for a season ticket. This struck me as remarkable, and I asked Besanceney if anyone ever tried to bribe him to get to the head of the line.

"Not at Alabama," Besanceney replied with a laugh. "But I wouldn't be surprised if it happened somewhere else."

Fans jockeying for season tickets take a number and wait to get called and, as at other football powers, it always helps to write a big check for a new weight room or practice facility to move up to the head of the line. Alabama also uses a point system to manage its scarce resource and to maximize revenue. This part of its seating program is called TIDE TOTALS POINTS and ranks fans according to how much they have given and for how long. Alabama uses the totals both to determine who gets the few available seats and as a tiebreaker if a seat with a better view opens up and more than one fan bids the same amount.

The seat donation program has its own name: TIDE PRIDE. (For some reason Alabama, like an angry blogger, puts everything in caps.) TIDE PRIDE sets the annual mandatory payment required above and beyond the cost of a ticket. Since Alabama introduced TIDE PRIDE in 1988, seat payments have swelled from $6 million to nearly $30 million a year. Most of that comes from football. Alabama takes in another $15 million annually from ticket sales. So just between these two, it collects about $45 million a year for its athletic programs.

I figured this was as good a time as any to slip in a question about seat donations and charity.

"Does any of this work without the tax deduction?" I wondered.

"That's a good question," Besanceney said.

•   •   •

Many schools claim that they were the first to successfully monetize their ticket programs. The seat-donation plans at Florida and Georgia, for example, have been in effect for decades. But if you really want to reach back to the beginning of athletic fund-raising—the seed of the "college football as charity" concept—you have to go all the way back to the Great Depression and Clemson University.

For years Clemson was a football power, winning titles and bowl games. However, by the early 1930s the team had fallen on hard times, scoring just one touchdown and winning only one game in 1931. Following a shocking 6–0 loss to a much smaller and less accomplished Citadel team, Head Coach Jess Neely and several other members of the athletic department huddled in a car outside the stadium, searching for ways to get Clemson back on track.

Neely said they needed a larger and more consistent source of funding to modernize facilities, recruit better athletes, and improve coaches' salaries. "If I can just get ten thousand dollars," he told the others, according to several histories of the meeting, "I can give Clemson fans a better football team."

Initially Clemson boosters considered starting a fifty-dollar club, with each fan asked to contribute that amount. But the idea was dismissed as too extravagant. It was the Depression, after all.

Three years later Dr. Rupert "Rube" Fike, a prominent radiologist and Clemson booster, came up with the idea for the IPTAY Club. IPTAY stood for "I Pay Ten a Year" to support Clemson football and "assist in every way possible to regain for Clemson the high athletic standing which rightfully belongs to her."

In IPTAY's first year Clemson boosters contributed $1.6 million. Some payments were made in the form of milk, sweet potatoes, and turnip greens. (Noncash gifts are still made at some schools. In 2012 Kansas State received farmland, mineral interests, grain, livestock, and gold coins valued at nearly $1 million, according to school documents.) The effects of IPTAY were immediate. In 1934 Clemson posted its first winning season in years and defeated its archrival, South Carolina. By 1940 Clemson again ranked among the elite football programs with a 9-1-1 record, finishing twelfth in the Associated Press poll.

The Clemson IPTAY Club still exists today and is incorporated as a charity, allowing donors to deduct their membership fees as gifts. Since its founding IPTAY has raised approximately $300 million for football and other sports. It now includes a full-fledged seat-donation plan and controls much of the seating in eighty-thousand-seat Memorial Stadium. In 2011 IPTAY collected $35 million in seat donations and ticket sales.

·   ·   ·

For years the University of California at Berkeley has ranked among the very best public universities in America—this even after state lawmakers slashed its funding by half. Its athletic program is one of the largest in the nation and has more in common with the Ivy League than with most other football powers. In 2011 Cal sponsored twenty-nine varsity sports and 872 athletes, the most in the Pac-12. One might fairly ask how smart it was to try to do more with less. But that is part of the bohemian appeal of Cal. Even in its approach to athletics there is something almost quixotic about the school.

"It is absolutely a philosophical thing," Cal's athletic director, Sandy Barbour, told me in 2013 when I called to ask about the athletic budget. At the time, Cal was in trouble financially and considering eliminating five teams to cut costs. "We absolutely believe the philosophy," Barbour said, "but we just don't have the economics to pull it off."

Actually, there were many things Cal athletics didn't have the money to pull off, because the economics no longer worked. Football didn't generate nearly enough cash to support all of the other sports at Cal and, from some angles, barely generated enough money to support itself, which is to say Cal was never going to be confused with Notre Dame, Oklahoma, or Michigan. It made only a few million dollars from its seat-donation program, not tens of millions. Given the desolate state of its crumbling, eighty-nine-year-old stadium in Strawberry Canyon—among other issues, the 72,000-seat stadium squatted on top of a major earthquake fault—it was hardly in a position to hit up its fans for more money.

The challenge for Barbour and Cal was to come up with an innovative new way to repair the stadium and turn its football program into an ATM. Adding high-end luxury seats was one part of the solution. Setting the football team on a winning path was another.

Football has always been aspirational at Cal. The school has had good years and bad. But even when the team has won, it has had trouble filling Memorial Stadium. One college football Web site ranked Cal's among the most lackluster fan bases in the country; the team was unable to sell out its stadium even when it was playing Stanford, its biggest rival.

Between 2002 and 2012 Cal won eighty-two games and lost only fifty-seven, and for a time the mood, if ever so briefly, was transformative. Barbour rewarded head coach Jeff Tedford with a new $1.5 million contract. And even with the economy in decline, Cal officials decided it was finally time to renovate Memorial Stadium. In January 2010 they approved a $350 million remodeling plan, a gaudy sum for a public university facing serious retrenchments. They couldn't very well ask lawmakers in Sacramento for the money or jack up Cal's already-hefty student fees. So they started looking to other, riskier alternatives.

In business terms Cal football was an undervalued product. It didn't sell nearly enough season tickets and it didn't charge enough for the seats it did sell. That forced the athletic department to rely heavily on walk-ups (fans buying tickets at the gate)—a volatile and unreliable approach. The biggest challenge, then, was how to best monetize the newly refurbished stadium. Cal officials devised a plan to tap its richest, most loyal fans. They would take the best seating—three thousand spots at the west end of the bowl—and supersize them, offering wide cushioned seats in climate-controlled settings, complimentary seatside service with catered food and premium beverages, individual flat-screen televisions to watch replays, and priority parking. They called their plan an endowment seating program (ESP) and charged between $40,000 and $225,000 per seat, depending on the location and the length of the contract. Fans paying the entire amount up front would be guaranteed a prime seat at Cal football for up to fifty years, marketing brochures declared. Plus, they would be able to write off most of the huge fee on the following year's taxes as a charitable gift.

This was seat donations on steroids, a kind of madness normally reserved for professional teams. How could this possibly be considered a form of charity? For that matter, how did this not constitute a seat license, in which people essentially owned their own seats? Under the terms of the plan, Cal fans even had the right to sell their seats to someone else.

I exchanged half a dozen e-mails and telephone calls with an assistant athletic director who promised to hook me up with the person in charge of the ESP, but after a month of delays I wound up with the spokesman for the university instead. Dan Mogulof told me he knew as much about the supersized seat-donation plan as anyone. He noted that the plan had been vetted by one of the school's math professors, who had reassured the athletic department that the numbers added up. The various models showed Cal making money and able to cover its $14 million annual mortgage payment on the refurbished stadium. The debt payments were also back-loaded, which helped, Mogulof said.

"We came up with a financial model for all of this. Like any model, it generates a variety of scenarios, depending on the return on investment. There are scenarios where ESP not only pays off the stadium but also ends up with a surplus. Whether that happens or not remains unclear. If it did, it would be used as an endowment for the [athletic] department," Mogulof explained.

I asked him what type of fans could afford tens or even hundreds of thousands of dollars for long-term seat contracts. Given the area, I imagined there had to be a few obvious examples, like Silicon Valley entrepreneurs and venture capitalists. But Mogulof refused to bite, offering instead a generic "people who have long-standing and deep philosophical relationships with the university. As the saying goes, they bleed blue and gold."

I pointed out that the plan sounded a lot like a personal seat license and, initially at least, Mogulof seemed to agree, but he later amended his comments in an e-mail. "The ESP is actually a pledge that allows fans to have access to long-term rights on seats. It is not a PSL," he wrote. Cal couldn't call it a seat license, I quickly realized. If they did, they would sound like the NFL, and someone would probably start wondering about taxes.

Mogulof stressed that the three thousand seats represented just 5 percent of the now-downsized sixty-thousand-seat Memorial Stadium. "We did not monopolize all of the best seats in the house. There are still very good seats for students at severely discounted prices," he explained.

The new seating plan should generate additional revenue for the Cal athletic department, though perhaps not as much as the model assumed. As of 2013, Cal had received $41 million in up-front seat donations from fans, an amount well below what the model had predicted. The less money Cal collected, the less it had to invest, the less interest it would earn, and the less it would be able to generate for the hoped-for endowment.

But even more worrisome was the fact that the football team was once again struggling. In 2012 Cal finished 3-9. Barbour fired Tedford, replacing him with an innovative but relatively unproven coach, Sonny Dykes. Dykes went 1-11 in his first season. The risk now was that such losses would drive down demand and make selling ESP seats even harder. Mogulof assured me that attendance was not yet a problem. "But you do ask yourself," he added, "if you lose your edge, do the fans stop coming at some point?"

Sandy Barbour put it more bluntly: "We need football to win." Several months after our talk Barbour stepped down as athletic director, saying it was time for a "change in leadership." No mention was made of the ESP plan. Barbour is now athletic director at Penn State.

Cal officials recently expanded their marketing efforts to include local businesses. Mogulof insisted that it was a natural evolution of the plan, not a panicked reaction. But the change only raised more questions. For example, would businesses treat their payments as gifts or as a cost of doing business? And if they sold their seats to someone else, would the new owners still get a tax deduction? The services of a tax lawyer were clearly required.

●   ●   ●

A few weeks later I flew to Chicago and drove down to the University of Illinois to meet with John D. Colombo at the law school. I have known Colombo since the midnineties, when we learned that we shared an interest in nonprofit hospitals and charities. Colombo had begun to publish scholarly articles on the subject. Among other things, he was fairly startled by how easy it was to win tax-exempt status from the IRS and then, once having acquired it, to hold on to it without necessarily doing much to merit the tax break.

"Many of the policies benefiting charities and nonprofits linger on for no particular reason," he once told me. "The reason is we don't like to ask deeper policy questions like What is the public benefit we get in return for awarding someone tax-exempt status? And are they still doing enough to deserve it?"

Colombo, fifty-seven, is funny, smart, and self-deprecating. He has the midwestern gift of not sounding harsh or critical even when he is being harsh and critical. He doesn't seem to mind speaking with reporters and has a rare ability to translate complex legal arguments into plain English.

Other than a relatively short period in Georgia clerking for a federal judge and practicing business law at an Atlanta firm, Colombo has spent most of his life in Illinois. He grew up in the southern part of the state in a coal-mining town near the Ozarks. His paternal grandparents were immigrants from Italy, and Colombo attended a Catholic grade school "where if you didn't have a vowel at the end of your name, the question was why you were there."

In 2009 he wrote a lengthy law-review article dissecting the tax breaks for college sports. In his opinion many of the exemptions were an artifact from earlier, quainter times and hardly reflected the overtly commercial nature of today's large football and basketball programs. "The idea that college football evokes a Greek ideal of well-rounded athletes—that's just nuts," he told me during my visit. "That's just crazy. The Greek ideal, if there is one, is intramural sports. Big-time college football is nothing more than the minor leagues for the pros, and everyone knows it."

When I asked him directly if seat donations could be considered charitable gifts, he looked at me for a moment as if I had lost my mind. "The easy and direct answer is that it's not charity," he replied. "If you receive a quid pro quo—that is, something tangible—it is not considered to be a donation. The IRS has held that position forever. But Congress decided to act on its own and call the payments charitable contributions."

"You are buying something of value," I clarified.

"It's a purchase transaction," Colombo confirmed. "You are getting something of value in return for your donation."

"And isn't the idea that a gift should be voluntary to be called a gift?"

"That is what the IRS has consistently maintained."

I could understand how, in the beginning, no one cared too much, as relatively little money was involved. But as with everything else in college football, the scale had changed dramatically in the last two decades; the once-modest seat-donation schemes had become an important part of the college-football economy and were even more lucrative than the football television deals. Why, then, hadn't tax policy been revised to reflect these new conditions?

One reason, Colombo suggested, was obvious: No one in Congress wanted it to change. The politics of college football were such that you never won an election by punishing your flagship university. Here I recalled a conversation I once had with the athletic director at a prominent football school. He told me that once a year he and several other athletic directors traveled to Washington to rub elbows with their representatives and senators. "We always bring along a football coach or two," he said, "because one thing you learn is that politicians like to slobber all over football coaches and make fools of themselves."

"Think about it," Colombo continued. "If you're from Texas, do you really want to piss off every University of Texas supporter? At the end of the day there is no political upside and an enormous downside to going after college football."

In February of 2015 the Obama administration proposed ending the 80 percent deduction of seat donations as part of the budget it submitted to Congress. It was a surprising—even important—move, Colombo suggested to me. The mere fact that Treasury officials thought it was a significant enough issue to include "means that someone thinks the issue isn't a complete nonstarter." Colombo put the chances of the proposal getting through Congress as low but not zero: "I'd handicap it at perhaps ten to twenty percent."

I am slightly less optimistic, given the importance of the exemption to the financial model underpinning football. Seat donations account for 20 percent to 30 percent of the athletic department budgets at Alabama, Texas, and other elite programs. It is not hard to imagine what would happen if that tax break went away. It would cripple the model, and college football along with it. I am betting that history holds.

•   •   •

In 1984 the Internal Revenue Service issued a document known as Revenue Ruling 84-132, covering the tax treatment of seat donations for college football. Revenue rulings are the agency's way of giving everyone a heads-up about its thinking on complicated or controversial issues. They are meant to serve as guidance for regulators and those being regulated—in this instance, athletic directors and universities with seat-donation plans.

Revenue Ruling 84-132 concluded that fans shouldn't be allowed a tax deduction on their seat donations because they weren't actually gifts, in the service's standard definition of that term. Not surprisingly, the ruling wasn't well received by the football powers, which predicted that it would destroy college football and staged an aggressive lobbying campaign to block the IRS and preserve their valuable tax break. The extent of the schools' lobbying efforts can be gauged by the volume of legislative memos, lawyers' notes, and university records I discovered in college archives. For example, an October 10, 1984, memo by a member of Pennsylvania senator John Heinz's staff noted: "While the revenue ruling is probably correct, it will have a severe impact on Athletic Associations, and athletic scholarships." The staffer advised Heinz that Joe Paterno, the head coach at Penn State, planned to call him shortly to discuss the issue. He added that Senator David Pryor of Arkansas had introduced a bill to repeal or postpone the ruling for a year and that he had prepared a statement for Heinz supporting Pryor's proposal. In pencil at the top of the memo, Heinz scribbled "agreed" and added his initials.

Pryor issued his own statement, contending, "The tragic result [of the ruling] would be a reduction in the pool of financial aid available to help promising scholar-athletes attend college. Without these scholarships, many students might not have been able to go to college." Pryor provided no data or examples to back up his claims—for example, the number of scholars who might actually be affected. And as best I could determine, none of his colleagues or members of the media asked him about the cost of the seat-donation plans or why taxpayers should be subsidizing college football.

In any event, the lobbying campaign was successful. Later that fall the Treasury Department backed away from the IRS ruling after being approached by Senator Bob Dole of Kansas. A hearing was arranged for testimony from the football schools.

That hearing took place in January 1985. The IRS insisted that Revenue Ruling 84-132 merely restated its long-held position that a gift is tax deductible only if nothing is received in return. Nevertheless, a top agency official promised to revisit the decision. A representative from the University of North Carolina encouraged the IRS to move quickly, because the ruling was causing "fear" that the payments would be disallowed, and then suggested that colleges would have no choice but to turn to the government to help pay for football scholarships if the IRS taxed the seat donations. Remarkably, no one questioned this claim. However, the panel did include one critic, Richard L. Kaplan, a colleague of Colombo's at the University of Illinois College of Law, who called the deduction for football seats "an entertainment subsidy."

On April 28, 1986, the IRS issued Revenue Ruling 86-63, its long-awaited sequel. Agency officials made some concessions but continued to question whether seat donations were actually gifts. The IRS now decided to put the onus on fans to prove their payments were true charitable donations and not quid pro quos. In order to do so, fans would have to place a value on their donations, calculating how much was the market value of the seat itself and how much was an actual gift. An attorney for the National Association of Collegiate Directors of Athletics predicted that the process would be a logistical nightmare.

On the same day that Revenue Ruling 86-63 was issued Senator Pryor drafted an amendment to overturn it. Shortly thereafter Representative Norm Dicks, a former linebacker for the University of Washington, introduced companion legislation in the House. In a floor statement Dicks called the new ruling "just as flawed as the previous ruling in its impact" and invited members of Congress to attend a "special breakfast" sponsored by the National Association of Collegiate Directors of Athletics and featuring Joe Paterno. A staff member for John Heinz suggested that Heinz cosponsor a bill to reverse the IRS ruling. "Considering the number of Penn State, and U. of Pitts fans, and the contributions to the athletic funds it is a good issue," he wrote.

It was at this point that the seat-donation saga took an unexpected turn. Even as the football powers were mounting a new campaign to block the IRS, a pair of lawmakers from Texas and Louisiana slipped language into pending tax-reform legislation to protect their alma maters. Senator Russell B. Long of Louisiana was a graduate of LSU and a powerful member of the Senate Finance Committee. He was a champion of tax breaks for businesses and once famously described tax reform as meaning "Don't tax you, don't tax me, tax that fellow behind the tree!" J. J. "Jake" Pickle was from the hill country of central Texas, a character straight out of *Lonesome Dove* and a graduate of the University of Texas, where he had competed for the swimming team. Pickle was a huge fan of everything Texas, including the university's football program. "He was beloved in Texas," DeLoss Dodds told me. "And of course, being a graduate, he would do anything for his university. If you had a problem, you called Jake. If you wanted something in Washington, you called Jake."

Dodds contacted Pickle after the 1986 IRS ruling came out. "Jake had a friend [Long] in Louisiana. Those two guys put a rider on bills: If you were from Texas or LSU you could use the full amount [continue to take a tax deduction on your seat donations]. That stirred up everybody," Dodds recalled.

In the mid-1990s I crossed paths with Pickle at a hearing he was chairing on tax abuses involving charities. I knew he was an old-time Texas populist, but for some reason college sports remained a blind spot for him. After the hearing I introduced myself and asked him what

he thought about the seat donations. Pickle smiled at me as if he imagined I had posed him a trick question, finally drawling, "Aw, Mr. Gaul,
it's just football is all it is. We can't go messin' with football, can we?
Why, they'd run me out of Texas if we tried."

As is often the case, their schools' names did not appear in Long and
Pickle's legislation, but it did not take reporters long to figure out which
they were. Allegations of favoritism erupted, and a senator from Nebraska
asked the obvious question: Why just Texas and LSU? Why not exempt
Nebraska and all of the other football programs? The sponsors of the
amendment quickly backpedaled, insisting that it had never been their
intention to single out just two schools.

In 1988, just before recessing for elections, Congress solved the val-
uation issue by passing legislation allowing a flat, across-the-board 80
percent deduction for the seat donations, retroactive to 1983. This ren-
dered the IRS's attempts to tax the payments moot. The only question
lingering was what to do about the proliferating luxury suites and skyboxes. Should the fans renting those suites for $100,000 a season also
be able to write off their payments as gifts? The question bounced around
until July 1999, when the IRS ruled that these payments should be treated
identically to seat donations.

"The 80 percent rule was nothing more than a straight-up giveaway to
college football," Colombo said. "There is no real argument or larger principle at play here. Congress simply decided to give the schools a gift."

It was one of many. Congress has effectively decreed that college football is exempt from paying taxes on billions in seat donations, television
broadcast rights, bowl-game payments, and corporate sponsorships. At
the same time, no one up on the Hill seems able or willing to acknowledge the role that these tax breaks have played in unleashing a tsunami
of spending that has transformed once-modest state universities into
sports entertainment factories.

To truly address the issue would require conditioning a university's tax-exempt status on how its athletic department behaves, Colombo said. For instance, Congress could link the exemption to graduation rates or other academic metrics. "Even if someone tried," Colombo conceded, "and I don't think they will, but if they did, the schools and their lobbyists would descend on Washington and hold a march. They have a long history of getting what they want."

I wondered what Jake Pickle would think, were he still alive. He died in 2005, even as the football powers were negotiating another round of lucrative new television deals. I managed to find his only daughter, Peggy, who lives in Austin. "My father bled orange," she told me. "He had a great sense of protectiveness and affection for the University of Texas. At the same time, I think Jake had no idea what this would mean for athletic programs. It seems to me athletics are now driving the bus. Athletics has become the business that no one anticipated. My father's last few years he was able to be a guest in those skyboxes [at DKR-Memorial Stadium], and he enjoyed that. But he did not pass that legislation with the intent of getting skyboxes a tax break. I'm sure of that."

•   •   •

I was left with the question of my mother-in-law's football tickets. Should she hold on to them, transfer them to her family, or give them up? For me, ultimately, the most troubling aspect of the situation was the surcharge that Penn State was levying on fans to share their tickets with loved ones. Even with the tax deduction, that simply didn't seem fair. Over the decades my mother-in-law and her late husband had paid thousands of dollars for the privilege of attending Penn State football games. Why should they be charged on top of that and then have that payment categorized as a gift? It felt almost Orwellian to me.

The seat payments Penn State fans made washed through something

called the Nittany Lion Club, which serves as the athletic department's
money-raising arm. It employs seventeen fund-raisers, including several
just for football, and also oversees the seating plan at 106,000-seat Beaver Stadium.

Over the years thousands of fans joined the Nittany Lion Club and
paid a fee to secure season tickets. Many, like my in-laws, had held their
tickets for decades. In many ways Penn State football defined their
lives. They traveled to home games in RVs and threw parties when the
team played in New Year's Day bowl games. Many of these loyal supporters were now in their seventies and eighties, which created a new
and important problem for Penn State: Their best fans were slowly dying
off. At the time my mother-in-law received her package in 2010, she was
eighty-two, which was not atypical of the graying fan base.

The idea that your oldest, most devoted fans could constitute a threat
seems counterintuitive until you realize that a graying population of fans
isn't necessarily a good thing for your product. In fact, it could be a bad
thing and could even threaten your fundamental financial model. Ideally,
you want a mix of fans, young and old, with a reasonable amount of turnover each year. But age by itself isn't precisely the problem. It is that all
of those sixty-, seventy-, and eighty-year-olds control a disproportionate
share of the seats. Many of the Penn State fans originally purchased their
seats back when seats were cheap and athletic officials were happy just to
be able to fill the stadium. A surprising number now controlled as many
as five to ten seats and were still paying at the older, cheaper rates. All of
which helped to explain how my five-foot-tall, now eighty-six-year-old
mother-in-law went from being viewed as an asset to being viewed as a
liability in the calculus of Penn State football.

In 2009 Penn State officials stared into the future and realized several things. They needed their fan base to get younger. And they needed
to recapture as many of their cheap seats as possible and repackage them

at the new, higher mandatory seat-donation levels. Separately, they needed to start rewarding their most generous fans by offering them a way to spend their way up to better, more expensive seats. If they failed to do so, an athletic department with a $116 million budget faced, however improbably, an impending crisis. The business types in the athletic department even came up with a color graphic to show their season ticket holders. The illustration depicted revenues increasing year after year, always a little faster than expenses, until the trend suddenly reversed around 2016, when expenses would top revenues. It was pretty basic stuff, but it got their message across.

"We saw a point where the black line and the red line crossed and realized we had to do something," explained Greg Myford, a Penn State associate athletic director for business at the time he spoke with me, now in the private sector. "We began looking certainly at football and the revenues associated with football and we began to consider current scenarios and what positive changes we could make."

Although many of the seats in Beaver Stadium had required a donation for years, the amounts were modest relative to what many other schools charged. And oddly, Penn State didn't distinguish between fans who gave a thousand dollars and fans who gave a hundred dollars. "As long as you gave the minimal donation required, you got to stay in your seat," Myford explained. "It was not uncommon for a fan who gave a thousand dollars to sit next to the fan who gave a hundred dollars."

Tim Curley, the athletic director at the time, referred to Penn State's awkwardly named Seat Transfer and Equity Plan as a way for fans to "embrace tradition while preparing for the future," according to marketing materials sent out to fans. He characterized the transfer portion of the plan as a "limited-time offering [that] will allow many of our longtime friends to pass the glory of game days on to others who can keep their traditions alive for years to come."

Myford insisted that Penn State fans wanted the right to share their seats. "They had been clamoring for a way to transfer their tickets," he said.

"Clamoring?" I asked, finding it hard to imagine anyone clamoring to pay a two-thousand-dollar surcharge.

"It was easily thousands as opposed to hundreds."

That still didn't explain the hefty charge to transfer tickets or why those payments were considered gifts instead of a penalty or a tax.

"Make no mistake," Myford said, "the primary reason for putting the plan in place was to generate increased revenue. We decided on the transfer donations because we could."

"And the deduction?" I asked.

"It's what the law allows," Myford answered.

The athletic department collected $3.8 million from fans who transferred their tickets to family members or friends. That represented a one-time gain in the 2012 budget, Myford told me. Penn State pocketed another $4 million from its higher seat donations. That additional revenue will presumably continue into the future, so long as fans keep coming.

Attendance took a hit after the Sandusky scandal in 2011 and, even with its higher fees, Penn State reported that revenues in its athletic program fell by $8 million in 2012, to $108 million. One fan writing in a local newspaper blamed the decline on the higher cost of attending home games. "Two main reasons for the attendance drop: 1. Greed! 2. Greed!"

On the face of it, Penn State appears to have miscalculated, increasing its fees at a time when its fan base was aging and the economy was tanking. Or maybe it was just bad luck, with the Sandusky scandal driving away thousands of fans? My best guess is that it was all of the above. The question now is whether the fans will come back and revenues will rebound. If not, Penn State could become Cal and be pressured to cut some of its teams.

My mother-in-law eventually decided to give up her tickets, which I assume went back into the general pool to be sold at a higher price. I think it was the best choice. Her daughters had no interest in football, and traveling to State College for games had become an ordeal for her. "I'll miss going," she told me, "but almost all of the games are on TV." After all, she could always watch in her den, surrounded by her Penn State pillows and blankets and the autographed photo of Joe Paterno hanging on the paneled wall.

Three

• • •

RETURN ON INVESTMENT: THE ART OF PAYING A COACH $23 MILLION NOT TO COACH

TWO WEEKS BEFORE CHRISTMAS OF 2004, Notre Dame University announced that it was hiring Charlie Weis to be its new head football coach. It was, in some respects, an occasion more for relief than for celebration. The allure of coaching football at America's most prominent Catholic university was not what it once was. Several leading candidates had passed on the job, choosing other schools or staying put. There was simply no way to gloss over the embarrassment. Notre Dame had gone from being the prom queen to waiting by the phone for someone to call.

A strong case could be made that Notre Dame's administration and fans had no one to blame but themselves. Their expectations were unreasonably high, and the base often turned on its coaches at the first sign of trouble. It wasn't enough to win at Notre Dame; you had to contend for national championships. And there was the rub. Notre Dame hadn't won a championship since 1988, when its biggest fan, Ronald Reagan, was in office. What the Fighting Irish needed was another Knute Rockne, All American, but what they got was Charlie Weis, an accomplished professional coach with relatively little college experience.

By this point Notre Dame had cycled through five coaches in ten years, including the leprechaun himself, George O'Leary, who was fired after just five days for fudging his résumé. Two other coaches—Bob Davie and Tyrone Willingham—had won six of every ten games they coached, but that still wasn't good enough. In 2004, Willingham's final season, the team finished with three ugly losses and a 6-6 record. A few days later he was fired, and Notre Dame again began scrambling to find a new coach, eventually selecting Weis.

You might think that the turmoil at Notre Dame was unusual, but really it wasn't. It was suggestive of one of college football's most enduring myths: that there was a rational, market-driven system for hiring head coaches and paying them unimaginably large sums of money. The truth was far less impressive. The truth was that the system was far less rational or efficient than the athletic directors believed and the fans and the media accepted as canon. By almost any reasonable measure, athletic directors at elite football schools wildly overpaid for coaches, convincing themselves that if they didn't come up with the money, someone else would. When you asked them why they were so willing to empty out their bank accounts, the stock answer was that there was only a shallow pool of coaches with the necessary discipline, skill, and intelligence to successfully compete at the highest levels of college football.

What the athletic directors actually meant was that there were only so many coaches who could reliably win enough games to keep their athletic departments in the black. So when you did find one, you had better pay him whatever he wanted and then rationalize it as the cost of doing business in the new, hyperinflated model of college football. Only the athletic directors never used words like "hyperinflated" or "irrational." Instead they argued that paying someone $5 million or $6 million to coach a college football team represented an efficient market because, as we learned in economics, efficient markets pay only what they can afford to pay. It was the same kind of blind faith and triumphalism that we have since come to associate with Wall Street bankers.

By nature athletic directors tend to be optimistic. Like a lot of people, they also tend to exaggerate their ability to identify talent. This is especially true when it comes to selecting and paying football coaches. They routinely overpay coaches based on one or two good years and then appear surprised when the team stumbles or is merely average. Not surprising, coaches take advantage of the gaps in this process to bid up their own salaries and win lengthy contract extensions. And why wouldn't they? They would be crazy not to.

Consider what happened in 2014 when Bill O'Brien decided to leave Penn State to become the head coach of the professional Houston Texans. After an eight-day search, Penn State announced it was hiring James Franklin to a six-year, $25.5 million deal. Franklin had only three years of experience as head coach. But because he had turned around an awful Vanderbilt team, going 24-15, he was considered an attractive hire and was on the radar of several elite schools.

Where it got interesting was Franklin's pay package. Penn State agreed to give him $4.5 million a year, or $1.5 million more than what it had paid O'Brien, who coached the team for two years following the Sandusky scandal. It was also $3.5 million more per year than what Penn State had paid Joe Paterno at his peak, according to published reports. That prompted an interesting question: Had Penn State underpaid Paterno, the most successful coach in college history, or was it overpaying Franklin, based on a small sample of years and the hope that he would return the football program to its former glory? It seemed like a good question to ask

Penn State's president, Rodney Erickson, but I was informed by the university's spokeswoman that he was too busy to meet.

Viewed at a distance the process of selecting coaches felt more like a leap of faith than logic. What were the metrics? Wins? Graduation rates? The cost of the program? And why were schools so quick to fire coaches and pay them millions? In all my conversations with athletic directors I had yet to hear one say "I am looking for a really good, inexpensive coach." The bias was always toward paying more. They seemed to see throwing mountains of money at a coach as inevitable, not to mention a confirmation of their good judgment.

"In other words," I asked Rob Mullens, the athletic director at the University of Oregon, "if everyone is paying a coach $3 million, you have to pay your coach $3 million to stay competitive?"

"Yes, more or less like that," Mullens replied. "You do research. You look at what other schools are paying, get comparables."

It sounded like buying a house, only in this case the buyers were all working against their own best interests to bid up the price. If there truly were a limited number of candidates (and, by the way, I think that is a specious argument), the agents and coaches would—and actually do—use that to their advantage.

"You never want to pay more than you should," Mullens said. "But being a college football coach is a tough job, and it is a very competitive market. The salaries reflect that."

When I visited Mullens in 2013, he had recently lost his head football coach, Chip Kelly, to the Philadelphia Eagles and had replaced him with Kelly's longtime assistant, Mark Helfrich. Kelly had been making $3.5 million. Helfrich was starting at $1.8 million, a salary that, for such a high-profile program, might even be considered a bargain. It was also one of the only times I am aware of that a school paid less for a new head coach. Usually, they jack up the price tag every time there is a new hire.

Alas, it didn't last. In January 2015 Oregon played for the national championship as part of the new, lucrative play-off system. It lost badly to Ohio State. However, a few weeks later Helfrich got a new five-year, $17.5 million contract—or an average of $3.5 million per year, the same amount Kelly had collected. "We want to make sure we retain him, given the profile he's created over the last two years as head coach," Mullens explained to the local media.

Helfrich's new salary was nearly six times what Oregon paid its president and thirty-nine times the average pay for its faculty. Still, it was about $1 million less than the average football coach was paid in the football-crazed SEC, where half of the coaches collected $4 million or more and the fourteen head coaches pocketed a total of $57 million.

DeLoss Dodds, the former athletic director at Texas, summed the situation up nicely: "Once you get a good coach and they're successful, you set the salary where they won't want to leave. If you pay them $5 million and they're generating $125 million, they're worth it."

Texas's coach at the time, Mack Brown, didn't come close to generating $100 million by himself, but I took the point: It was a high-stakes job. But after Texas gave Brown a $2 million raise in 2009, bringing his total pay to $5 million, plus bonuses, the team went into a tailspin. When the 2013 season ended with another loss, Brown either quit or was pushed out, depending on what you read. Texas hired a new coach, Charlie Strong, at $5 million and agreed to cover his $4.375 million buyout at Louisville, bringing the true cost of hiring the new coach to $9.75 million.

What Dodds and the other athletic directors seemed to be acknowledging was that college football was at least as much a business as a game. It was a tricky position to take. If college football was a business, what kind of business was it? Was it a private one, in which case it might have to pay taxes? Or was it a not-for-profit, and if it was, could a nonprofit pay its CEO millions of dollars in salaries and bonuses and still be a nonprofit? The athletic directors appeared to be arguing both sides, claiming to be private businesses when it suited them and non-profits when anyone brought up the subject of taxes. Either way, they won, or at least appeared to win, until they became victims of their own faulty logic.

•   •   •

Football is critically important to the Notre Dame brand. For better or worse, millions of Americans know the university not for its outstand-ing academics but for its iconic football team. These two endeavors are not mutually exclusive, of course, but it is football that dominates the school's profile and is far and away the largest source of revenue in its financial model for athletics, generating about $80 million a year. One example of Notre Dame's power and appeal is that it has its own con-tract with NBC to televise its games. Not even Alabama or Ohio State has this sort of deal. The contract brings in $15 million a year—essentially found money for the athletic department.

Given the cultural, emotional, and financial stakes, one can appreci-ate the anxiety, if not panic, that must have gripped the Notre Dame community in 2004 as the team searched for a new head coach. The school wanted Urban Meyer, the promising young coach at Utah, badly. Meyer had worked at Notre Dame as an assistant coach in the 1990s. But even though he had called the school his dream job, he opted to take the head coaching position at Florida, where he guided the team to two national championships and compiled a 65-15 record before eventually moving to Ohio State and winning the 2014 national championship.

Several other prominent coaches' names surfaced in the weeks lead-ing up to Christmas, but they either withdrew or decided that they were happy where they were. That left Charlie Weis, who at forty-eight was probably the most intriguing but unconventional candidate. Weis was a Notre Dame alumnus, class of 1978, but hadn't played football there. After graduating with a degree in speech and communications, he spent a decade coaching at New Jersey high schools and as a graduate assistant at the University of South Carolina. In 1990 Bill Parcells hired Weis as an assistant offensive coach for the New York Giants. Later Weis moved to the New England Patriots as the offensive coordinator for Bill Belichick and helped the team win three Super Bowls.

Weis was a North Jersey guy, which is to say, no one would ever mistake him for shy. He was big, loud, and funny. Some considered him an offensive genius, and Weis didn't go out of his way to disabuse them of the notion. Still, he had spent most of his career in the pros, which was a completely different model from college football, one less encumbered by distractions like academics.

Notre Dame introduced Weis as its new coach on December 13, 2004. School officials stressed his great pedigree and personal ties to the university. Weis, for his part, said he was awed by the opportunity and acknowledged that it was "obviously a high-profile, big-time job," according to press accounts of his hiring. Brimming with confidence, he told reporters that he hadn't been hired to put a mediocre team on the field. If games came down to the tactical decisions of designing plays (X's and O's, as football coaches call them), he asserted, "I have to believe we're going to win most of the time."

Notre Dame gave Weis a six-year, $12 million contract, a record for the school, and initially Weis delivered impressively. In his first season the team got off to a 4-1 start, including wins over Michigan and Pittsburgh. It can be argued that to some degree Weis was riding Tyrone Willingham's coattails—after all, it was Willingham who had recruited the players Weis was now coaching—but the administration and fans were euphoric. In the sixth game of the season, the Fighting Irish nearly upset the number one–ranked USC Trojans. Then, in an act of what can only now be viewed as magical thinking, Notre Dame athletic director Kevin White tore up Weis's original contract and gave him a new one for ten years, guaranteeing Weis millions of dollars if he was fired.

"In a very short period of time, Charlie has clearly and impressively demonstrated the ability to take the Notre Dame program where we all want it to go," White said in announcing the new deal.

Weis's agent, Bob LaMonte, sounded almost giddy discussing the contract. "Charlie Weis doesn't own the Golden Dome," he told Teddy Greenstein of the *Chicago Tribune,* "but he has the keys to it for the next 11 years."

To recap: Notre Dame extended Weis's contract by four years, guaranteeing him additional millions, after he *lost* a game and had been the head coach for only six games.

Notre Dame finished the season 9-2 but then lost to Ohio State in the Fiesta Bowl. The following year the team finished 9-3, but once again the season ended badly with blowout losses to USC and LSU.

By the third season it was unquestionably Charlie Weis's team, staffed with his recruits and guided by his system. Notre Dame opened with five straight losses. Then, after managing a win against UCLA, it lost four more games, including to Air Force and Navy, matches once viewed as guaranteed victories. The next two seasons were marginally better at 7-6 and 6-6.

Speculation was now rampant that Weis would be fired. As he himself had said when he was hired, he wasn't being paid to go 0.500, let alone 16-21 over the last three years. But addressing the problem wasn't as simple as just pushing Charlie out the door. Weis still had six years remaining on his extended ten-year contract, and Notre Dame stood to take a huge hit if it let him go.

As the 2009 season stumbled to an end with four straight losses, the normally buoyant Weis appeared deflated. Following a loss to Connecticut, he told reporters he would have "a tough time arguing" if the school decided to fire him. Apparently the new Notre Dame athletic director, Jack Swarbrick, was thinking along similar lines. A few days later, on December 1, Swarbrick announced that Weis was finished. "He'll add some Super Bowl rings to the ones he already has as a successful coordinator in the NFL, and we will miss him," Swarbrick said. "But for us it's time to move forward."

Weis, in fact, eventually went on to the University of Kansas and, in keeping with the school's policy, Swarbrick declined to discuss his buyout. However, as a tax-exempt university, Notre Dame is required to file public tax returns annually detailing salary and severance data. Notre Dame's filings are based on the school's fiscal calendar, which starts on July 1 and ends on June 30. The first Notre Dame tax return including Weis's severance was for fiscal year 2010 and revealed that Weis received $6,638,403. He collected a total of an additional $6,165,327 over the next three years, tax returns show, bringing his buyout as of June 30, 2013, to $12,803,730. Assuming he continues to be paid at the same rate through 2015, the final year of his ten-year contract, Weis will collect an additional $4,109,488 from Notre Dame, bringing his total severance package to nearly $17 million. (Some writers have used estimates of as high as $19 million, but those appear to include the actual salary that Weis was owed from coaching. I am opting for the more conservative estimate.) That, of course, is in addition to the estimated $10 million that Weis was paid to actually coach. Overall, then, Notre Dame gambled nearly $27 million on Charlie Weis. Even by the standards of one of the biggest and richest football programs in the country, it was a spectacularly expensive investment.

•   •   •

It probably goes without saying that paying someone $17 million *not* to coach your football team isn't the most efficient way to go about your business. How Notre Dame got to that point reveals a great deal about the mind-set of big-time football schools and how far they will go to protect their financial models and brands. In that sense the Notre Dame example feels extreme only because of the school's repeated coaching miscues and its willingness to buy out its mistakes at retail rates.

Charlie Weis or the other coaches can hardly be faulted for taking the university's money. Theirs is probably the only rational response in an otherwise irrational system. For its part, Notre Dame appears to have more than enough cash in reserve to cover the buyout, with billions in its endowment.

What is interesting, though, is how common lucrative buyouts have become in college football and what that reveals about the hiring process. At one point I started to add up all of the buyouts, but I stopped after reaching $50 million. A weird thought crossed my mind: If I were a coach with a big contract, why would I care if the team won or lost? The model appeared to value failure as much as wins. I couldn't help questioning the assumption that there are only a handful of coaches who can manage big-time programs like Notre Dame, and that you have to overpay to hire them.

Consider the fact that there are approximately sixty schools in the five power conferences that control most of the money in college football. Each school has a head coach and at least nine full-time assistants. That makes for a pool of 600 potential head coaches. If, say, only 10 percent of the 540 assistants are qualified to be head coaches, that would mean 54 potential coaches are available at any given time. In 2014 there were approximately one dozen openings for head coaches at major football schools. Was it really so hard to find even a few candidates in that pool of 54 assistants willing to take $1 million to coach, instead of $2 million or $3 million? And this didn't include hundreds of other potential coaches at lower levels.

When you study coaches' pay, what you quickly observe is that there is a great amount of dissonance in the most important metric: wins. Coaches who consistently win are sometimes paid less than you might imagine, given the parameters of the system. Conversely, coaches with mediocre records are paid far more than they probably should get.

The other thing you notice is the unusual willingness of athletic directors to lock coaches into long-term contracts. The theory seems simple enough: Protect your most valuable asset. If you have a coach signed to a long-term deal, no one can come along and steal him without paying a hefty penalty. This approach usually works well, until it doesn't, as was the case with Notre Dame and Charlie Weis.

When Notre Dame extended Weis's contract after just six games, it was reacting emotionally, not logically. It assumed that Weis would continue to win at the same rate in the future, which it couldn't possibly know. It was also overvaluing optimism and discounting the role of luck. The difference between a winning record and a losing record can turn on a few mistakes—a fumble here, an intercepted pass there. But there is no way of accounting for luck, and Notre Dame wound up paying an extraordinary premium for its unwarranted optimism.

That kind of irrational exuberance pervades college football. In 2009 the University of Iowa signed its coach, Kirk Ferentz, to a ten-year, $39 million deal following an 11-2 season. Over the next three years the team underperformed, going 19-19, and the fan base was furious, demanding that the coach be fired. Ferentz had a clause in his contract requiring Iowa to pay him 75 percent of his contract, which worked out to about $15 million, if he was let go. Iowa officials apparently decided they couldn't afford such a big buyout and kept Ferentz. Since then Iowa has gone 15-11.

The University of Tennessee is another example of a football power with an uneven history of picking coaches and then overpaying them.

In 2008 it fired Phillip Fulmer after just one disappointing season. Fulmer had been Tennessee's head coach for seventeen years, winning 152 games and a national championship in 1998. But when the team got off to a rocky start in 2008 and then lost to 26-point underdog Wyoming, the fan base grew restless. Even with his impressive record, Fulmer was a marked man.

It cost Tennessee $6 million in severance to jettison Fulmer. But as it happens, that was only the start of the school's troubles. Tennessee replaced Fulmer with Lane Kiffin, a thirty-three-year-old boy wonder who had won accolades as an assistant at the University of Southern California but had no head college-coaching experience. His initial salary was set at $2 million but scheduled to rise to $2.7 million.

Kiffin lasted just a single year in Knoxville. After finishing 7-6, he announced that he was returning to USC to be its head coach. Angry students dragged mattresses out of their dorm rooms and set them on fire to protest. A mob blocked one of the exit routes from the auditorium where Kiffin was holed up. No arrests were made, but the headline in the local newspaper the following morning seemed to sum the situation up succinctly: LANE KIFFIN FIASCO LOWEST NOTE OF A LOW TIME FOR UT FOOTBALL.

It is unclear how much USC had to pay Tennessee to hire away Kiffin, but presumably it was not an insignificant sum. Kiffin went on to have a 28-15 record at USC but was fired midway through the 2013 season after the team was throttled by Arizona State. According to published reports, he was owed $10 million on his contract. So in the strange case of Lane Kiffin, the University of Southern California apparently got hit coming and going.

Tennessee, meanwhile, replaced Kiffin with another unconventional hire: Derek Dooley, the son of a legendary Georgia Tech football coach. Dooley Junior's only experience as a head coach was at Louisiana Tech, where he had compiled a 17-20 record. Undeterred, Tennessee signed him to a six-year deal worth $1.8 million per year and paid off his $500,000 buyout clause at Louisiana Tech. "How can you ask for anything better than the University of Tennessee?" Dooley gushed at his introductory press conference.

Dooley went 15-21 before being fired at the end of the 2012 season. He had three years remaining on his contract and was owed more than $5 million. Tennessee also owed $2 million to Dooley's assistants, according to newspaper reports.

When you added it all up, Tennessee had spent approximately $1 million for each win since firing Fulmer back in 2008. It was also on the hook for approximately $13 million in severance, less whatever it got from USC. But there was more. The upheaval in Knoxville was driving away fans. Attendance dropped by 12,000 per game at 102,000-seat Neyland Stadium. And the athletic department's reserves were dwindling— so much so that Tennessee's chancellor, Jimmy Cheek, agreed to let the department forgo millions it had pledged to share with the university. "We've got to get football healthy," Athletic Director Dave Hart bluntly told the SportsBusiness Journal.

In December 2012 Tennessee hired Butch Jones as its next coach, awarding him $18.2 million over six years—a significant increase over Dooley's salary—and agreeing to pay his $1.4 million buyout clause at Cincinnati. Still, Tennessee officials believed they had finally found the right man. Jones, who was considered a relentless program builder, had gone 55-34 at Cincinnati and Central Michigan, his previous two jobs.

His first season in Knoxville didn't go quite as well. Though the team was competitive, it finished 5-7, including a loss to archrival Vanderbilt, never a good thing. Jones told reporters it was wrong to measure the season solely by wins and losses, which was possibly the wrong thing to say when you were being paid $3 million a year to deliver victories to a victory-starved fan base.

In 2014 Tennessee improved to 7-6, including a win over Iowa in the TaxSlayer Bowl, named for an online software program. Tennessee rewarded Jones with a $600,000 raise, lifting his salary to $3.6 million a year. At the same time, it extended his contract by two years, through the 2020 season. If Jones leaves before 2017, he will owe Tennessee $3 million. If he is let go, the school will owe him nearly $11 million.

● ● ●

For weeks now I had been thinking about Bobby Petrino, one of the more successful but enigmatic coaches in college football, whose recent coaching history seemed to best capture the absurdities of the money culture now ruling college football. A *New York Times* columnist once referred to Petrino as an "ethical train wreck." *Sports Illustrated* titled a 2014 profile of Petrino "Lather, Rinse, Repeat." Those may have been a tad harsh, so let's leave it at this: Loyalty has never been Petrino's strongest suit.

One thing Petrino is clearly good at is winning college football games. His record as a head coach is 92-34. In the mid-2000s at Louisville he led the Cardinals to 41 victories and just 9 losses in four years. In July 2006 Petrino signed a ten-year, $25.6 million contract and told anyone willing to listen he wasn't going anywhere. But just days after guiding his team to a school record of 12 wins and a number 6 national ranking, Petrino announced he was leaving to coach the professional Atlanta Falcons, which had agreed to pay him even more—$24 million over five years.

Things did not go as hoped in Atlanta. The team's starting quarterback, Michael Vick, pled guilty to bankrolling an illegal dogfighting operation near his Virginia Beach home and served twenty-one months in prison. Left with a backup, the Falcons struggled to a 3-10 record.

Once again Petrino decided the future looked better from the rearview mirror, bolting the Falcons with three games left in the season to become the head coach at the University of Arkansas.

Arkansas agreed to pay Petrino $2.85 million a year for five years. After going 5-7 his first season, the team averaged 10 wins over the next three years and in 2011 finished 11-2. But again the spool quickly unraveled. In April 2012 Petrino crashed his motorcycle while cruising down Highway 16 near the unincorporated community of Crosses, Arkansas. He initially claimed to have been alone, but it quickly was revealed that he had been accompanied by a twenty-five-year-old former Arkansas volleyball player with whom he was having an affair, according to numerous published reports. Petrino had recently hired her as his assistant. Arkansas fired him for trying to hide the fact that he had a passenger in the accident. A university investigation also revealed that Petrino had given his new assistant twenty thousand dollars in cash as a Christmas gift. For his part Petrino expressed remorse and told reporters he was working hard to rescue his marriage.

At this point you might conclude that Bobby Petrino was such damaged goods that he would never coach again. Just six months later, though, Western Kentucky announced it was hiring Petrino as its next head coach and paying him a school record $850,000 per year over four years. The athletic director, Todd Stewart, acknowledged that he might be criticized. "But this is the United States of America, and we're a country of second chances," he told The Associated Press.

In 2013 Western Kentucky finished 8-4, and everyone seemed happy enough. But then things got not just confusing but truly and inexplicably weird. In early January the University of Texas hired Charlie Strong away from Louisville to be its head coach. And then, a few days later, Louisville held a press conference announcing that Petrino was returning to head its football team. The contract called for Louisville to pay him nearly $25 million over seven years, or $3.5 million a year—a raise from his prior salary.

Tom Jurich, Louisville's athletic director, told reporters that he had sat down with Petrino and found that "he's a changed man." But just to be safe, he included a $10 million buyout and a morals clause in Petrino's new deal. Louisville's president, James Ramsey, appeared focused on maintaining the upward trajectory of the football program. "There's no question we've got the very best person to lead our Cardinal football team forward," he said. "It's Tom's recommendation, but it's supported by the university."

At the time, Petrino acknowledged that he had made professional and personal mistakes. Then, with no apparent irony, he added, "I want everyone here to know this is my destination job. I'm home."

For Western Kentucky there was one upside to Petrino's brief fly-over. In early January of 2014 Louisville wired the school $1.2 million to satisfy Petrino's buyout clause, Stewart, Western Kentucky's athletic director, told me in an e-mail. So, in effect, Petrino hadn't cost Western Kentucky a dime. Better yet, the school actually *made* $350,000 on the deal—the balance after accounting for Petrino's $850,000 salary. This was one instance where a buyout clause actually worked.

•   •   •

Years ago the prominent sports agent Jimmy Sexton told me he was surprised when college football coaches cracked the $1 million barrier. Then he explained how it was all tied to revenue: The more college football grew, the more athletic departments took in, and thus the more money they had available to pay celebrity coaches. It sounded like a simple enough formula, which I suppose it was: Size equals pay.

Sexton was right in at least one respect, as salaries for celebrity coaches did continue to expand—dramatically so. When we spoke in 2000, there were only a handful of football coaches drawing $1 million in salary. By 2004, when Charlie Weis was hired at Notre Dame, it was closer to thirty. Today seventy-five coaches collect at least $1 million—and most are paid considerably more, according to university records and various databases on coaches' salaries. Five coaches have pay packages topping $5 million annually. Another fifteen collect between $3 million and $5 million. Thirty-four others receive $2 million or more.

One of Sexton's most successful clients, Nick Saban, is paid $6.5 million by the University of Alabama to coach football. To put this in perspective, Saban collects the equivalent of what fifty full professors at Alabama earn for teaching and doing research, and twelve times what the university's president, Judy Bonner, is paid. And that doesn't include hundreds of thousands of dollars Saban can collect in bonuses or earn from outside sponsorship deals.

In Alabama Saban's extravagant pay isn't considered unusual. On the contrary, he is seen as a bargain, considering all of the reflected glory and championships he has delivered, not to mention the $82 million a year that Alabama football brings in for the athletic department. In November 2013 the chancellor of the university, Robert E. Witt, told the news program *60 Minutes* that Saban was the "best financial investment this university has ever made." Witt's comment was revealing on several levels, not the least of which was that the university's top educator referred to his football coach as a financial investment. Saban himself routinely refers to college football as a business, and when asked about his salary he uses business terms to defend it, telling reporters they have to look at the return on investment to gauge his value.

It is hard to argue Saban isn't a great coach. Since 2007 he is 85-16 at Alabama, including three national championships. Football revenues have increased by 43 percent. And the program has generated a combined $209 million in profit, according to university records.

But when you study the numbers, you also notice this: Nick Saban and his football program generate a lot of expenses too. Since 2007 the cost of coaching and equipping the Alabama football team has swelled from $16 million a year to $38 million a year, which suggests Saban is spending money nearly as quickly as it comes in. A lot of that goes toward salaries. Saban's nine assistant coaches alone are paid nearly $6.5 million. Saban has also spent millions building up the back-office and support staff, so that Alabama now resembles an NFL team more than it does a college team. He has added directors of player personnel, specialists who track high school recruits, and a cadre of "analysts" to break down film and study data, some of whom happen to be former coaches.

As a result, the Alabama football program's profit margin has steadily eroded during Saban's tenure: from 72 percent in 2007 to 54 percent in 2012. Granted, 54 percent is still a highly impressive number, and no one is suggesting hiring Saban was a mistake. The point is that while Alabama is making more money, it isn't by any stretch of the imagination a model of efficiency. Even as the school has piled up victories, the cost of each of those victories has increased, not gone down, as you might expect in any other business. Viewed one way, Alabama is basically spending its way to the top.

Saban would be the first to tell you he didn't always make the big bucks. He grew up not poor but modestly in the West Virginia coal country, where his father ran a gas station. After playing defensive back at Kent State in the early 1970s, he began coaching, at which he was quickly successful. In the mid-1990s he took over a then-middling Michigan State team and built it into a winner. In 1999 the team went 9-2, finishing second in the Big Ten. At the time, Saban was paid $697,000 but felt underappreciated. He thought he deserved more, according to former Michigan State administrators. He also was dismayed that the administration had placed limits on his outside income. When LSU approached him about coming to Baton Rouge, Saban was receptive.

LSU was in the SEC and was a big football school with a big history, but it had stumbled and needed someone to help restore its glory. To illustrate how much it wanted Saban, LSU flew out its chancellor, Mark Emmert (now the president of the NCAA), on a private jet to assure Saban that he would have his back. Then Emmert dangled a check for $1.2 million, doubling Saban's salary with the wave of a hand. Saban, nobody's fool, quickly said yes.

And thus began perhaps the most remarkable trajectory in the history of college football coaching. In 2003 Saban delivered a national championship to LSU, and the school responded by bumping his salary to $3.5 million—about seven times what Emmert made and thirty-five times the salary of a full professor. Again, no one blinked.

Still, by the end of the 2004 season, Saban was once again restless. That year the Miami Dolphins offered him a chance to be their head coach, and he jumped. Saban swore it wasn't because of the money, though his salary climbed to $4.5 million.

Saban's time in Miami is probably best summed up as difficult. The older, entitled pro players reacted badly to his highly disciplined style, and the team went 15-17 over two seasons. Saban told reporters he realized in Miami that he wasn't cut out for the pros; he was better suited to being a college coach.

In a scene reminiscent of his LSU experience, Alabama sent a plane down to Miami on New Year's Day of 2007 with an offer of the head coaching job—an eight-year, $32 million contract that would grant Saban complete control over arguably the nation's most fabled football program.

His salary would drop to $4 million a year, but the deal included opportunities to boost his pay with bonuses, twenty-five hours of private use of a university jet, two luxury cars, a country-club membership, and free use of a skybox atop Bryant-Denny Stadium.

Saban was now the richest coach in college football and, by definition, the one setting the ceiling. But other coaches would soon benefit from his good fortune, with salaries escalating across the board. Indeed, the bottle-rocket trajectory of coaching salaries has helped to create a new if unexpected class of millionaires. Saban, for example, has invested in real estate and auto dealerships. In 2001 he purchased a $2 million vacation home on a lake in north Georgia and then added a second investment property with six bedrooms, nine bathrooms, a wine cellar, and a panoramic view of the lake, which he sold in 2013 for nearly $11 million. That same year Saban sold his Tuscaloosa home for $3.1 million to a university foundation established to boost athletics. Saban and his wife continue to live in the 8,759-square-foot residence, though the Crimson Tide Foundation pays the property taxes, according to published accounts. A spokesman for the foundation told the Web site AL.com that it wasn't unusual to provide coaches with university housing and that Saban could continue to live there after he retires: "We want to keep him happy," Scott Phelps explained. "We think he is the best coach in America."

The question I was left with was this: Was Nick Saban really that much better? Was he worth nearly $6 million more now than he was in 2000; fifty-four times more than what Robert Bentley, the Alabama governor, was paid; twelve times more than the university's president, who is responsible for a budget seven times the size of the football budget? I posed the question to Bill Battle, the athletic director at Alabama, who pointed to Saban's larger effect on the university as a whole. "Nick's impact on this campus and this program is everywhere," Battle said. "He has just changed the entire culture here."

CASHING IN: NICK SABAN'S STARTLING TRAJECTORY

TEAM	CONTRACT YEAR	ANNUAL SALARY
Michigan State	1999	$697,000
LSU	2000	$1,200,000
LSU	2004	$3,500,000
Miami Dolphins	2005	$4,500,000
Alabama	2007	$4,000,000
Alabama	2012	$6,000,000
Alabama	2014	$6,500,000*

Source: NCAA filings, newspapers, author's interviews.
*Does not include bonuses and payments for completing contract.

•   •   •

One effect of the sharp escalation in coaching salaries is that it has reframed the definition of "public employees." As a rule, college football coaches are now the highest-paid public employees in virtually every state in the nation. They earn far more than governors and chief justices and are generally paid five to ten times what college presidents collect—and to put this in perspective, the salaries of presidents have been rising at two to three times the rate of inflation in the last decade.

Recall that college football is considered to be a charitable activity, and recall the earlier argument that size should equal pay. The CEO of the American Red Cross, Gail J. McGovern, is paid $500,000 to oversee a $3.2 billion organization. Nick Saban is paid $6.5 million to run an $82 million football business. Ask yourself whether coaching college football is really that much harder than running a huge, complex charity that supplies half of the nation's blood and responds to hurricanes, fires, and other disasters. Or, in the entertainment-driven economy that now prevails, do we simply value college football more?

One of the standard defenses of million-dollar coaches is "Look at all of the money football brings in." True, football is often the biggest and richest department on campus. But college football coaches are paid far more than CEOs of similarly sized private companies, salary data show. In some cases their cash payments exceed those of CEOs of Fortune 500 firms. In 2013 Saban collected more than the CEOs of Costco, Procter & Gamble, Starbucks, and Delta Air Lines, according to salary data published in the *New York Times*. While many CEOs also receive valuable stock options, the underlying point is still revealing. Saban's salary alone accounts for 8 percent of the football budget, a far higher percentage than the salaries of the CEOs of private firms.

As a group, the top one hundred college football coaches are paid a staggering $200 million. And then there are the many perks of the job: luxury cars, country-club memberships, free tickets, skybox suites for families and friends to watch the games, accountants to help with taxes, extra pay to cover (gross up) taxes, and tens of thousands of dollars or more in bonuses for winning championships or finishing among the top twenty-five teams.

Most of the top football powers now also include bonuses for meeting academic goals. However, these rewards pale in comparison to what coaches get for winning titles. According to a copy of his contract, Florida State's head coach, Jimbo Fisher, earns a $25,000 bonus if 65 percent to 84 percent of his players graduate in six years. On the other hand, if Fisher's team wins the Atlantic Coast Conference, he collects $100,000. And if the team wins the national championship, he gets $400,000 ($200,000 for qualifying and $200,000 for winning).

Here you might ask: Why doesn't the NCAA do something to address this situation? The short answer is that it can't. In the mid-1990s the NCAA tried to place a cap on the salaries of assistant coaches, but the coaches filed an antitrust claim and won a $66 million judgment. Since then the NCAA has been reduced to the role of bystander. Besides,

Mark Emmert, the organization's president, is paid $1.7 million, which doesn't give him much standing to tell the coaches they are overpaid.

•   •   •

One of the less visible impacts of paying football coaches as if they were corporate titans is the cascading effect it has had on the salaries of assistant coaches and athletic directors. Not surprisingly, when the head coach gets millions, his nine full-time assistant coaches want more too—which is exactly what has happened in the last decade: Pay packages for assistant coaches at elite football programs have ballooned from $100,000 to $1 million or more at some schools. Athletic directors' paychecks have also soared and now average $500,000 at elite football schools. In 2013 nine athletic directors collected $1 million or more, according to public tax returns and university records.

It is one thing for the largest and richest schools to overpay their coaches. With the vast wealth they accumulate from television deals, tickets, and seat donations, they can probably afford to be overly generous. But there are only sixty or so schools that fit this description. The remainder—the sixty-plus other schools that play Division I football—don't have the luxury of these income streams. Most operate on a shoestring and lose millions of dollars each season. In the last decade, though, pay for head football coaches at these schools (Ohio University, Florida Atlantic, Western Kentucky, Toledo, Eastern Michigan, and Florida International, among others) has doubled in many cases, to between $500,000 and $1 million.

"A lot of these schools can't afford it, but they do it anyway because they want to compete at a higher level, and in order to get there they think they have to pay their coaches like the larger schools," said Jeff Smith, an instructor of accounting and finance at the University of

South Carolina Upstate, who has written about the effect of college sports on rising student fees and subsidies.

In October 2013 I flew to Ohio to visit with the president of one of these aspirant schools, the University of Akron. Akron has played football since the late 1800s. It has enjoyed its moments of glory but has struggled lately. The Zips are 59-107 for this century, meaning they have won just one of every three games. Still, Akron keeps trying. A few years back it opened a shiny new football stadium that cost $62 million. The stadium is often half filled, so, like many of the schools in the Mid-American Conference, Akron has to give away or buy its own tickets to meet minimum NCAA attendance requirements for playing Division I football. In 2012 the football program lost $4.2 million.

That year Akron hired Terry Bowden to help revive its program. Bowden, the son of former Florida State head coach Bobby Bowden, was once the head coach at Auburn, where he lost his job despite posting a 47-17-1 record. He is by all accounts a good coach. After years out of the game, he landed at Akron, where he was rewarded with the biggest contract in the school's history: $2 million over five years. Bowden and the Zips stumbled the first season, going 1-11, but improved to 5-7 his second year.

"We consider ourselves lucky to have Terry. He brings a huge amount of excitement to the campus and is making progress," Akron's president, Luis Proenza, told me.

"Did you have to pay him more than the last coach to hire him?"

"Yes. That's just the reality. It costs a lot for a good head coach."

"How do you measure whether he's worth it?"

Proenza paused to look around his spacious office, which was decorated with many kangaroos, Zippy the Kangaroo being the school's mascot. "It's hard to measure," he said. "There's a level of value that's tangible but fickle."

I had no idea what "tangible but fickle" meant, so I suggested, "What about wins?"

"Yes, that is the ultimate goal," Proenza replied. "We want to be successful at football. We have made a significant investment. It's here to stay."

I had one last question. "So if Terry does manage to turn it around," I said, "what's to stop him from leaving for a bigger school and more money?"

Proenza smiled at me and said it was a good question. "He has told us he wants to stay here," he said. "I am taking him at his word."

•   •   •

One measure of any market is the talent it overlooks. I was thinking about this as I drove across eastern Ohio under a flag blue October sky on my way to meet Larry Kehres, the best football coach you never heard of and maybe the best college football coach ever. Kehres won a staggering 332 games and lost only 24 as the head coach of Mount Union College (now University of Mount Union). In twenty-seven years his teams won eleven Division III national championships—or nearly a championship every other year. He surely would have won more, but at the age of sixty-four Kehres decided he had proved whatever he needed to prove and retired as football coach while keeping his "second job" as athletic director.

Kehres named his son Vince as his replacement. Lest you think this was favoritism, Vince had worked as a Mount Union assistant coach for twelve years, and he had gotten that job only after writing his father a detailed letter explaining why he should be hired. Vince went 28-2 in his first two seasons as head coach, losing only in the Division III championship each year.

It was not easy finding Larry Kehres. I rolled down one Blue Highway after another, cutting across withered cornfields and flyspeck towns ruined by time. One minute it was Norman Rockwell, the next it was *True Detective*. Alliance, Ohio, the home of Mount Union, tilts toward Rockwell, a picturesque merger of old and new, which was the case with the college campus as well. Larry Kehres was waiting for me in his office in the athletic complex. He is a big man with piercing gray blue eyes and a rough flattop. I'd been warned not to expect much—Larry wasn't a big talker and especially didn't like to talk about himself—so of course we hit it off immediately and wound up talking for several hours.

For the last thirty-nine years Kehres had been either an assistant coach or head coach at Mount Union. He'd also gone to school there and played quarterback. In fact, the only time Kehres hadn't been at Mount Union was when he was a graduate assistant coach at Bowling Green University for two years in the early seventies and then when he was a high school coach for one year. Otherwise, his life had been defined by Mount Union, family, and football. The question I had was why, with all of his success, had he never left?

In a sense, the answer was right there in front of me. Kehres had a spacious office, but apart from a picture of Larry on the sidelines and a pigskin scrawled with names, there was almost no evidence of football. Kehres loved football but he wasn't owned by it. If a star player's sister planned her wedding for October, he didn't make a fuss but urged the player to attend. Kehres followed a no-cut rule, as did all of the other sports at Mount Union: If you came out for the team and practiced, you suited up on Saturday. His squads were bigger than those at Ohio State, and Mount Union didn't give out athletic scholarships. The previous year the team had started out with 198 players and finished with 160. It still functioned the way college sports were supposed to before they became a commodity and a brand.

"I lived for backyard football growing up," Kehres told me. "Creating plays. Do you have to count to three before you can rush? We played Sunday-afternoon football. At church I used to use the back of those prayer cards to create some plays." Here Kehres laughed as if he were revealing a secret. "I loved the creativity of what football allowed. That's what I always loved about football."

Kehres grew up fifteen miles from Alliance in a town of three hundred. His dad worked in a nearby factory, and his mom took care of the kids. He was a good enough high school football player to get "some recognition," but not good enough to get recruited by the bigger schools. Kehres was okay with that, just as he was with attending Mount Union. It was a good school with good football and close enough that his parents could watch him play. It did not hurt that his sweetheart, Linda, was studying nearby to be a teacher. Part of the answer as to why Kehres never left was the role of geography and his deep sense of place. "I was just always comfortable here. It's where I grew up, what I knew. It was a good place to raise a family."

Still, there must have been offers, I suggested.

"Some," Kehres said, "but it was never as if my phone was ringing off the hook."

The previous day I had visited the president of Akron University, who, in the middle of our conversation, had casually informed me that he'd tried to hire Larry Kehres. When I mentioned this to Kehres, he merely shrugged. Maybe Akron had and maybe it hadn't. Imagination and age have a way of coloring memories. No doubt a lot of college presidents wished they had hired Kehres.

The one school that did come close was Kent State, a Division I football school that plays in the Mid-American Conference and made a serious run at Kehres in the early 2000s. The money was certainly better, and while it would have been a step up in competition, Kehres thought he could make his system work there and be successful. It was as close as he would ever get to a boast, which he quickly followed with an equivocation: "It's a little presumptuous to think that you can do okay at any level."

"So you don't think you can just jump to the next level?"

"No. Maybe you can be a successful assistant, work your way up."

"Did anyone try to hire you as an assistant?"

"No one else came after me."

This was still shocking to me, but Kehres didn't seem bothered. "When I didn't take the job and announced I would be staying, I felt really, really good," he said.

I asked about money. When Kehres started at Mount Union, he earned $9,300 a year. In addition to his job as an assistant football coach, he was also the swimming coach. "It was for no extra pay. They gave me a choice. I could either coach swimming or tennis. We had no swim team. I had to start the team. I liked that notion."

Mount Union raised Kehres's salary after he turned down Kent State. He also took over as athletic director. At his peak he earned about $200,000, which is a lot in Alliance, Ohio, but still one third of what he would have made as an assistant coach at Ohio State or another big-time program and one tenth of what he would have made as a head coach.

"Honestly, I've realized for a long time that increased salary doesn't necessarily bring better family unity or contentedness, or the success of your children," Kehres said. "Money just won't do that. My wife was always working. She liked her job. Together we didn't lack for anything. And I still feel that way. I wouldn't change anything."

A few days later I called Linda Kehres to get her take on her husband's choices. One of the first things she told me was "We've had a great run—no regrets."

Then she shared something I found revealing about Kehres and coaching. She told me that when they would travel to coaches' meetings, she would sit by the pool with the other wives while Larry was at a work session. "One time I was talking with a woman whose husband was an assistant at a Division I school, and she was talking about all of the distractions and how hard it was. She was envious when I told her we were at a D-III school. 'You know, that's really football,' she said. 'It's football first. You play for the love of football.' She said that, and it was kind of like I understood. Our guys play for the love of the game. I think that's why Larry loves it so much. It's always been about the game first and none of the other distractions."

•   •   •

Charlie Weis didn't exactly wander off into the wilderness after losing his dream job at Notre Dame. He spent a year directing the offense for the Kansas City Chiefs, then one season as the offensive coordinator at the University of Florida, where at $800,000 he was the highest-paid assistant coach. Then, in December 2011, a surprising thing happened: The University of Kansas called, asking Weis to be its new head football coach.

It would be nice at this point if the story of Charlie Weis became a redemption tale. But if Weis was indeed looking for redemption, Kansas wasn't necessarily the best choice. For one thing, it wasn't a football school—it was a basketball school. In fact, Kansas was one of the only Division I schools that made more money playing basketball than football— this even though it belonged to one of the largest and richest football conferences in the nation, the Big 12. It was rare that Kansas basketball didn't rank in the top ten. The football team, on the other hand, hadn't won a conference title since 1968, the year Richard Nixon was elected to his first term. And only one of the Jayhawks' last eleven coaches had posted a winning record.

Its recent history was even less encouraging, if possible. Since 2000 Kansas had won fewer than 40 percent of its games. Not surprisingly, the fans didn't bother going to the games, and ticket sales were in a tailspin—all of which helped to explain why Kansas hired Weis in the first place. It was looking for a name, someone who could give its sagging program a boost.

Kansas's athletic director, Sheahon Zenger, told reporters that he "set out to find the best and I found Charlie Weis." Zenger certainly paid Weis as if he were the best, awarding him a five-year deal at $2.5 million a year. Weis could earn an additional $50,000 for winning five Big 12 Conference games, $100,000 for a conference championship, $50,000 for appearing in a bowl game, and another $50,000 for being named conference coach of the year. All of this, of course, was in addition to his generous severance from Notre Dame.

The Jayhawks had churned though four head football coaches prior to hiring Weis. Turner Gill, who preceded Weis, was fired after just two seasons and a 5-19 record. Kansas owed him $6 million for the remaining three years of his five-year, $10 million contract. His assistants were owed another $2 million, according to published reports.

The question now was whether all of the money that Kansas had agreed to pay Charlie Weis would translate into wins—and how quickly. The initial results weren't encouraging. In 2012 the team finished 1-11. Always blunt, Weis characterized the program as "downtrodden." The following season the media picked Kansas to finish last in the Big 12, and Weis didn't bother to argue the point, observing, "We've given you no evidence or no reason to be picked anywhere other than that," he told reporters at a preseason media gathering. The Jayhawks finished 3-9. So in two years Weis was 4-20, with just one more win than Gill.

This time, Zenger said, Kansas was going to stay the course. "Wins and losses aren't always indicative of the effort put in by this coaching staff and these players over the past couple of years," the athletic director told the *Kansas City Star.*

It was hard to tell if it was apathy or panic in the air in Lawrence. Instead of recruiting high school players to slowly build the program, Weis was now leaning heavily on junior-college players for a quick burst of success. His 2013 recruiting class included fifteen players from junior colleges. Another eight arrived the following year. This wasn't an entirely surprising approach, as Bill Snyder at archrival Kansas State had been successfully mining junior colleges for years. There was a lot of talent playing at these smaller, out-of-the-way schools. But it was a risky tactic, as most of these players were in junior colleges for a reason: They had flubbed their high school studies and were desperately trying to reboot and become academically eligible for a Division I scholarship.

In any case, the strategy didn't work. Kansas stumbled again in 2014, barely beating lower-division Southeast Missouri State in its opener and then losing to Duke—Duke!—41–3. After being shut out 23–0 by a struggling Texas team, Zenger suddenly reversed himself and fired Weis four games into his third season with a 6-22 record.

"I normally do not favor changing coaches in midseason," the athletic director said in a prepared statement, "but I believe we have talented coaches and players in this program, and this decision gives our players the best chance to begin making progress right away." Kansas replaced Weis with one of his assistants and went on to lose its next four games, including a 60–14 blowout by Baylor, leaving it in last place in the conference.

None of which meant Charlie Weis wouldn't get paid. With two and a half years left on his contract, Kansas owed Weis $5.625 million, due by December 31, 2016. That meant the school owed nearly $12 million for its last two football coaches alone, who, combined, had won just 11 games while losing 41.

An athletic department spokeswoman promised to pass along my interview request to Weis. But I never heard back from either of them. I don't doubt that Charlie Weis is a good football coach. He just wasn't especially lucky at college football. Apparently Kansas officials didn't see it that way when they gambled millions on him. Or maybe they didn't look very hard. Maybe they overlooked his shortcomings because of his pedigree. They wouldn't be the first football school to make that mistake. After all, how else can you explain a system in which two schools were now paying Weis nearly $23 million not to coach?

Four

·   ·   ·

WALKING WITH MR. BALDWIN: IN THE LAND OF ACCIDENTAL STUDENTS

BY THE TIME I ARRIVED in Lawrence, Kansas, in April 2013, spring was already vaulting ahead to summer. The change occurred so suddenly that it was disorienting, with the temperature surging nearly thirty degrees in a few hours. Students poured out of their dorm rooms in large, noisy clusters and sprawled across the quads, luxuriating in the warm sun with bare legs and arms, a few even shirtless, others in baggy neon shirts and shorts.

I'd come to Lawrence to hang out with the walkers, or, as the athletic department chose to call them, class checkers. Their job was to make sure athletes got to their classes, log them in, and then report back to the coaches. "Athletes" in this case was largely understood to mean football and basketball players. Those two groups were by far the most efficient at avoiding class, though occasionally the walkers might have to shadow a runner or a softball player. But generally the athletes in the poor sports—those that didn't make money or appear regularly on television—weren't the problem. Also, there was only so much money to go around, and given that football was picking up the tab, it only made sense that their players got special attention.

I preferred the term "walkers" because that was mostly what they did—walking from one end of the thousand-acre campus to the other, taking up their stations outside designated classrooms, and waiting for football and basketball players to show up. On an average morning the walkers might cover four miles and climb hundreds of steps. It was one small piece of a costly and elaborate system the University of Kansas used to keep its athletes eligible to compete. The athletic department also employed more than one hundred tutors, reading and writing specialists, disability experts to deal with players with attention deficit and other learning disorders, psychologists, and other specialists. For all intents and purposes the athletic department was operating a charter school exclusively for football players and other athletes, which was even housed in an athletic-department building. These efforts cost the Kansas athletic department $3 million a year.

Every school in the five superconferences that dominate college football effectively has its own version of Kansas's program. These are typically called academic support centers, and while it's hard to say what it costs in the aggregate to keep thousands of football players eligible, a conservative, back-of-the-envelope estimate would be north of $100 million annually. That does not include the debt associated with building the separate schools and stocking them with computers, books, and other supplies. That would add another $100 million, give or take a few million.

From the universities' perspective, opening charter schools for football players was the responsible, even moral thing to do. Why wouldn't they help players adjust to college life, negotiate their courses, pick majors, and arrive for class? After all, football is a demanding sport. Athletes put in forty hours a week lifting weights, practicing, and playing games, and it's understandably hard getting out of bed for class when they're so exhausted. And because the players generate so much money for their athletic departments, it seems only right to help them achieve a degree in return.

Wait, that's not fair, I remember thinking the first time I heard a version of this argument, which seemed to me a matter of covering up a failure by calling it a success. These schools accepted athletes who didn't come remotely close to meeting their admissions criteria and then spent millions propping them up. What about all of the other students who might benefit from tutoring and special classes—the real students, in other words? Where were their walkers? Their learning centers? Didn't they have trouble getting out of bed in the morning too?

It is now generally accepted as a given that some elite football players are seriously unprepared to handle the academic requirements of college and/or aren't especially interested in learning. At a number of football powers, it is considerably more than "some." According to internal reports from those schools, scores of football recruits arrived with SAT scores 200 to 400 points below those of other incoming freshmen. A surprising number read at grade-school levels. Given that, the schools had to do something, so they hired reading and writing specialists who coached players on how to sound out words and construct a simple paragraph.

Prize recruits have come to expect—in fact, *demand*—the assistance. After all, they could go to any school, and they aren't likely to pick one that will let them slip through the cracks, lose their eligibility, and ruin their chances of going pro. A tour of the academic support center is now a critical piece of recruiting: Okay, you showed me the state-of-the-art weight room; now show me the new and improved academic facilities.

And if a phalanx of tutors, advisers, and learning specialists isn't waiting for them when they arrive, they are gone, tour over.

An arms race has now arisen to see who can build the biggest, most lavish learning center—part of a larger, billion-dollar arms race in college athletics. So far the University of Oregon is winning, hands down. A few years back it unveiled a $42 million, three-story glass and steel cube known as the Jaqua Academic Center, exclusively for athletes. The money came from Phil and Penny Knight. Phil, a onetime 1:53 Oregon half-miler, is the founder of Nike, the multibillion-dollar shoe and apparel company that has helped to transform college athletics from an activity to a brand. There are many impressive features in the Jaqua Center, including white oak floors and a large flat-panel screen on the first floor that lists tutor times. One of the more unusual flourishes is a neon profile of Phil in the women's bathroom on the second floor; one of Penny hung in the men's bathroom. "It's a little weird," an Oregon official shrugged when I asked about them. But then again, "a little weird" is okay when someone is writing you a check for $42 million.

•　　•　　•

One of the questions I had was whether football players received a real education—meaning an experience mirroring that of actual students with real majors and real career paths—or something less than that, a form of faux education. There are, after all, ways to get through college without learning very much.

As I combed through football media guides profiling each player, it quickly became apparent that football players tend to cluster in certain majors at much higher rates than the general student population. Four of the most popular included communications, general studies (which, as it sounds, is more of a primer than an actual major), public administration, and sociology. In many cases these majors required less work: fewer credits, labs, papers, or math and science courses. Fifty-two percent of Baylor University football players, for example, were enrolled in general studies, which I learned was not an accident.

"It allows you to be a little more flexible with [their] academic plan," Baylor's athletic director, Ian McCaw, explained to me during a visit. "Our goal is to graduate athletes. We've got some taking premed and prelaw. Some tend to be in general studies. Some move into other majors. It's a popular major, and those kids seem to do well."

Texas A&M offers 120 different majors, according to the school's Web site. Among the more popular are business, management, engineering, and biology. Forty-seven percent of the varsity football players listed in the 2013 A&M media guide were enrolled in agriculture leadership and development. Another 13 percent of the players were majoring in recreation, parks, and tourism. One brave soul was majoring in physics.

Athletic directors argue that at least the players get a degree, which is better than no degree at all, and, not surprisingly, the NCAA appears to side with them. It even has a number of metrics to gauge the progress athletes make toward graduation. The data are valuable up to a point but really don't tell you much. In 2006 the NCAA started to collect data on majors, but its analysis is only inches deep. It does not, for example, break out results for the problem sports of football and basketball, let alone publish university-specific numbers, which might embarrass individual schools. More broadly the most important measure—how football players actually do after they graduate—is nowhere to be found.

"What you really want to know are the later life outcomes," William Bowen, the former president of Princeton University and the author of several books on athletics and academics, told me. "What you want to focus on is not so much what students look like when they come. You want to look at when they go out and what they look like ten years later."

Athletic directors argue that they don't have that luxury, as they are too busy looking at now to worry about what happens a decade in the future. Another unspoken concern is that they need to ensure that the money keeps flowing, and the way they do that is by keeping their best players on the field. For them, then, it is not only morally correct but also logical to spend millions of dollars ensuring that football players get up for class and attend mandatory study halls and tutoring sessions.

But to someone outside the bubble, it feels dangerously close to making a mockery of the university's purpose and seems like possibly another symbol of the absurd privilege and excess of college football. The system feels inverted: Schools are rewarding the wrong students, heavily investing in athletes with inferior academic skills at the expense of their brightest, most ambitious students.

Paul Buskirk, the director of Kansas's academic support program, takes a pragmatic approach to the issue. "It's not my proudest moment that we have class checkers," he told me. "I wish we didn't have to, that students would go to class. But the coaches believe it is an appropriate thing to have, and I have to admit it is efficient." The idea, he added, was not to hide in the bushes and yell, "Gotcha!" "The class checkers stand out in the open and greet the students. I refer to them as our varsity ambassadors."

The situation seemed almost normal the way Buskirk described it. And I liked that he used the word "efficient." However, I couldn't help wondering what an *inefficient* class-checking system would look like. Years ago Kansas used students to keep tabs on its athletes, but that got messy in a hurry. The athletes didn't like being followed and came up with what I like to think of as an innovative solution: They began bribing the students with free tickets to their games. It got so bad the athletic department had to hire a retired cop to follow the student checkers. Finally, about a decade ago, Kansas abandoned student checkers in favor of its current system, which uses retired teachers and truck drivers, among others, to keep track of the athletes. The older walkers are harder to manipulate and aren't particularly expensive, earning minimum wage.

· · ·

The following morning I arrived at the Hale Center for Academic Achievement at 8:00 A.M. Ken Baldwin, my walker/escort, had already been there an hour handing out laptops and logging in athletes for prearranged tutoring sessions. The sessions run continuously from sunup to sundown and sometimes later. Many but not all involve football players. One player who showed up late began to work on Baldwin to mark him as being on time. His excuses were a version of "the dog ate my homework": His alarm didn't go off. There was a power outage at his dorm. The exchange went on awkwardly for five minutes, but Baldwin stood his ground—all five feet six inches of him. "I love these kids," he told me after the player finally retreated, "but I can't do it. I can't change the time."

Baldwin is sixty-six years old, fair, and trim. He has thinning gray blond hair and a scant gray beard. His eyes are milky blue. This morning he was wearing cargo shorts, running shoes, and a blue KU athletic jersey. In many respects he looked like a smaller, older version of the athletes he was paid to chase around campus. When I mentioned this, he laughed and informed me he had been a mediocre high school student and "couldn't get within a mile of this place. Now I probably know every square inch."

After high school Baldwin served in Vietnam and then went to work at Hallmark Cards as a printer. He stayed at that job for thirty-seven years, until he retired in 2002. One day a friend of his, Don Gardner, a retired cop, asked if he wanted to work as a class checker. The KU athletic department was in the market for more retirees.

"I needed something to do," Baldwin recalled. "I had tried a couple of part-time jobs. They were okay. I enjoyed them. This seemed really ideal. I'm up early. I get some exercise. I get to be with kids. I have my afternoons off to do what I need. I have a little extra money. We can go out to eat on Friday night." Baldwin had been a class checker for eleven years at the time of my visit and estimated he had logged ten thousand miles roving the hilly campus.

A little before nine we headed outside. The wind was furling and unfurling the flags, strong and warm off the plains. Baldwin started off at a brisk pace toward the student center, where other class checkers gathered for coffee and gossip before starting their rounds. There were fifteen, he informed me, including at least one PhD. When we arrived at the food court, Baldwin introduced me around, but as soon as he told them I was writing a book, coffee hour abruptly ended and the checkers scattered to the wind.

Baldwin and I headed northeast toward the football stadium, which squats in a bosky glade below campus. "When the weather is nice, like today, I like to stick to the pathways," he said. "But in winter, or when the weather is bad, I use the underground tunnels. I can pretty much get anywhere on campus that way."

Each morning around 8:00 A.M. one of the academic advisers gives Baldwin and the other walkers a list of athletes they want tracked that day. The schedule includes the name of the student, the classroom building and class number, and a place for the student to sign in when he arrives. "I like to get there about fifteen minutes before class starts, and I stick around ten minutes after that," Baldwin explained. "If the athlete hasn't shown up by then, I'm gone."

The first building we stopped at was the administration building, a long limestone rectangle that vaguely resembled the Pentagon. We settled on the third floor outside a classroom where a freshman-level math class was starting in a few minutes. The football player we were waiting for—let's call him G—arrived a minute or two before class and wordlessly signed in. A basketball player, on the other hand, never appeared, but Baldwin didn't seem surprised. "This time of year I don't expect him to show up."

I was curious what Baldwin thought about shadowing football players and the elaborate infrastructure KU had set up exclusively for athletes. "It's part of the guarantee that we make to students is the way I look at it," he said. Especially in the summer months, when football recruits arrived to train, take a few classes, and get adjusted, he liked to "start a relationship and get to know them. We try to show them we're not just a bunch of old people with blue books. We are your friends."

Even so, some of the athletes "try to work you," Baldwin said. "If there are multiple doors to a classroom, they will come in one and want to go out the other. Sometimes they will get flagged by the instructor. But some are just going to try. They always try."

One of the auditoriums we visited had more than one thousand seats with seven doors on the first floor alone—and there were three floors. "The more doors, the harder it is to check," Baldwin said. "It becomes a game of cat and mouse. When we catch them, they'll say something like 'Aw, I'm just funning with you.'" Baldwin's solution was to arrange a designated meeting place. "That way, they know where we are supposed to be. You can fool us once in a while, but we're going to get you sooner or later."

We ended the morning outside another auditorium in Budig Hall. It was here I noticed an engraving on a curved wall that seemed to nicely capture the purpose of the academic-support enterprise at Kansas. It was a takeoff on the old Hillary Clinton "It takes a village" maxim: "It takes a campus to graduate a student."

Later I asked Paul Buskirk, the director of academic support, if he had seen the inscription, and he told me no. "But I like it," he said. "It makes a lot of sense."

I could practically hear the gears spinning in his head.

*   *   *

The previous night I'd met Buskirk and several of his colleagues in a large auditorium at the Hale Center. They had invited me to sit in on a session where they were debriefing the tutors and settling up at the end of another academic year. Most of the discussion involved paperwork and when the tutors' final checks would be issued. There was also an obligatory reminder about ethics, including a warning about not accepting gifts from athletes. Roughly fifty tutors attended the meeting—half of the total. One of the directors told me they ranged from undergraduates to retired professors. Pay was commensurate with experience but generally ranged from ten dollars to fifteen dollars per hour. At any given time roughly 350 athletes were being tutored, including most of the football and basketball players.

"What does that work out to in terms of weekly sessions?" I asked.

"We average fifteen hundred to sixteen hundred sessions per week," the director of tutoring, Michelle Martin, said.

For some reason I was taken aback by the number, which sounded too big, but when I asked for confirmation, Michelle said, "No, that's right."

Over the years there have been many scandals involving tutors and athletes, including most recently one that deeply scarred the University of North Carolina and cost the school its football coach and its chancellor. According to one academic adviser, some of the North Carolina players arrived on campus unable to read or write. They were cutting and pasting entire papers from the Internet. At least one tutor was reportedly writing the players' papers for them. Scores of football and basketball players were also enrolled in so-called paper classes, which required only a single paper to pass. To date a tutor and a professor have been indicted, and the school has spent more than $1 million defending itself. Recently an independent investigation found that the cheating had been going on for eighteen years. And the truly damning detail was that North Carolina had been considered a model for how to balance education and sports.

I asked Martin how the Kansas tutors protected themselves against cheating and other abuses. "We are constantly reminding the tutors about doing too much work for the student athletes and about ethics," she said. "It's tricky. There is a line: What can they do and not do for students? What can they give and accept? The tutors are there to guide, not to do the editing. They try to walk the students through the process. It's the Socratic method."

"How much does all of that cost?" I asked.

Martin and Buskirk looked at each other, as if trying to decide whether the figure was secret. "About four hundred forty thousand dollars," Buskirk finally said, and Martin nodded in agreement.

* * *

The Kansas athletic program has not been without its challenges. The football team in particular has struggled over the years to meet the

NCAA's minimum graduation rate and has been targeted on two occasions for special interventions—what Kansas called football improvement plans—to improve its dismal academic performance.

In 2003, following a 2-10 season, the school recruited a dozen junior-college players with the aim of quickly boosting its record. Several of the players arrived on campus without enough credits to play and enrolled in correspondence courses through Brigham Young University to cover their deficits. According to a subsequent NCAA investigation, some of the players received improper assistance, and two were purportedly given test answers by a graduate assistant. Buskirk told NCAA investigators it was a "stressful" time with a lot of pressure from the head coach to help the players. "Here comes this demand from an intimidating and occasionally verbally abusive head football coach saying they will get it done and they will get it done on our campus, boom," he stated, according to the NCAA report.

Kansas was placed on probation for five years and lost a number of football scholarships. Since then the football team's academic performance has improved. But now the new head football coach, Charlie Weis, was again recruiting large numbers of junior-college players in an attempt to reverse a 4-20 record in his first two seasons. I wondered if the program was at risk of repeating its previous mistakes.

Buskirk acknowledged that the junior-college players present "more complicated profiles" than other students. They often arrived on campus with giant holes in their transcripts. Many of them had loaded up on easy electives in junior college while avoiding tougher courses like math and science. But now, with their electives maxed out, they had nowhere to hide. "It makes it tough," Buskirk granted. "They are training, trying to make the team. Now they have to take math."

Buskirk couldn't afford to judge; he was, above all, a pragmatist who recognized the challenges and tried to solve them. In any case, he explained, Kansas has a lot more experience today dealing with junior-college players than it had a decade ago. "We don't treat them differently," he said, "but we work with them differently."

Inevitably this includes more hand-holding. Junior-college players spend the summer in Lawrence taking classes, getting tested, and polishing their library and research skills, as well as being schooled in life skills. In this respect Kansas is hardly alone. Most if not all football powers now bring their recruits and transfers to campus in the summer to train and study. It is a way to help them adjust, pile up credits, and stay out of trouble. But it too comes with a hefty price tag. Kansas spends more than $1 million on summer school, and if you multiply that figure by fifty or a hundred schools, you are talking about real money. "It's expensive," Buskirk says, "but we think it is a good investment."

•   •   •

At first glance Paul Buskirk seems like an unlikely candidate to do battle with burly football coaches over issues regarding recruits, eligibility, and academic performance. He is a slight, gentle man, with a neatly kept graying beard and glasses. His father and grandfather were both Presbyterian ministers, and for a time Buskirk thought he might follow them into the ministry. In 1987 he left his job as a counselor at the university and enrolled in a seminary in Austin, Texas. But after one semester he decided it wasn't for him and he returned to Lawrence.

Buskirk had previously worked with the athletic department but in a less formal role. When a position opened for a full-time academic support director in 1989, he "swung for the fences," he said. One of the first things he did when he got the job was bring the tutoring program in-house. From there he slowly built up the staff and added more services.

"Initially the budget might have been a few hundred thousand dollars," Buskirk recalled. "We got a big bump in the early 2000s when the athletic budget grew from $22 million to $45 million." Today the athletic-department budget is just south of $90 million; the budget for academic support: $3 million. There are six full-time counselors and three full-time tutor coordinators, as well as several learning specialists. "We clearly have students who have been passed along," Buskirk said. "We've got to teach them how to read and write. Some are ju co [junior college], some high school."

In the late 2000s Kansas built the two-story complex that now houses the Hale Center. There are dozens of rooms for tutoring, a large computer lab, space for advisers and specialists, an auditorium, even a lounge where players can relax. Kansas now graduates 85 percent of its athletes. "My best day of the year is May 19, when we watch them gather at the top of the hill . . . to walk down to commencement" in the football stadium, Buskirk says proudly.

Listening to Buskirk it was easy to get swept along in his narrative. Certainly it is better to graduate football players than to not graduate them. It is only when you take a few steps back that some of the inspirational notes wash away. Why would a school accept someone who can't read or write in the first place? And what does it say about a university that it is willing to spend millions of dollars and erect an entirely separate academic infrastructure to hand-hold its athletes for four, five, or even six years? Is this really the new normal in athletics?

Buskirk didn't seem to mind the question and even appeared to welcome it. However meek he may look, you don't survive in his job for twenty-eight years without some intestinal fortitude and smarts. It wasn't his role to decide if what he is doing is right or wrong, he explained. "My role is to deliver part of the promise every coach makes. And I know what they say: Come to Kansas, and we will give you every chance to succeed athletically and academically." Then he considered the other side of the argument: "I know what the provost will say: If only we had the same resources to do for every kid what we do for the five hundred [Kansas] athletes. We have a program that is not available for every other kid. So they are being disadvantaged. Yeah, you can argue that."

•   •   •

The day after I left Lawrence, a blue norther roared across the plains, and the temperature plummeted back into the fifties. I was reading a "confidential memorandum" about Kansas athletics that had been written by the provost in 2001. It was a startling document in many respects. A large percentage of football players were failing out of school at the time, and recruits were being accepted even though they read at a fourth-grade level. The most popular fields of study then were communications and human development and family life. I pulled out my spreadsheet with the current majors and, sure enough, fifteen years later, communications was still the most popular major. Nearly one of every four football players was enrolled in the field.

Buskirk told me via e-mail that communications is a "very solid" major. "For all the students who don't want to weather the accounting and calculus requirements for [a] degree in business, this major is marketed as good preparation for [the] real world of business," he wrote. So if you wanted to go into business without the math, communications was the way to go.

More encouragingly, the spreadsheet did show that there were a few football players studying engineering, history, and math. And one was premed. The lesson I took away from all of this was that some things do change, but at a steep price. Also that a fair number of football players will always major in the sport and be students on the side. Whatever the Kansas athletic department was paying Paul Buskirk, I decided it wasn't nearly enough.

• • •

A few months later I flew out to Eugene to visit the University of Oregon's $42 million academic support center, which its director, Steve Stolp, once called "the Taj Mahal of academic services." The three-story, forty-thousand-square-foot glass and steel cube was located across from the main entrance to campus. In many respects it looked and felt like a museum of modern art. The exterior facade consisted of two giant glass frames separated by thin, vertical shades made out of steel. The shades were designed to resemble rain falling, and from across the street that was exactly the effect they produced: rain slowly cascading down a gray bank of fog. The shades automatically opened and shut depending on the outside temperature. If you listened quietly, they made a shivery hissing sound, like lawn sprinklers coming to life on an early-summer morning.

There were two main doors, but not just any glass doors. Each weighed 820 pounds. When the center opened in 2010, visitors could push the doors and they would automatically slide open. But apparently some of the athletes pushed too hard, and the doors broke. "The German engineers were here every week," Stolp recalled. Now visitors push a button, as at a handicap entry, and the doors unwind very, very slowly.

The interior space was airy and bright and abounded with dramatic flourishes, from the names of athletes laser-etched onto the walls and floors to a three-story mural of Albert Einstein dangling in the atrium. When you studied the mural closely, you saw that it was actually a collection of five thousand images of Oregon athletes stitched together on forty stainless steel panels. Stolp explained that it was supposed to depict a day in the life of the athletes. The walls were also covered with many inspirational slogans carved into them, including a line from a philosopher about courage and wisdom, as well as a sillier one that exclaimed: "Ducks Are Quacking to Learn." Oregon, after all, being the Ducks.

The architects and engineers had simply outdone themselves. And why not? They were playing with house money. In this case the money belonged to Phil and Penny Knight, who took control of the project, set up a limited-liability company, Phit LLC, paid for all of the design studies and construction, and then handed the finished product back to the university. It was how Phil liked to do business, several people at Oregon informed me. He didn't like to mess around with bidding requirements or have to wait while bureaucrats debated what to do next.

Knight and Nike have transformed Oregon in the last two decades from a regional university with middling academic and athletic programs to a nationally ranked power in sports, especially football, and improved but not-yet-stellar academic offerings. Following an embarrassing loss in a bowl game in the mid-1990s, Knight devoted himself to hauling Oregon athletics into the future, spending an estimated $300 million to expand Autzen Stadium, build extraordinarily lavish training facilities, help finance a new basketball arena, and, certainly not least, construct the John E. Jaqua Academic Center for athletes, named for Knight's friend, a former Nike attorney, who died shortly before the center opened in 2010.

Nike's involvement in Oregon athletics has only deepened in recent years. It lends designers, marketing, experts, and advisers on major projects while also supplying the school with its latest envelope-pushing equipment and shoes. The company uses an algorithm to help decide which uniforms the football players will wear on Saturdays. There are more than one hundred possible choices, I was informed. Nike employees play with the combinations of jerseys and helmets, mixing and matching colors for each game, going all black one week and neon yellow the next. Some weeks the players don't know what color they will wear until hours before the game. "They kind of enjoy it. It is a surprise," a spokesman for the football program told me.

At odd moments it has all felt a bit much to critics, who complain that Nike and Knight have effectively taken over the university. The company's presence does seem to loom over the school to the point that there are even Nike swooshes on some of the trash cans. It is all part of the art of Nike and the extraordinary reach of Knight and his personal brand. You can argue this a lot of ways, the earnest efforts of a dedicated philanthropist or the branding strategy of a wily business-man being just two of them. What you cannot argue is the impact Knight has had. His brilliance, or overreach, is everywhere. (I tried to interview Knight, but Nike officials did not respond to my e-mails or phone messages.)

It had taken me months to get an invitation to Oregon, but once it arrived I found officials there to be generally open about their athletic juggernaut. Unlike many football powers, Oregon doesn't try to fudge the excess. On the contrary, officials appear to celebrate it. "It helps to set us apart," said Jim Bartko, an assistant athletic director who works closely with Knight, "and it definitely helps with recruiting. The kids see us on TV, see the Nike swoosh and the cool uniforms, and they want to be part of that."

Many believe that Oregon is the future of college football, but in fact it feels like the future is now, and Oregon is it. Intercollegiate sports is all about branding—and monetizing the brand, especially football—and no one does that better than Oregon. No major football school has grown as much or as quickly. In less than a decade its athletic budget has exploded from $40 million to $115 million, and the school currently ranks ninth in size among the major football powers. Football alone generates $60 million, with $39 million, or 65 percent, falling to the bottom line. What makes this all the more impressive (or suspect, if you prefer) is that Oregon is a relatively modest-sized school with one of the smallest football stadiums among elite programs, seating just 54,000 fans, or roughly half the number that squeeze into the Texas, Ohio State, and Michigan stadiums. Even Louisville is bigger.

Oregon makes up for its lack of size by outperforming other schools financially, which is another way of saying it maximizes its revenues by charging higher ticket prices and ramping up the mandatory payments required to secure premium seats. The average price of a season ticket has soared by 300 percent in the last decade, to $451. Oregon can get away with these steep hikes because the team is wildly popular and doesn't have a lot of competition—over the last thirteen years Oregon has sold out ninety games in a row.

Bartko said Oregon has considered expanding the stadium, but it comes down to a question of geography. The nearest city of any size, Portland, is a couple of hours to the north. The population of metropolitan Eugene is only 351,000, or half that of Boise, Idaho, which isn't enough to justify adding ten thousand or twenty thousand seats. "So the question for us is do we want to have a smaller stadium that is always sold out or a larger stadium that maybe isn't always full?" asks Bartko.

Oregon also has the luxury of belonging to the Pac-12 Conference, which recently signed a $3 billion television deal with ESPN and FOX to broadcast its football and basketball games. The deal essentially doubled Oregon's annual conference payout to $22 million, with up to $32 million a year possible if the Pac-12's in-house regional network takes off as expected.

Although Oregon's athletic program is relatively small, with only nineteen varsity sports and 450 varsity athletes, it outspends many larger schools by significant margins. Some of this covers the cost of staffing. The athletic department has 221 employees, or one staff member for every two athletes. Coaches' salaries, meanwhile, have tripled since 2005 and are nearly double the national median for major football schools. The cost of putting Oregon's nationally ranked football team on the field is also climbing sharply. In 2011 Oregon spent the equivalent of $181,498 on each of its eighty-five football players on scholarship—double what it had spent just six years earlier. The most dramatic increase, however, has been in the debt on its athletic facilities. As of 2013 Oregon owed $233 million on those facilities—up from about $35 million in 2005. The annual mortgage payment alone has ballooned from $3 million to more than $19 million—a 537 percent rise.

Nathan Tublitz, a biologist who studies the nervous systems of squid, octopuses, and other cephalopods, believes the extraordinary investment in football is damaging Oregon's academic standing: "It has pushed the university in the wrong direction, away from investing in academics in favor of investing in athletics." Observing that the university now attracts fewer graduate students and does less research than before, Tublitz said, "The real tragedy is you have a lot of really smart people making really bad decisions." According to Tublitz, a faculty member who wins a summer research award—twenty are given out each year—receives $8,000. "Compare that with a football award of full tuition, room and board, food, and books, which is worth $45,000 to $50,000. There is a real disconnect."

Tublitz met me in the coffee shop on the first floor of the Jaqua Academic Center. "This is the only public space in the building," he laughed. "The second and third floors are off limits even to professors. You need a secret key code to get up there." But it could have been worse, he said. "The original design didn't even allow the general public into the building. I was the Senate Faculty president at the time and complained bitterly. I said it was contrary to the purpose of a public university. So they added a coffee shop and café. I said: Do you know how many coffee shops there are on campus? Oregon, I think, ranks number one in the nation for coffee shops. We need another coffee shop like a hole in the head."

Tublitz is a slight sixty-year-old with a long gray ponytail. I noticed his hair was wet, and he explained that he'd just come from a vigorous game of squash. "I don't dislike sports," he said. "I just don't like when they take over the university."

Tublitz has been at Oregon for twenty-six years and spends part of his time in Eugene and the other part in Italy doing research. For more than a decade he has belonged to the Coalition on Intercollegiate Athletics, a national group of similarly minded academics who are trying to reform intercollegiate athletics. "This is not an issue of jealousy," he insisted. "I don't give a shit if the administration gives every one of their coaches fancy rooms and leather couches." Tublitz's own office is a small cinderblock bunker. "What I care about is we maintain our academic integrity."

Tublitz said he worries about the athletes. "It's very hard even for a student with good academic study habits to perform well under circumstances where they are working the equivalent of a full-time job. It's incredibly stressful, especially for football players." The Jaqua Academic Center "fills a role in theory but in practice is very unrealistic," he added. "Every athlete has individual tutors for every class. They have mandatory study halls, people who look at their homework every day. They get free computers. And then the administration trumpets the fact that student athletes are graduating at the rate of the [regular] student body. I say to them, the rest of the student body doesn't get all of these perks. It's a sham. The athletes are living in a different parallel universe."

Tublitz prods me to ask about the tutoring program for other students. "It's a joke," he explained. "They've publicly admitted that there is a tenfold difference between what they spend on athletes and what they spend on other students. They put them in the basements of these 1960s-era buildings in these tiny, overheated rooms with one or two tutors. And the athletes get all of this," he said, waving his hand in the direction of an open gas-fire pit, one of the other signature strokes of the first-floor design.

"Do you know what the other students call this place?" Tublitz asked in a sharp professorial tone. "They refer to it as the Jock Box. It's beyond crazy," he said, standing to leave, "and most of the students get that."

•   •   •

In Steve Stolp's view the new academic center was helping Oregon meet its obligations to the athletes—graduation being the end goal of athletic departments everywhere. The football team, for example, had recently posted its best academic progress report in years. "Was it because of the center?" Stolp asked rhetorically. "I can't say yet. But I do know we are able to serve all of our athletes in a better way."

I had arranged to meet with Stolp in his second-floor office at the cube. I'd expected to get maybe an hour, but we ended up talking for three. Stolp was at all times generous, enduring my bollixed questions and openly sharing information.

Stolp grew up in the Bay Area and played basketball in high school. At fifty-one he still has the build of a competitor, tall and wiry, like a triathlete. (When I observed as much, he laughed. "Actually, I couldn't do the swim," he said. "I'd be so slow the sharks would eat me.") After graduating from high school in 1980, Stolp played basketball for two years at Cal State–Hayward. Then he transferred to UC Berkeley, where he did not play, to study physiology, with the intention of becoming a medical researcher. But when a doctor asked if he really wanted to spend his time humping grants, he decided to look elsewhere. After getting a master's degree in speech and a PhD in curriculum and instruction, he migrated to Oregon, where he met his wife, started a family, and veered into academic advising.

In 1998 Stolp accepted the job of director of services for student athletes. It was an interesting choice and in some respects a step backward. What passed for a tutoring center at the time was located in the annex of a musty old basketball gym. "It was just a really nasty office space," Stolp said. "It was more triage than real advising. I mean, essentially, we could only provide services and academic support to the neediest of athletes. We were not functionally able to provide the support or services that were needed." He added that the coaches didn't bother to show the center to recruits because "it was a liability."

Everything changed when Phil Knight agreed to pay for a new center in 2007. But Knight being Knight, he had a few requirements, which were spelled out in the licensing agreement between Phit LLC and the athletic department. First, he wanted control over the design, including how the center would be used, the number of professional positions, even the number of laptops—225, with an estimated price not to exceed two thousand dollars per computer. Second, the university would have to cover the salaries and operating expenses—now $2 million annually—out of general revenues. The latter provision continues to be controversial, and critics on the Senate Faculty believe the wealthy athletic department should pay its own way. In 2008 they approved a resolution calling for an end to the subsidies but, like many such resolutions, it drifted along in a kind of academic limbo. In 2012 Oregon president Michael Gottfredson endorsed the idea in concept but said "more analysis" was needed, according to Senate Faculty documents.

Stolp accompanied the planned facility's architects during their visits to study other academic support centers. They looked at Michigan, Mississippi, Georgia, LSU, and Texas Tech. They were all "impressive," Stolp says, but Knight didn't want merely impressive; he wanted the very best, which is how Oregon got the biggest, most lavish academic center for athletes in the country.

The Jaqua Academic Center opened in 2010 with a professional staff of nineteen, including six academic advisers, six learning specialists for students with ADHD and other learning deficits, a director and assistant director of life skills, and a wellness psychologist, among other positions. Initially there were forty tutors, but the figure has since doubled to eighty-five. These include juniors and seniors with exemplary grades, retired teachers, law students, and graduate students. Pay starts at ten dollars an hour and rises to fourteen dollars an hour. During the school year the center averages 1,700 sessions a week, Stolp informed me. Freshman athletes are required to put in eight hours of "structured tutoring," which generally means face-to-face sessions. If they do well enough, the number goes down. If they don't, they keep coming.

The new space and expanded services prompted Stolp and his colleagues to "reimagine" how they might provide the most useful form of assistance. In the past they had relied on large, mandatory study halls to get football players and other athletes to do their homework. "But a lot of the time they were using their time to check their draft status on ESPN," Stolp said. "It didn't work very well. Now when athletes are in study hall, they are either in one-on-one or small-group study."

Like Kansas, Oregon runs a Summer Bridge program for incoming football players. It offers a variety of classes ranging from how to use the library to managing social media. One offering, Issues of Intercollegiate Athletics, or FHS 199, caught my eye. The three-credit course was billed as an introduction to university life for athletes and required, among other assignments, watching a film about Oregon "heroes" and reading a handout: "101 Things to Do in Eugene." Students were encouraged to "do one thing on the list and respond to the discussion board." Additional topics included stress management, drugs and alcohol, and healthy relationships. Following complaints from the faculty, the class was canceled in the spring of 2013.

Oregon accepts fifteen to twenty athletes each year who do not meet university requirements—so-called special admits. Football probably accounts for the largest share. The question, Stolp said, is how do they survive in an academic environment? "A lot of these kids don't feel like they fit in or don't come to the university for academics," he said. "They come to play a sport. Selling the academic side of the institution to these kids is a big part of what we do. I think we're successful in some cases. In some cases we aren't."

Each Oregon athlete is given an Apple laptop. There is also a computer lab on the third floor with fifty-four cubicles. The room is divided into quiet areas. A flat-panel screen on the wall enables the tutors to follow along. Down the hall there is another lab with foggable glass where athletes can drop by "to have a paper assessed or get help with editing," Stolp said.

Inevitably, two questions come to mind. The first is about the return on the $42 million investment. Stolp says it is too soon to tell its effect on graduation rates, but he does think Jaqua is helping Oregon to attract better student athletes. Oregon encourages athletes to major "in whatever they want and are passionate about," Stolp added. However, as at other football schools, the players tend to cluster in a handful of majors. For example, 44 percent are majoring in sociology or general social sciences, which require fewer credits to graduate. Another 18 percent are majoring in sports marketing.

The other question goes back to something Tublitz had said earlier about Oregon athletes living in a parallel universe alongside students who do not have access to Jaqua or Oregon's many other lavish athletic facilities. How is that possibly fair or acceptable?

"There shouldn't be a wide disparity," Stolp agreed. "The goal should be for everyone at Oregon to have access to outstanding facilities and services. I think if you ask, that's what we are striving to achieve."

•   •   •

One of the best ways to experience a university is to walk it end to end. And one of the best ways to understand what it values is to see how it treats its most ambitious undergraduates. Because I was already in Eugene, I decided to visit the Robert D. Clark Honors College, which serves approximately one thousand of the University of Oregon's brightest students. Clark might also be viewed as a charter school—only a much poorer charter school than the one run by the athletic department.

I had been talking on the telephone with several professors and administrators at Clark for several weeks before I arrived at the campus, and they had all told me a version of the same story: The honors college was one of the university's greatest assets but was underappreciated and short of cash. Typical of the comments was one from Andrew McNall, Clark's director of development: "Clark is the jewel in the crown of the University of Oregon, yet our facilities don't reflect that," he said. "We educate thousands of Oregonians, but people in Oregon don't know us. And for all that we accomplish, we have a very modest budget."

"How does the honors college compare with the Jaqua Academic Center?" I asked at one point.

There was a muffled cough on the other end.

"That bad?" I asked.

"You really should see for yourself," McNall told me.

Chapman Hall, home to Clark Honors College, was easy enough to find, as it was one of the oldest buildings on campus. When it was built it was considered state of the art, but that was seventy-five years ago, in 1939, as part of the Depression-era Works Progress Administration. There are no interior staircases to reach the second and third floors. There is an elevator, but for some reason it doesn't go to the basement.

Renée V. Dorjahn, a graduate of Clark who now serves as its director of finance and administration, agreed to give me a tour. Like Andy McNall and all of the other Clark officials I spoke with, Dorjahn loves the college and everything it represents. But even so, she told me, "It is a challenged building."

For years the first floor of Chapman Hall served as a bookstore, Dorjahn explained. The third floor was the location of the home economics department. We poked our heads into a small library with a wooden wall filled with tiny drawers. Back in the day the drawers were used to store sewing projects. Pull-down ironing boards lined another room. "There is no air-conditioning except for the first floor," Dorjahn said. "It gets a little toasty on the third floor when the heat is on."

Surprisingly, there were only two classrooms in the honors college, and one was used part time. Dorjahn explained that the students take most of their classes elsewhere. One of the two classrooms was called Fireside, though that was misleading, as the fireplace hadn't worked in years. I counted six computers in the computer lab, fifty or so fewer than in the lab at Jaqua. As best I could tell, there was no cache of laptops to loan to the students.

The first floor of Clark was renovated in 2012 and is now used for administration. Dorjahn declined to say what the renovation cost, only that the money had come from a private donor. The rest of the building needed a serious upgrade. McNall put the cost at $8 million to $12 million. As recently as three years ago, Clark was near the top of the governor's list of capital projects to be funded with money from Oregon's state lottery. "We were, like, number two or three on the list," McNall said, but then the governor came out with a new list, and Clark was nowhere to be found. As of my visit, McNall had raised approximately $4 million earmarked for a major renovation.

It was here I asked what seemed like an obvious question: Why didn't Clark officials go to see Phil Knight? But apparently it wasn't that simple. You did not ask Phil, several Oregon employees told me. He liked to come up with the ideas himself.

Despite its outdated accommodations, students continue to apply to Clark in record numbers. In 2013 the honors college received 1,400 applications for 230 freshman slots. The majority were from Oregon, but that proportion was shifting as talented students washed across the border from California, where the state legislature had slashed public funding for the state university system.

"Our students can hold their own," Dorjahn proudly informed me. "We have many Fulbright scholars. We had one Rhodes scholar. Last year we had three Goldwaters. Stanford only had two."

A large percentage of Clark students qualify for academic scholarships, and some even receive full tuition. But Clark students are charged higher tuition—about three thousand dollars more—than other students, under the assumption they are receiving a more challenging and costly education. It took a moment for this to sink in: If you netted the three thousand dollars from the five-thousand-dollar grant that typical Clark students receive, Oregon's smartest students received a two-thousand-dollar scholarship in real terms. Two thousand dollars is certainly better than no dollars, but it pales next to a fifty-thousand-dollar football scholarship.

When I pointed out that it seemed as if the Clark enrollees were being penalized for being smart, McNall said, "I think there are people on our advisory council who are asking the same question," and added that there was a plan in the works to help the students, but for the time being it was still a plan.

Back in 2004 the Senate Faculty recommended that the athletic department make a voluntary contribution to help cover the cost of more generous academic awards, the idea being to establish a meaningful link between academics and athletics. But ten years later students and faculty are still waiting.

Bill Harbaugh, an economics professor at Oregon, told me the athletic department didn't want to part with its money. "The egos over there really hate the idea the academic side would get anything," he said. "They particularly hate the idea they would be forced to give anything. They see that as a loss." Harbaugh told me he liked Athletic Director Rob Mullens and thinks he is a smart guy. "But there's still no money," he said.

"Wouldn't it make sense for them to give a token amount, say, a million dollars?" I asked. "Think of all the goodwill that would generate."

Harbaugh had been down this road before. "We met with the athletic director," he said. "We were very blunt. We said, give us one percent of your budget. For very little money you can get the academic side to support you. We told him we're really cheap; you can buy us off real cheap. So we said, how about a ticket surcharge? They didn't like that idea at all. We finally said how about a penny?"

Harbaugh told me he had also met with Michael Gottfredson, but the president wasn't any more receptive. "I don't think the administration likes us faculty. They think we're freeloaders and overpaid," Harbaugh said.

Tublitz, for his part, told me the resolution was still "under consideration." But truthfully, he didn't sound all that optimistic.

•   •   •

It has become fashionable lately to argue that playing big-time college football makes your school smarter—the implication being that you would be crazy not to invest tens of millions of dollars in your football program. I suspect part of the appeal of this argument is that it goes against almost everything we know about football's effects—soaring costs, celebrity-level coaches' salaries, dumbed-down majors, cheating scandals, recruiting distractions, and so forth. But let's forget all of that for the moment and concentrate on what is, admittedly, a counterintuitive idea.

If I am understanding it correctly, I think the argument goes something like this: If you have a dynamic football team, like Oregon's, that plays on television a lot, it makes for an exciting atmosphere on campus, and the exposure helps to pump up your brand. When your brand is inflated, more students want to come to your school. By the law of large numbers, some of those students are going to be smart. And the more smart students you attract, the smarter your school.

In 2011 Oregon experienced a bump in attention when it played in the national championship, losing to Auburn. Interest in the university "just skyrocketed," Oregon's president exclaimed, and the following year's freshman class ranked among the strongest in school history.

What Oregon officials didn't note was that the growing influx of students from California was also helping to boost its profile. In recent years students who couldn't get into California's highly competitive public universities were crossing the border in large numbers to attend Oregon. In general they arrived with higher test scores and GPAs than those of the in-state pool of applicants. Today more than 45 percent of

Oregon's students are from another state, and so many come from California, the joke is that Oregon should now be called the University of California at Eugene.

So was Oregon truly smarter because of its nationally ranked football team or because thousands of students were fleeing California and its overburdened state colleges in search of a relatively cheap education? How did you separate the two? For that matter, how did you separate the impact of football from a dozen other possible explanations for Oregon's rising pool of applicants? And, even with the increase, Oregon ranked just 106th in *U.S. News and World Report*'s 2013 ranking of national universities.

Five

• • •

WHY THE SOUTH LOST THE WAR
BUT WINS AT FOOTBALL

PART ONE: MEDIA DAYS

It was now summer in the Deep South, a July day so washed out that the sky was the color of yellow wax beans. The receptionist at the hotel where I was staying in Hoover, Alabama, insisted I was lucky to have such good weather. It was very unusual, she said.

"You mean it gets hotter than this?" I couldn't imagine how.

"Oh, yes, sir. This isn't bad at all. We hardly have any humidity to speak of."

The humidity level that morning was approaching 90 percent, which is basically the same as taking a shower.

Not that I had time to debate the finer points of humidity levels. I needed to find my way to a different hotel where more than one thousand members of the media, new and old, were gathering to dissect the upcoming season in the most powerful conference.

"You can't miss it," the receptionist said, drawing a map in the air with her finger. "Just take a left out of the parking lot."

I'd decided months ago that if I was going to write about the financial madness that is college football, I needed to go to the center of that madness. I needed to go south.

I knew college football was different in the South. There are entire books on the subject, many of which concern the disproportionate pride that southerners take in their teams. A few even examined the unrivaled dedication of the base. For example, there were stories about devoted fathers abandoning their daughters on their wedding days to catch the last quarter of a game, widows sneaking onto the fifty-yard line with baggies containing their husbands' ashes, and lately the practice of sending off the deceased with the rally cry of Alabama fans everywhere: *Roll Tide!*

Over the decades, history, culture, and college football had so thoroughly bled together in the South that they were now nearly indistinguishable, tangled up in the many strands of the southern genome—part mythology, part loyalty test, part obsession. Marino Casem, a former coach at several southern schools, possibly put it best when he once said: "On the East Coast, football is a cultural experience. In the Midwest, it's a form of cannibalism. On the West Coast, it's a tourist attraction. And in the South, football is a religion, and Saturday is the holy day."

Then there was the craziest story of all: that of Harvey Updyke Jr., a sixty-two-year-old former Texas state trooper who loved Alabama football so much he poisoned two iconic oak trees belonging to Alabama's archrival, Auburn. The thirty-foot-tall, century-old oaks were located at a place called Toomer's Corner near Jordan-Hare Stadium. For decades, after victories Auburn fans liked to parade there and celebrate by rolling the trees in toilet paper. In 2010 Updyke got it into his head to douse the oaks with herbicide. He then phoned in to a wildly popular sports talk radio show in Birmingham to take a victory trot. The host of the show, Paul Finebaum, asked if the trees had died. "Not yet," Updyke exclaimed, "but they definitely will." Finebaum then inquired if it was against the law to poison a tree. "You think I care?" Updyke shouted. "Roll damn Tide!"

Finebaum's show (he has since decamped to ESPN and its new SEC-themed network) was uncommonly popular in the South. On any given day one quarter of the males in Birmingham reportedly tuned in to debate the latest SEC developments and other outrages indigenous to the football-limned culture. Therefore it wasn't entirely surprising when the poisoned-oaks story exploded across social media. Updyke, who for some reason called himself Al from Dadeville on the show, was soon unmasked and charged. He pleaded guilty and spent several months in the county jail. On some level he appeared genuinely remorseful for his actions. Things had gotten out of hand, he told Finebaum during another call. He just had "too much"'Bama in him.

As the statisticians might point out, the South's preoccupation with college football is several standard deviations from the mean. Or to put it in slightly gentler terms, the fans down south are unusually distracted by their teams, which isn't always a bad thing but is nevertheless fascinating to an outsider like me.

I figured I could learn something by heading south. The problem was the South didn't seem to want anything to do with me. For months I had been sending e-mails and leaving increasingly desperate phone messages at the SEC's headquarters in Birmingham, inquiring how I might get credentials for its three-day celebration of all things football. But for some reason attending SEC Media Days is harder than getting a White House pass. You have to submit a personal dossier and explain at length the reason for your visit. *What the hell?* I thought. I had been a reporter for thirty-seven years. Wasn't that enough reason? The answer was emphatically no—or, more truthfully, the answer was "So what?" Who *hadn't* been a reporter for thirty-seven years? I made a stack out of the unanswered messages. After a while they began to pile up like losing lottery tickets.

Finally, from mounting paranoia as much as anything, I called an assistant athletic director at one of the SEC schools. The conversation that followed wasn't so much a disquisition as a brief but fertile inquiry into the state of mind of the South and college football.

ME: *"I thought southerners were supposed to be polite."*

HIM, LAUGHING: *"We take great pride in our politeness."*

ME, SOURLY: *"Except when it involves northerners."*

HIM: *"No comment."*

ME: *"Help me out. What am I doing wrong?"*

HIM: *"Southerners don't like to talk about college football with folks like you. They think all you want is to make fun of them. You're going to call us a bunch of yahoos in your book for being passionate about a game."*

I assured the assistant athletic director that I had no interest in deconstructing the psychology of Harvey Updyke or the many other preternaturally consumed fans. What I wanted to understand was the money: the tsunami of television dollars, advertising, royalties, licensing fees, and booster gifts that had transformed towns like Baton Rouge, Tuscaloosa, and Auburn into formidable football economies. Part of my interest included the power and sway of college football and the way it appeared to mesmerize the South, certainly, but I was also curious about more mundane questions, such as why no one blinked at paying a man $6.5 million to coach a college football team—an amount equal to what fifty or so full professors earn at the University of Alabama. Or why it was not merely tolerated but considered normal to spend a small inheritance on season tickets to watch a handful of games.

•   •   •

After one more request, I was finally approved for Media Days. Shortly thereafter I received a package of helpful information by e-mail advising me that I was one of 1,200 "credentialed" media representatives who would be attending the gathering this year. The word "largest" came up a lot, I noticed, scale apparently being of great importance to the nation's preeminent college football conference. Even in the throes of the worst economic downturn since the Great Depression, the annual extravaganza had doubled in size, drawing reporters and television personalities from media outlets as far away as New York and Boston. SEC football was now so big it was effectively its own economy, with hundreds if not thousands of employees and a budget that dwarfed those of many cities in the South.

"There is just a huge appetite for college football in the South," Drew Roberts explained when I called to ask him about the appeal of college football among the kudzu and live oaks. "It's almost a Civil War mentality—civic pride."

In 2010 Roberts and several of his buddies created a Web site called Saturday Down South, which I stumbled across in my research. The site is devoted exclusively to SEC football. It covers recruiting heavily but also reports on which schools have the nicest locker rooms and players lounges and once a year runs a photo spread called "Wives of the SEC Coaches."

"We try to be a little more classy than some of the other sites," Roberts said. "Lots of Web sites show women in bikinis. We drew a line in the sand and said we're not going to do that."

"Is there really enough interest to keep going?" I asked.

"We have one point one million followers on Facebook," Roberts replied. "We have two hundred fifty thousand fans on our Alabama Facebook page alone. Our choice to cover SEC football is purely just a business opportunity. We built our brand by tapping into the natural conference pride. This is a growing marketplace with a lot of potential for revenue. The demand for information from people who are so heavily invested in their team, especially in the South, is pretty extraordinary."

"Do you ever commit acts of real journalism?" I asked.

Roberts laughed. "We're not quite *Sports Illustrated*. The way I view it, we're not traditional journalism. We're entertainment. We don't have to be objective. But our view is that is the way media has gone. We want to have fun. We admit: We're SEC homers."

•   •   •

Shortly after 8:00 A.M. I arrived at the Wynfrey Hotel, a large tower of tinted glass attached to an even larger glimmering mall and galleria. The main parking lot was already overflowing with Jeeps and vans bearing the logos of TV and radio stations. Thick cables snaked across the parking lot, and satellite dishes pressed against the whitewashed sky. More than once I wandered into the path of some impossibly young reporter practicing a stand-up. "Sorry, sorry," I apologized, something I found myself doing a lot over the next three days.

A tour bus idling near the hotel entrance announced its presence like a giant Peter Max poster: **DIRECTV: THE ONLY WAY TO WATCH ALL OF COLLEGE FOOTBALL.** Another message exclaimed: **ESPN: DRIVE TO THE NATIONAL CHAMPIONSHIP.** ESPN makes nearly $5 billion a year in profit, and not a small chunk of that comes from broadcasting college football games—and, more to the point, SEC football games specifically, which helped to explain why dozens of ESPN suits were here in Hoover, Alabama.

I made my way into the main lobby. A rope had been set up, red-carpet style, to keep the more rabid fans away from the coaches and players who would shortly start arriving. The fans were dressed in team jerseys, and a few were even wearing helmets. Several had stashed posters under their chairs. The SEC had a very clear one-item-per-person policy regarding autographs, but some of the fans clearly had other ideas. I watched them for a moment and saw that they weren't just ambitious; they were also clever. They were using hand signals and had positioned children near the rope to act as their proxies. One way or another these posters would soon appear on eBay or other electronic trading posts. It was just how things worked now: There were the genuine fans, and then there were the enterprising fans in it for the commerce.

After a while I slipped behind the rope and slowly made my way down a long, dimly lit hallway known as Radio Row, where the talk radio shows set up. There were dozens of tables, somewhere near forty in all, tucked elbow to elbow, each with its own banner brazenly announcing: **THE FAN** or **THE ZONE** or **THE GAME**. I had learned from my research that Radio Row was part of the ritual of Media Days. Each head coach was expected to drop by for a few minutes to chat with the hosts. For the most part, these conversations were anodyne. The hosts asked how the team looked, and the coaches, being coaches, responded with the expected bromides before moving along to the next table.

When I arrived the Radio Row hosts were already talking about Johnny Manziel, the mercurial quarterback of the Texas A&M Aggies. Over the weekend the Internet had blown up with reports that Manziel had been kicked out of the Manning Passing Academy, which is a summer camp for high school quarterbacks run by the Manning family— Archie, Peyton, and Eli, the American royalty of quarterbacks. The stories were like nearly all Internet stories: attributed to impeccable, high-level sources who demanded anonymity. The lack of identifiable sources didn't seem to bother the radio hosts, who offered various versions of the Manziel narrative: Johnny Football had (a) been caught drinking; (b) overslept and missed camp; (c) disrespected the Mannings; or (d) all of the above. With Manziel due at Media Days the following day, it was all the hosts could do to keep from frothing.

•   •   •

Later that morning I joined a long, sluggish line of media types waiting to pick up their press packets. An older gentleman in a faded John Deere cap was impatiently tapping his foot. "It was never like this before," he complained to no one in particular. "You'd come and say your name, and that was that."

I looked around uncertainly. "You mean the line?" I asked.

"There was never a line," he said, tugging at his cap. "I've been coming to Media Days for twenty-two years, and it's only gotten like this the last few."

His face was a diorama of age: dark, sunken eyes; liver spots and deep lines radiating from his eyes and mouth. He informed me that he was seventy-three years old and worked part time for a small newspaper in Mississippi, covering college football. He'd once landed a one-on-one interview with Peyton Manning at Media Days when Manning was the star quarterback at Tennessee. "That'd never happen now," he sighed.

"No," I said. "I imagine it wouldn't."

I told him that I was writing a book about college football and wanted to see what all the fuss was about.

"I bet you do," he replied. "Well, you should interview the coach of Ole Miss, Hugh Freeze. He is an ordained minister. He is a great man, a character man. He is teaching his boys the right way to play. You know him, don't you? He's the one who coached Michael Oher in high school— the one from that movie *The Blind Side*. He's teaching his boys that it's not about exhibitioning themselves. It's about playing for one another."

By now we had inched inside the press room, where four separate lines funneled toward a long table, organized by last name, like at the motor vehicles department. The woman who helped me couldn't find my packet, so I waited as she leafed through several single-spaced pages. Finally she found me in a column headed "Author." "You are the only one," she said, eyeing me with amusement. "I guess that explains why I couldn't find you."

•   •   •

The real action was on the second floor—real action meaning television. ESPN had erected an improbably large stage outside the main conference room and was broadcasting live feeds back to the mother ship in Bristol, Connecticut. Three young men in white linen jackets sat around a curved desk. Every so often, one of them would toss his hands in the air to make a point. And then, as if on cue, a verbal brawl would erupt. I wondered if ESPN scripted its shows, like reality television? It felt that way from a distance. Or maybe "practiced" was a better way to describe the back-and-forth. In any case, it felt familiar, like I had seen this exchange many times before, and I probably had.

Two smaller stages were set up near the escalator, where more ESPN personalities were doing interviews. The cable network has multiple platforms devoted to college football, and apparently it can never have too much live content. Meanwhile, CBS, FOX, and any number of other media outlets were camped out in the smaller meeting rooms that flanked the main conference hall. As soon as a coach finished speaking in the main hall, he was ushered in and out of these smaller rooms. One door would close and the next one would quickly open, revealing a scrum of handlers

with clipboards and mikes. It was weirdly entertaining to watch and reminded me of a fun house where you stumble around in the dark, bumping into things.

After lunch I headed into the main conference hall, where I slid into
one of the back rows and fired up my laptop. An older man with a pink
face and a generous smile leaned over to introduce himself. "Bill Powell," he said, slipping me a business card identifying him as the executive director of the Hoover Area Chamber of Commerce.

Hoover is a suburb of Birmingham. Like many suburbs, it sprawls
across wide and varied swatches of land and is defined by clusters of big
boxes and chain restaurants. Bill Powell eagerly filled in a few of the
details. "When Hoover was formed in 1967," he said, "it had four hundred and ten residents. It now has eighty-five thousand. That's pretty
good growth in forty-six years, don't you think?" This was followed by
the random yet equally intriguing fact that Hoover had more than two
thousand hotel rooms. "It's why we attract so many conventions, including SEC Media Days," Bill explained. "We can accommodate all of the
teams and fans."

I noticed a well-groomed young man sitting next to Powell. "This is
Griffin Hamstead," he said, by way of introduction. "He wanted to come
along and take in Media Days."

I couldn't help noting Griffin's wrinkleless jacket, clean white shirt,
and carefully knotted rep tie. He was easily the best-dressed man at
Media Days, where, except for the television talent, the standard-issue
outfit consisted of cargo pants, Nikes, and a rumpled polo shirt. Griffin's
laptop was open to a screen saver for the University of Tennessee football
team: a flickering checkerboard of Volunteer Orange.

"Are you working here?" I asked.

"Bill helped me get credentials," he replied.

"Griffin's grandparents live here in Hoover," Powell explained when he saw my confusion. "They asked me if I would help him out, which I was happy to do."

Later Griffin and I fell into a conversation that was interesting but also a little bewildering. Like me, Griffin Hamstead had come to Media Days to see what all the fuss was about. He was a big fan of SEC football and the Tennessee Volunteers especially. When he'd learned that Media Days were in Hoover, it only made sense to come. "I really wanted to get the experience for my blog," he said. "I figured it would help me get my name and my product out there."

"Wait," I fumbled, "you have a product?"

"Yes, sir," he said, "my blog."

Thus began my education in the cascading effects of technology and youth. Griffin explained that he authored a blog called *Teens for Tennessee*, which was an occasional compendium of opinion, statistics, and random musings on the University of Tennessee football team. "For example, I'll see something in the paper and write about it," Griffin explained. "I do give recaps of games, but I also include a lot of my personal opinion, because it is a blog. I don't want to be completely objective, black and white. I figure they can read the stats anywhere. But they can't read Griffin Hamstead's opinion unless they read my blog."

It sounded convincing enough. But I was having a hard time picturing the audience. Weren't most teenagers chasing one another around at parties or busy firing off inflammatory texts?

"It's not so much like ESPN," Griffin said. "It's pretty much for my friends and some of their friends who follow the team. I have had over four thousand unique visits since I started. I also have fifteen to twenty e-mail subscribers and one hundred Twitter followers."

Griffin explained that he started blogging at the age of twelve when his mother "was annoyed with all of my talking about sports. She told me to find a creative outlet. I thought a blog would be great. My dad graduated from UT, and he's a big fan of the football team. And then I became interested when I was in sixth grade. And now I am a huge fan."

"How old are you?" I said. "If you don't mind my asking."

"I'm fifteen."

I tried to recall what I was doing when I was fifteen. Whatever it was, it wasn't nearly this ambitious. I certainly wasn't attending conferences, taking notes, and catapulting my thoughts out to the world.

More details followed: Griffin was a sophomore in high school, where he was a straight-A student in a demanding International Baccalaureate program, in addition to periodically blogging.

"Do you consider yourself a journalist?" I asked.

Here Griffin shyly smiled and handed me a business card. It read "Teens for Tennessee. Griffin Hamstead. Journalist/blogger."

"It looks very professional," I said, palming the card.

The cynic in me imagined that this must be part of some plan to add to Griffin's already-impressive résumé. Wasn't that what enterprising high school students did these days to gain an edge? But Griffin didn't strike me as the least bit conniving. He was simply an extraordinarily earnest and focused young man who, like nearly everyone else in this giant conference hall, was enamored with SEC football.

·   ·   ·

After lunch Mike Slive, the seventy-three-year-old commissioner of the SEC, began to recount for the assembled crowd the conference's many accomplishments.

"SEC teams have won seven straight national championships in football," Slive proudly reminded us. "Last year six SEC teams ranked in the top ten. Sixty-three SEC players were drafted by NFL teams— twice as many as the next conference. And for the fourth time in six years, an SEC player won the Heisman Trophy."

In other words, no other conference had come close to achieving such complete, unrelenting domination. Which, of course, irritated the hell out of the four other major football conferences—the Atlantic Coast Conference, the Big Ten, the Big 12, and the Pac-12. All of them had grown immeasurably in the last two decades, adding new members, signing lucrative television deals, and otherwise padding their bottom lines. Together they now funneled about $1 billion a year in television fees and other royalties to their members. But still, none of them was as big or wielded as much power in college football as the almighty SEC.

Since 1980 the SEC has distributed $2.2 billion to its members. Under Slive, a former judge who took over the conference in 2002, the scale and rate of these payments has only accelerated, from less than $100 million annually to $293 million. In 2014 SEC revenue was expected to top $300 million—or more than $21 million for each of its fourteen schools.

One way or another most of these riches come from television. The networks and cable companies can't seem to get out their checkbooks quickly enough when the SEC has a few spare games to auction off. You want $3 billion? No problem. We'll wire it right over. That's pretty much what happened in 2009 when the SEC signed a new long-term deal with CBS and ESPN to broadcast its football games. ESPN alone paid $2.25 billion for the right to broadcast the SEC's games for fifteen years. And last year it agreed to extend those rights as part of a new twenty-year deal.

There are now so many SEC games on television that it's hard *not* to watch one. CBS broadcasts one of the conference's marquee games on Saturday afternoon; ESPN then jumps in with two more games at night. In 2014 rival schools complained that ESPN was biased toward the SEC, but the complaints seemed to miss an important point: ESPN is in the entertainment business, and the SEC is its business partner. Why wouldn't it broadcast as many SEC games as it could?

In 2013 six of the ten most popular football games on television featured SEC teams. Alabama alone drew an average of 6.5 million viewers, a viewership roughly equal to that of the wildly popular television show *The Walking Dead*. Collectively, on any given weekend, about 50 million SEC fans watched their favorite teams.

Shortly before Media Days, Slive had announced still another new deal with ESPN, this one to create a premium SEC-themed channel to rival the networks now offered by the Big Ten and Pac-12. The SEC channel debuted in August 2014 and offered an additional forty-five football games. The conference has yet to disclose the economics involved, but with thirty million potential subscribers in eleven states, it's hard to see how the channel won't generate tens or even hundreds of millions in additional revenue for SEC schools.

For years the SEC has also led the nation in attendance, with roughly one million fans attending games each Saturday in the fall. Not surprisingly, the conference also showcases many of the largest stadiums in the nation, with Alabama, Tennessee, Texas A&M, and Louisiana State each accommodating more than 100,000 fans. Georgia has 92,000 seats; Florida has 88,000. On game days some SEC towns are the largest cities in their states, if only for a few hours.

All of this translates into absurd amounts of cash for the schools' athletic departments. Five of the ten richest athletic departments in the country are in the SEC. In 2013 those schools alone reported $232 million in profits from football, or an average of nearly $50 million each. And, like everything else connected with the SEC, the numbers are only growing. For example, in 1999 the University of Florida reported earning $7.7 million from its football program, financial records show. In 2012 it made $52 million.

"I don't think anybody saw it happening quite like this," University of Alabama athletic director Bill Battle said, referring to the conference's extraordinary wealth. "We have been blessed in our success."

"You mean no one anticipated it?" I asked.

"Not like this. It sort of snowballed is what I would say."

The availability of cash gives SEC schools startling advantages in recruiting, hiring coaches, and adding to their already-lavish facilities. Simply put, the conference outspends everyone else. In 2011 SEC schools reported a staggering $1.2 billion in debt on their football stadiums and other athletic facilities—double what they had reported only five years earlier.

At its core this is a matter of values, and the SEC clearly values football above everything else. In 2013 the Knight Commission on Intercollegiate Athletics released some remarkable data on the gaps in spending between college football and academics. Among other things, the data showed that Auburn University spent the equivalent of $14,000 on each of its students but about $400,000 on each football player. Similar gaps were the case at other SEC schools.

I imagined at least a few of the SEC presidents might be embarrassed by these revelations. Instead the Knight report was met with thundering silence—apparently shrugged off as one more misguided attack by do-gooders who just didn't understand the importance of college football to the South.

PART TWO: THE COLOR OF MONEY

For nearly a year I had been following the story of an artist who made his living depicting famous plays from University of Alabama football games. Truthfully, I had no idea there was even a market for oil paintings and prints of football players crashing into one another, let alone one as seemingly robust as this one. Some of the artist's original paintings sold for fifty thousand dollars, and more than a fair number hung in museums and private collections.

Daniel A. Moore had been making art from football since 1979 and, by his own account, earned a good living from it—maybe too good a living. In 2005 the University of Alabama sued him, contending he was misappropriating its intellectual property with his renderings of Alabama football players. Among the alleged infringements cited by the university's lawyers was that Moore was using its crimson-and-white color scheme in his prints and paintings of players' uniforms and helmets.

It is indisputable that Alabama is known as the Crimson Tide and that its football players wear white pants, crimson jerseys, and egg white helmets. As for the rest, let's just say I had no idea a public university could own the colors of its football team or that the legal terrain of logos and trademarks could be quite so fascinating or baffling.

Like most nonlawyers, I assumed that because Alabama is a public university, the citizens of Alabama owned the rights to the team's colors. But the school and its lawyers argued otherwise: The colors belonged exclusively to the University of Alabama and its football program. If Daniel Moore wanted to use them, he had to pay up, like everyone else who uses the university's logos and marks for commercial purposes. The market is not insignificant. Nationally, sales of college athletic merchandise, including everything from T-shirts to coffee mugs to calendars to prints, generate about $5 billion annually, with several hundred million of that returned to the schools in royalties and licensing fees. Directly or indirectly football is responsible for most of that bounty.

I imagine the university's lawyers expected Daniel Moore to fold when the lawsuit spat out of his office fax machine in 2005, but they clearly underestimated the sixty-year-old artist. In addition to being a talented painter, Moore is a tenacious defender of his work, which is to say his livelihood. Moore hired a Birmingham attorney and dug in for the long haul. The long haul, in this instance, took eight years and wound up accumulating $300,000 in legal fees. Finally, in June 2012, a federal appeals court in Atlanta held that Daniel Moore's artwork was, well, art, and as such was protected by the First Amendment. It was a resounding, if bitter-sweet, victory for Moore, a 1976 graduate of Alabama, whose license plate on his crimson SUV reads: ROLL TIDE.

At this point Alabama could have appealed the ruling to the U.S. Supreme Court, but by now the lawsuit had morphed into one of those David-versus-Goliath stories, and because no one roots for Goliath, the university wisely decided to cut its already-significant losses—$1.5 million in legal expenses alone, according to published reports.

Here you might pause to ask what seems like an obvious question: How could a university, of all places, drag an artist, of all people—and one of its own graduates, no less—through eight years of legal hell and think it would turn out well? As with most good questions involving college football, the answer inevitably flows back to the money.

Because I was already in Alabama for SEC Media Days, I arranged to meet Daniel Moore and tour his gallery, which happens to be in Hoover. But before I did so I needed to make a quick detour down I-20 to Tuscaloosa to learn a little more about the University of Alabama and its trademarks.

•   •   •

As recently as the 1980s the University of Alabama didn't invest a lot of time or energy protecting its logos and marks. For one thing, there wasn't a lot to protect. The market for school-themed merchandise was relatively modest, valued in the millions as opposed to billions, as it is now. And Alabama had more serious issues to worry about: The athletic department was several million dollars in debt, and many of its facilities were outdated.

At the time, no one seemed to think that the two things were related—that if you charged more and higher licensing fees, you might make enough to cut into the deficit or help to remodel the football stadium. Then again, it was a different era. Football was still a relatively modest enterprise, and many of the elite football powers were still largely unaware of the money they could make off their marks.

Enter Bill Battle.

The seventy-three-year-old athletic director at Alabama, who bears a striking resemblance to the actor Peter Graves from the original *Mission: Impossible,* recalled wandering from one office to another in the fall of 1981 searching for the person in charge of licensing. "What I found," he told me, "was that no one was in charge of licensing at the University of Alabama. I don't think they even knew they had anything worth licensing."

Battle was in private business at the time, working as the president of a large window company. But he had strong ties to Alabama. He'd played tight end on the university's 1961 national-championship team coached by Bear Bryant. Later he'd become friends with Bryant and had invited him to sit on the board of the window company. "He wasn't particularly active on the board, but he did come to some of the meetings . . . and we became pretty close over time," Battle recalled.

One day in 1981 Bryant informed Battle that he was looking for someone to help manage his speaking engagements. At the time, Bryant was only nine wins away from becoming the most successful coach in the history of college football. Battle quickly grasped that the milestone would generate lucrative business opportunities for Bryant and offered to take over as his agent. "We started to put together some pretty cool deals," he recalled, including some involving the school's logos, "which is when I went looking for the licensing department."

There were thousands of things you could stick a logo on and charge a licensing fee for doing so: key chains, pens and pencils, baby clothes, T-shirts, calendars, coffee mugs, prints, footballs, you name it. But Alabama and the other big football schools were either too busy or unprepared to take advantage of this untapped market. So Battle and his business partners proposed managing it for them. Universities warmed to his idea, and Battle's Collegiate Licensing Company (CLC) not only helped to create an entirely new industry but also soon dominated it.

Initially Battle figured he needed fifty schools in order for CLC to operate profitably. But with college football experiencing a huge uptick in popularity in the late 1980s and 1990s, Battle wound up signing two hundred clients, collecting millions in fees, and generating millions more in royalties for CLC's clients. For Alabama and the other football powers it was like found money.

"It was silly to leave money sitting on the table," Battle said. "I knew a lot about universities. I knew they had something valuable: their brand and their marks. But it takes a lot of money and work to protect those. What happened was I ended up talking to a lot of assistant purchasing agents who told me they had been thinking about this for a long time but weren't sure how to go about it. I knew if we could sign them up, we could eventually get this thing up and running."

In 2012 the Alabama athletic department collected $10 million in licensing fees, royalties, and sponsorships, financial records show. That amount was second only to that earned by the University of Texas. Winning three national championships in football didn't hurt. All those students and fans walking around in T-shirts with the Alabama logo are effectively kicking a little something back to the athletic department.

All of which helps to explain why CLC and Alabama have become so aggressive in protecting its marks. In the past Alabama could afford not to care, but now the $10 million it makes off those marks accounts for nearly one of every ten dollars the athletic department takes in.

According to the university's Web site, Alabama charges a "standard royalty rate of eight percent" to use one of its marks. It trademarks words and slogans, including "Crimson Tide" and "Roll Tide," as well as "any other designs, symbols, art, seal words, or groups of words that have come to be associated with the University." The list of relevant items takes up two pages. The football team's helmets, with the famous script letter *A*, are trademarked, as is the school's fight song, the word "tide," and thirty-six other logos, seals, and symbols.

Defending all of those marks takes effort, Battle explained. Alabama has gone to court to put counterfeiters out of business and has also challenged small mom-and-pop businesses, including a coffee shop and a nonprofit Christian group selling T-shirts with the word "'Bama" on them, according to newspaper reports. In some quarters the perception is that the athletic department has lost all sense of proportion. But Battle, who sold CLC in 2007 to the marketing giant IMG for a reported $100 million, told me, "The university has no choice; we have to defend our marks. You would be surprised how sophisticated some of these outfits are. We try hard not to go after people frivolously. Do we occasionally miss the mark? Maybe."

Battle was right, I suppose, but I was still struggling to sort out the opposing roles of public universities as proprietors of free speech and as commercial businesses. The upside of having a fabulously rich athletic program is that you don't have to count every penny. The downside is that all too often you end up spending a surprising amount of time and money protecting those pennies.

In the last decade Alabama has sent out 153 cease-and-desist letters to companies and individuals for allegedly violating its marks. In some cases it has instructed them to destroy their inventory. In others it has ordered small businesses to pay damages for products they sold years ago. Perhaps the most inflammatory case involved Daniel Moore, who, in the eyes of many fans, is an integral part of the Alabama football experience. To own a Moore painting or print is to own a moment in history. Thus the notion that the university would turn on one of its own seemed to many almost sacrilegious.

•   •   •

Growing up, Daniel Moore played football and baseball and had a strong interest in sports generally. "But in high school I figured out I was a decent enough [football] player but not good enough to play in college," he recalled. Moore studied graphic design and painting at Alabama. After graduating in 1976, he worked as a commercial artist for a utility company while continuing to paint on his own. One of his paintings of a marathon runner was made into a popular poster and sold thousands of copies.

"I began to think this might be a way to do something I loved," Moore said. "That's how it started. I quit my day job in 1979 and started painting football scenes. And now I am able to merge two loves—sports and art—and together turn it into a career."

Football was "a perfect subject to paint," Moore explained. "In terms of superrealism, sports and football were ideal, especially football, with the shiny helmets and the reflections of texture and color."

For years Moore was able to obtain a sideline pass to Alabama home games. He photographed plays and then used them as the basis for watercolors, oil paintings, and prints. The work featured photorealistic renderings that featured the team's uniforms, helmets, jerseys, and crimson and white colors. Moore's first iconic work was of an Alabama linebacker hurling himself at a Penn State fullback trying to leap into the end zone. It was fourth down in the 1980 Sugar Bowl and preserved Alabama's 14–7 lead while helping to secure another national championship for Bear Bryant.

The painting was a huge success, and Moore saw the opportunities widening ahead of him. Other paintings and prints followed. In 1986 Moore captured a violent hit in a game between Alabama and Notre Dame in a painting he called *The Sack*. Alabama linebacker Cornelius Bennett had broken through the Notre Dame line to crush the Irish's quarterback, Steve Beuerlein. It was Alabama's first-ever victory over the Fighting Irish.

Moore donated the painting to the campus's Paul W. Bryant Museum, which serves as a kind of shrine to Alabama football and its late, exalted coach. "They had that one and one or two others in the museum," he said. Several of his prints and paintings also hung in the athletic department. Between 1980 and 1982 the university ordered twenty prints from Moore that it later resold. It also sold more than twelve thousand dollars' worth of Moore's calendars at its campus store, court records show.

Moore worked for years without a formal agreement with the university. That changed in the 1990s, when the school asked Moore to produce a series of prints memorializing the centenary of Alabama football. Moore said he was always careful to keep the university seal and other trademarks out of the main body of his paintings. Because the new project would push the margins of protected work, he entered a series of licensing agreements with the university. But even though he signed those agreements, Moore maintains he wasn't giving up his right to make other paintings and prints that didn't contain seals or trademarks. "I absolutely was not giving up my First Amendment rights," he said. "That goes all the way back to my training as an artist as a student at the University of Alabama."

Moore continued to create paintings and prints and to sell his earlier work without paying licensing fees or royalties. Nor did the university request them. Then, in January of 2002, Moore received a letter from the university informing him that, henceforth, he would need to license *all* of his Alabama-themed work. It also notified him that he needed permission to portray the team's uniforms, including its iconic jerseys, helmets, and crimson and white colors.

Moore believes he had become too good at what he did. "The university saw that I was popular and had a following, and I think they saw the additional money they could make," he explained. "As far as I am concerned, it was always a money grab for them."

Initially, Moore thought he was going to be able to work out his differences with the school, and a meeting was set up. According to Battle, the university's lawyers "were nervous that Danny Moore was going to sue them, so they jumped the gun and sued Danny Moore first." Moore offered a different version of events. In his account the university reneged on the "crucial meeting and filed the [2005] lawsuit out of the blue instead."

The lawsuit meandered through the U.S. District Court for the Northern District of Alabama. At various stages seven different judges were involved. Bills piled up, and news stories appeared, most critical of the university. "Danny Moore beat the crap out of us in the media," Battle said. "He and his attorney had everyone against us. We didn't have a chance at that point."

In November of 2009 federal judge Robert B. Propst ruled that Moore's depictions of Alabama's uniforms in his paintings and prints were protected by the First Amendment. In addition, the fact that Moore had prior licensing agreements with the university didn't mean that he now needed university permission to portray the team's uniforms, Propst ruled.

The university appealed the decision to the Eleventh Circuit Court of Appeals in Atlanta. The university contended that Moore was violating its trademarks while producing commercial art. Moore countered that his work represented artistic renderings of historic events and was protected by the First Amendment. The court sided with Moore, writing in 2012 that his "paintings, prints and calendars very clearly are embodiments of artistic expression, and entitled to full First Amendment protection."

On the critical issue of colors the court said Moore's prior licensing agreements were "ambiguous." And "despite the public notoriety of Moore's work, the University never requested (until this litigation) that he pay royalties" on his previous unlicensed paintings and prints. After nearly a decade Moore had won on all of the key issues.

When I asked Battle why the university and CLC thought the case was worth litigating, he insisted it was important to clarify the First Amendment issue. "We were concerned about the art and images. Obviously, we wished the court agreed with us that Danny's work was commercial in nature. But they came down on the side of the First Amendment."

The lawsuit has complicated Moore's relationship with his alma mater. "My entire family went to the university. My three daughters are graduates," he said, swiping an errant lock of brown hair from his forehead. Moore stressed that he still loved the university but believed "certain individuals" maligned his character during the long, costly lawsuit.

Moore once had eight season tickets to football games. He no longer has any. If he attends a game, he uses a friend's ticket. The university, for its part, no longer allows Moore a sideline pass. That felt small to me, and I asked Battle if the university might ever allow Moore back. He smiled but didn't respond.

Moore still produces prints and paintings of historic Alabama football plays, but these days he is trying to branch out. When I visited his gallery, he was working on a painting of Johnny Manziel, the Texas A&M quarterback and Heisman Trophy winner, in a scene from A&M's 2012 upset victory over Alabama in Tuscaloosa.

"It almost feels sacrilegious," I observed.

"Do you think?" Moore asked, grinning.

In the picture shafts of late-afternoon light form a halo around Manziel.

"It was the college football game of the year," Moore said. "Johnny Football is doing something heroic."

Later that afternoon Moore took me to Aldridge Gardens, a thirty-acre oasis of pine and fir trees not far from the hotel where Media Days was being held. A collection of his watercolors and oil paintings was on display in the conference center. While we were slowly making our way from room to room, Moore asked if I had heard about "the cookie lady," Mary Cesar, and her own problem with the University of Alabama licensing juggernaut.

I told him I planned to drive down to Tuscaloosa the following morning to meet her.

"My attorney offered to help her. But Mary decided she didn't want that. She's a strong woman, from what I hear. I think you'll enjoy her story."

Here Moore rolled his eyes. It was his way of saying, *Just when you think things can't get any crazier, they always do.*

$\bullet \quad \bullet \quad \bullet$

Mary Cesar is probably not the first person you would suspect of stealing the University of Alabama's trademarks. The morning we met she was wearing baggy pinstriped pants and a pink T-shirt with the logo of her boutique bakery: Mary's Cakes & Pastries. Her long, dark hair was pulled back in an artful braid. I immediately thought but didn't say: *ex-hippie.*

It was an easy mistake to make. In her wry, bohemian humor and gentle, forgiving spirit there is about Cesar a halo of the sixties. Perhaps she had fallen forward in time and become a foodie? Cesar had in fact grown up in northern California and attended a small, wildly liberal college near Los Angeles before vagabonding in Europe for several years. And she just had the look of someone who had seen the foolishness of the world and decided she would be better off writing her own life story, which is exactly what Mary Cesar had done.

After returning from Europe she married an accountant and lived in Tarrytown, New York. For years she worked as a secretary but eventually decided that wasn't enough and earned an MBA from Fordham. She then worked in management, got divorced, moved to Atlanta, and joined a large paper company doing market research. Later she ditched the corporate job and joined an Internet start-up, trading a six-figure salary for the promise of stock options down the line. That job enabled Cesar to choose where she lived, and she opted for Northport, Alabama, a suburb of 24,000 located across the Black Warrior River from Tuscaloosa, home to the University of Alabama.

"There is a paper company there, so I had been to Northport as part of my work in the forestry [paper] business and I liked it," Cesar said. "Tuscaloosa was a reasonably civilized place, and it's just a few miles across the river. Housing is also cheaper here than Atlanta. I thought I would actually be able to afford something."

It was a few years before the economy imploded, but the tech boom was already flattening at the edges. Four years after she joined the start-up, the company still hadn't gone public and Cesar wasn't making much money. It wasn't exactly an existential crisis, but it was a turning point. Ever since she'd lived in Paris, working as a food handler, Cesar had dreamed of opening her own restaurant or bakery. "I peeled a hell of a lot of vegetables," she laughed. "But that was when I became interested in learning cooking and baking. I spent a lot of time watching and wondering. And someday, I thought, I'd like to do that."

Here was a second chance. She enrolled in a small culinary school in Birmingham, about an hour from Northport. After graduating, she worked her way through a series of restaurant and catering jobs, discovering that she loved baking. When she heard that the owner of a local Northport bar was looking to rent out a small storefront, Cesar leaped at the chance and opened Mary's Cakes & Pastries in July 2006.

Cesar's bakery is located in an alley a mile or two from the main highway that passes through town. It takes work to find, which is why I was surprised when she said she chose the location for its potential walk-in trade. "I wanted a place where people came to me," she said, "instead of having to haul my cookies and cakes to stores."

The bakery is an old wooden storefront with tight spaces. It has a small eating area with wobbly tables. Cesar also sells baking books and cooking supplies and runs baking camps for schoolchildren. She has four employees and by her count makes "just enough to not go bankrupt."

When she opened, Cesar concentrated on wedding cakes. But that changed quickly enough. The bakery was, after all, only a stone's throw from Tuscaloosa and its vaunted football team.

"Customers started asking for Alabama-themed cakes and cookies," she said. "They wanted them for their tailgate parties before big home games and just to have. So I started putting [script] *A*'s on cookies and cupcakes and making Alabama-themed cakes [red velvet cakes in the Crimson Tide's colors]. I made a cake of the stadium and one of the National Championship Trophy [in 2012]. People really loved them. So we added a little more each year. If it's Alabama related, people want it.

"The money in baking is in wedding cakes, but we sell a lot of cookies," she explained, sweeping her hand past a glass case containing all manner of colorful cookies. "In fact, it turns out we make more money from cookies, which is probably how we got in trouble with the university."

A local artist made Cesar a cookie cutter in the shape of Bear Bryant's signature houndstooth hat. Then she got one in the shape of an elephant, the Alabama mascot. Someone asked for a cookie shaped like Nick Saban's straw hat. Another requested a yellow hammer, part of a famous Alabama football cheer: "Rammer jammer yellow hammer, give 'em hell, Alabama!"

Sales peaked during the football season. "The first home game is always huge," Cesar said, "Homecoming as well. And if there are home games against rivals like LSU and Georgia, I always sell extra cookies. And Auburn! There are always big orders for the Auburn game, because everyone is having a party." For families with split loyalties—one graduate from Alabama, the other from Auburn—Cesar divides the colors: Half of the cookies are crimson and half are orange, to capture the "house divided" theme.

Cesar estimates that she sells 250 to 300 dozen cookies for big matches, nearly all of which are picked up on the Thursday or Friday before the game. "You can hear a pin drop in here on Saturday," she said. She will occasionally haul a cache of cookies up to the quadrangle on game day, but only to make a delivery. The university has made it clear that it doesn't want her selling cookies on campus.

Cesar charges $1.75 for a cookie. "I probably make ten cents per cookie," she said, or about $360 per game. Still, the cookies add up over the course of a season, and the orders keep increasing, especially when the team plays for national championships, which Alabama has three times in the last eight years under Nick Saban.

"We call it Sabanomics," Cesar chuckled.

Saban's wife, Terry, has placed orders. "She buys cookies for the new coaches' wives and she bought red velvet cupcakes for her son's wedding rehearsal dinner," Cesar said. The football offices and athletic department have also been customers, placing orders for visiting recruits and on National Signing Day, the day in early February when recruits announce which schools they will play for the following year.

All of which adds to the confusion about why the university and its agent, Collegiate Licensing Company, would accuse Mary's Cakes & Pastries of abusing Alabama's trademarks and ask for hundreds if not thousands of dollars in damages.

"For seven years I never heard a thing," Cesar said, sitting across from me in her bakery. "From the beginning we did cakes and cookies for the president's office. We did cookies for the Sugar Bowl. The athletic department ordered from us. Not ever, ever, did they ask if we had a license."

Cesar was in California in 2012 visiting her parents when, checking her phone, she saw a message from Collegiate Licensing Company. It was a cease-and-desist letter advising her that she was in violation of the university's trademarks and instructing her to stop immediately. It also ordered her to calculate the number of Alabama-themed cookies and cakes she had sold over the years, so CLC could assess damages. Attached to the e-mail were several images of Alabama-themed items from Cesar's Web page, including a gingerbread man in a houndstooth pattern.

"I thought it was a joke," Cesar said. "But then I started reading it and thought, *Oh, shit.* It ordered me to immediately cease and desist." As it happened, Mary's Cakes & Pastries was scheduled to deliver ten dozen elephant-shaped cookies with script *A*'s for a wedding party that very day. "I called the shop and canceled those orders."

Cesar remembers thinking: *How could this be happening? Why would they possibly be coming after someone as small as me?* "It made no freaking sense. I wasn't rich. It was cookies with *A*'s on them!" And how did they expect her to determine how many Alabama-themed cookies she had sold? "That was absurd! Cookies are often mixed together. Some might have an *A* and others might not. I didn't keep records. I was the definition of a small business."

Even as Cesar was sorting through the fog of accusations and making plans to fly home, an interesting legal defense formed in her head. It wasn't as if she were making anything permanent, she thought. She wasn't producing T-shirts or coffee mugs with Alabama's logo. She was making cookies that people ate—"ate" being the key word. Her products didn't last; people gobbled them down. Where was the lasting damage to Alabama's marks? It was in the stomachs of Alabama fans.

Here it got interesting. People were already angry with the university over its lawsuit against Daniel Moore. When news about Mary's Cakes & Pastries leaked later that day, customers were incensed. A few took to the streets to protest, while others notified the local newspaper. The *Tuscaloosa News* jumped on the story and devoted three-fourths of its front page to Mary Cesar. The clear impression was that Alabama and CLC were bullying one of Alabama's own.

"This is a small town," Cesar said. "We're kind of like family. When you pick on us, you're picking on them. They saw the little guy getting picked on and they were indignant."

Daniel Moore's attorney, Stephen Heninger, offered to represent Mary's Cakes & Pastries pro bono. But Cesar didn't want to get dragged into a lawsuit. She just wanted the problem to go away. And, as it turns out, so did the University of Alabama.

Say what you will about the Alabama athletic department: It is a big bureaucracy tripping over itself, money obsessed, a hugely profitable entertainment division, and maybe even a bully at times, but one thing it is not is stupid. As soon as the complaints started lighting up their switchboards, officials realized their mistake and went into crisis-management mode.

Early the following morning Finus Gaston, one of the senior employees in the athletic department, called Cesar as she was boarding a plane to rush back home. "He had called the shop earlier and apologized profusely," Cesar said. "He told me, 'I am sorry. We will work something out.' He sounded very genuine. I think they realized what a mistake they'd made."

The university issued an apology and offered mea culpas to the many reporters who called for comments. As best anyone could tell, it was genuinely an unfortunate mistake. Someone had called over to the athletic department to complain, and an "overzealous" secretary had passed along the complaint to CLC. "And someone at CLC told her they would take care of it," Battle said. "To this day I don't know who made the initial complaint."

After Battle was hired as athletic director in March 2013, one of his first official acts was to pay Mary Cesar a visit. "I wanted to go see her," he said. "I walked in. I said, 'I know you. I'm not coming to arrest you. I'm coming to be your customer.'"

Battle was in town with his wife looking for a house. They also were putting the finishing touches on their daughter's upcoming wedding in Atlanta the following month and ordered several dozen Alabama-themed cookies for the reception. The following April a thank-you note arrived from Battle. "The cookies were a big hit at our daughter's wedding," it read. "They definitely added some ALABAMA flavor to a Georgia wedding—Bill Battle."

Cesar couldn't afford the several thousand dollars that Alabama demanded for a license, so the university charged her only ten dollars. She sent over a check, "but they never cashed it." She expects to pay one hundred dollars for one of Alabama's newly created discount licenses for small businesses like hers.

As far as I can tell, Cesar holds no bitterness toward the Crimson

Tide. After the team was thrashed by Auburn in the final game of the 2013 season, ending any chance of playing in a third straight national championship, she sent over two big trays of cookies to cheer the players up.

"If it hadn't been so crazy and surreal, you couldn't have invented a better story," Cesar said. "If somebody had thought of this as a marketing plan, it would be freaking brilliant—but only if you knew the end."

• • •

The next morning I headed back to Media Days. I wanted to be there when Nick Saban arrived. As the rock-star head coach of the back-to-back national champions, he was the unquestioned headliner, and the lobby overflowed with fans attired in all manner of crimson and white.

Around 11:00 A.M. Saban appeared, surrounded by a phalanx of security guards in dark blue suits and tinted sunglasses who rushed him into an elevator and then cordoned it off. It all seemed a bit much, but then again I hadn't been cornered by a woman asking me to sign her houndstooth bra, as Saban had at Media Days a few years back.

I was suffering from a vague sense of unease at this point, though I couldn't say why. Saban has that kind of effect. Even when he is being nice he seems to rub people the wrong way. Years ago I had a conversation with Saban when he was the coach at LSU. He was holding one of his son's composite baseball bats when I walked into his office, so I tried for a joke.

"You aren't going to hit me with that?" I asked, grinning foolishly.

"It depends on what you ask," Saban said, which I later figured was his own idea of humor.

The Alabama fans in the lobby had begun swaying back and forth with oceanic force. Every so often, a roar of "ROLLLLLLLLLL TIDE" washed up the escalator to the second floor like spindrift. Then someone would inevitably break in with "SABAN . . . SABAN . . . SABAN . . ." until another thundering "ROLLLLLLLLLL TIDE" drowned him out.

A little later Saban told the reporters in the main conference hall that this was his seventh trip to Media Days and that he was among "1,200 of my closest friends," which drew awkward laughter. Then he reminded them that in twenty-one years they had accurately predicted the winner of the SEC just four times. "If I were 4-17 I would be pumping gas at my daddy's gas station," Saban smirked. "I just think it's crazy to speculate."

And yet wasn't that why 1,200 media types had jammed into this auditorium—to listen to Saban speculate about his team? It was no secret that Saban didn't want to be here. After all, Saban isn't stupid; no doubt he understood the absurdity of Media Days. But unlike a lot of smart people, he didn't seem to know how to hide his irritation.

When one of the reporters asked if Alabama was scheduling more home games to make more money, Saban appeared to interpret the question as a criticism. "It's not just what the coach wants," he said in a strangled voice. "It's about the business of college football. I'm not really comfortable with that question."

After Saban finished his presentation, his security detail hustled him downstairs to visit Radio Row and sign a few autographs. It was then I noticed the fan wearing an oversized championship ring on his head. I couldn't tell for certain, but the elaborate headgear appeared to be made out of cardboard and foam. It was a very good copy of the rings that Alabama players had received for winning the title the previous January. It had a large Alabama script A in the center, surrounded by the words "National Championship" and numerous faux diamonds. Just for a moment I wondered if the university would sue him for violating its trademarks.

A few days later I read that the twenty-three-year-old fan had paid three hundred dollars for the ring online. He was hoping to get Saban to autograph it. But when Saban passed by it was so loud he apparently couldn't hear the fan's cries and signed his football instead. The fan told the local newspaper he was disappointed, but at least he'd gotten Saban's autograph. It was the kind of risk 'Bama fans gladly take to get near a legend.

Six

• • •

HOW WOMEN'S ROWING SAVED COLLEGE FOOTBALL: WORKING THE BAR SCENE FOR RECRUITS

IN THE MID-1990S KANSAS STATE University's athletic department had a problem. The problem wasn't unique to Kansas State and in fact was shared by dozens of large public and private universities. But it was a problem nonetheless.

The problem was football. Football was becoming so big and rich it was getting in the way of everything else. A federal law known as Title IX, passed in 1972, required schools to offer women equal opportunities to participate in sports. Equal didn't *exactly* mean equal, which is another story, but schools at least had to make an effort. In some cases that meant upgrading locker rooms and training facilities. In others it meant adding new sports to their athletic programs. The law also mandated that schools keep statistics on scholarships, spending, and the number of athletes in each sport, parsed by gender. And if it appeared they were favoring men, which happened often enough, the government could—and sometimes did—step in.

Where it got complicated for Kansas State and scores of other large football schools was for the most part in the numbers. Large football schools typically had between 100 and 135 football players. Kansas State, a prairie school sometimes referred to as Silo Tech by the locals, counted about 120 players on its roster. Most received athletic scholarships covering tuition, room and board, books, and meals. Women, for their part, didn't have any sport nearly as big as football. The basketball team had 5 players; golf had 10; track and field, the largest women's team, had about 35 runners and throwers. The athletic department needed to do something to balance the numbers, and quickly. And so in the fall of 1995 Kansas State officials announced that they were starting a rowing program exclusively for women.

Here you might be inclined to ask, reasonably enough: A rowing program on the *prairie*, the site of biblical droughts and tornadoes? And wasn't rowing something they did at elite schools like Harvard and Yale, back east? Finally, where did Kansas State expect to find its rowers?

While these are all logical questions, they do not take into account any number of relevant facts. For example, there *was* some rowable water in Kansas. The western end of the state had the Ogallala Aquifer, and Manhattan itself had the Tuttle Creek Reservoir, a fifteen-mile-long plug of deep blue water about three miles from the Kansas State campus. In any case, geography and elitist notions about rowing weren't really the issue. The issue was those pesky numbers. There were simply too many football players monopolizing too much money and space and not nearly enough sports or money for women.

Rowing was, when you think about it, a brilliant solution. It wasn't particularly expensive—all you needed was some water, a boathouse, and a few boats. Each boat would hold eight athletes, plus a coxswain.

Add a few fours and pairs, and hire a head coach (at a fraction of the cost of a football coach) and maybe an assistant or two. Before you could shout, "Rowers ready!" you were in compliance.

As improbable as it sounds, this is how rowing became the sport of choice for women and saved college football in the process. In 1995, the year Kansas State announced its new team, there were forty-four Division I women's rowing squads with 1,804 athletes. Five years later there were eighty-four teams and nearly 5,000 rowers—almost exactly the number needed to offset football and comply with Title IX.

This was no accident. Without women's rowing, football would have been forced to shrink its squads, which, in turn, would have threatened the financial model underpinning college sports, including everything from the size of the stadiums to the multimillion-dollar pay packages lavished on the coaches. While it was exciting that women got a new sport, even if it happened to be the redheaded stepchild of football, and the women eagerly welcomed the opportunity, it made for a tricky balancing act—or, put another way, an awkward sort of codependency.

Because the football schools now had to rely on women's rowing to offset their big numbers, part of the job description of rowing coaches was to effectively become used-car salesmen and meet a quota by producing enough bodies. The big football schools even had a formula: Each year, before the season started, the athletic directors sent their women's rowing coaches a target number they needed to balance the football number. It might be fifty rowers or it might be a hundred, but in any event it was a big number and critical to maintaining the balance between men's and women's programs. But there was still a problem: The women got only twenty scholarships. Where were the rowing coaches supposed to find scores of unpolished athletes willing to rise before dawn and push themselves through relentlessly grueling workouts for little or no money?

The short answer was wherever they could: at freshman orientation and class sign-ups; waiting in line for lunch; walking around campus. The coaches looked anywhere they might find a tall, rangy woman with a little muscle on her. And when they saw one, they shadowed her until the right moment. Then they leaped forward and made their pitch: *Hey, have you ever thought about women's rowing?*

"It's a little bit like dating, like the singles bar scene," explained Bebe Bryans, the head coach at Wisconsin, which has one of the largest women's rowing programs in the country. "You have to get up your nerve and just go for it."

That's because, in the end, it *is* all about the numbers. If the coaches don't hit their target, nothing else matters. And while their job description doesn't say they are there to save football from itself, the truth of the matter is never far from their minds.

"Really, it's all built around football, and we just play along," said Megan Cooke, a former champion rower and one of Bryans's assistants. "The flip side is all of these women get a chance to compete in a really challenging sport, which is a good thing."

●   ●   ●

I first became interested in women's rowing by accident. At the time, I was studying reports that the major football schools were required to file annually with the NCAA. Among other data, the reports included a breakdown of the athletes participating in each sport. The first thing I noticed was the odd correlation between football and rowing. Any time I looked at a report for one of the big football powers, I inevitably found it also sponsored a large women's rowing program.

The second thing I noticed was the sheer size of the rowing squads. Wisconsin, for example, reported having 205 women rowers on its roster. *Really?* I thought. *How do you chase around two hundred and five rowers?* But it wasn't only Wisconsin—UCLA, Michigan, Ohio State, Washington, and many other football schools also reported surprisingly large numbers of women rowers. It was hard to tell if the numbers were real or a fiction— some kind of trick or artifact embedded in the reporting. Rowing, it seemed, was the most ecumenical sport of all.

Another thing that jumped out of the numbers was the huge gap in funding between the two sports. Many schools were spending the equivalent of $100,000 to $200,000 on each of their football players but just a few thousand dollars on each rower. I understood that football was paying for the rowing programs. That was how the financial model worked; football underwrote all of the sports with little or no revenue of their own. But how was it possible to spend so much on one team and so little on another?

A large part of the gap was explained by salaries. The head coaches in women's rowing programs were paid between $60,000 to $130,000, while the football coaches at elite programs collected $3 million on average—even though the rowing coaches were responsible for overseeing nearly identical numbers of athletes.

Here the head coach at one major rowing program—a woman—told me an interesting story. "When I was at my last school," she said, "I added up my salary and the salaries of all my assistants and compared it to what the football coach got. He was paid more in one month than we got for the entire year! When I asked the athletic director about it, he told me it was the market."

As it happens, the legislators who invented Title IX more or less gave football a pass on its extraordinary expenses. It was one of those weird, circular arguments—football is expensive, therefore, it can spend whatever it needs—that managed to completely skirt the most basic question of fairness. Unless, that is, you bought into the idea that football was a separate business, not really part of the university's educational mission, and thus free to spend whatever it wanted.

The last thing I noticed was the unlikely geography of a surprising number of rowing programs. They were scattered across Oklahoma, Texas, Alabama, Tennessee, Iowa, and Kansas, among other locations. This fact seemed as good a place as any to start to investigate. So I called the head coach of Kansas State, a wry sixty-year-old former Olympian named Patrick Sweeney, and asked him if I could come out for a visit.

"I'll be at the reservoir at six thirty in the morning," Sweeney said in a lilting accent. "If you can find me, you're welcome to ride along in the launch."

"Is it hard?" I asked, meaning finding him.

"It's a little tricky," he said. "You have to drive across the dam and then down a long dirt road until you get to the boathouse. We're sort of stashed away on the side of the hill there."

Sweeney asked me what I wanted to know, and I explained that I was interested in the numbers. "Really, what I want to hear is how you manage to find eighty or ninety women rowers in a state that has no rowing," I said.

Sweeney laughed and told me I was coming to the right place. "I've been asking myself the same question for ten years," he said. "How do you convince someone to come and row in the middle of nowhere? I'm not sure I have a good answer but I'm happy to tell you what I've learned. Just make sure to turn right at the dam. Otherwise, you're going to be wandering around in the dark awhile."

•   •   •

Up until the moment in 2003 when he heard there was an opening at Kansas State, Patrick Sweeney didn't realize Kansas State even *had* a rowing program. In that regard he wasn't alone. Although women's rowing had been introduced nearly a decade earlier, it had largely operated under the radar, having won no championships or national acclaim. Now Sweeney found himself studying a map of the United States in an attempt to locate Manhattan, Kansas. "I truly had no idea where it was," he said. "All I knew was that it wasn't the other Manhattan."

Where it was, was in the middle of the country, in the middle of nowhere, really, in a sparsely beautiful, windswept landscape of rolling flint hills interspersed with farmland. Sweeney was pleasantly surprised when he looked out of the airplane carrying him there and saw trees and hills. *It's not that flat!* he remembers thinking.

Sweeney had literally grown up around the sport, two blocks from an Oxford boathouse in the United Kingdom, and was at various points in his athletic career considered a star. He was small: barely five feet tall and one hundred pounds, the perfect size for a coxswain, which he was on the Junior National Team and later in two Olympics, winning a silver medal as a member of the men's eight in 1976 in Montreal. After retiring from competition, Sweeney took on a series of high-profile coaching jobs, overseeing national teams in the UK, Canada, and Belgium, as well as serving as the head coach of the women's team at perennial power Cal-Berkeley.

The day Sweeney showed up for his interview at Kansas State, one of the assistant athletic directors drove him out to Tuttle Creek. It was sunny and calm, and Sweeney remembers thinking: *This is great water; it's flat.* When he asked if the conditions were always like this, the assistant athletic director paused before answering: Yes, of course. "She lied to me," he laughed. "I guess I shouldn't say 'lied.' Anyway, I learned soon enough."

Tuttle Creek Reservoir is essentially a wind tunnel. Imagine a fifteen-mile-long dishpan of water rimmed on either side by thirty-foot-high flint walls. The wind roars down the tunnel from the north, generating currents and waves, the enemies of all rowers. By the time of my visit in April 2013, Sweeney's team had managed to practice on the water just seven times in the previous five months.

"I didn't realize how much of a challenge it would be when I took the job," Sweeney told me in the gravel parking lot overlooking the reservoir. A sliver of moon still hovered in the black-blue sky. "Honestly, you shouldn't be able to put a crew out of this program. The water is bad. Winters can be horrendous. The amount of water time is minimal. You can't recruit people who have rowed before [in high school or for clubs]. We have no tank [indoor practice facility]. No real facilities."

Despite these obstacles, Sweeney had grown to like Manhattan and enjoyed the challenge of building something from scratch. "We probably aren't going to win the NCAAs, and I'm okay with that," he said. "We have a different philosophy around here. It's all about teaching and giving these women an opportunity to get a good education and be part of a sport. Given all of the hurdles, I think the girls have done an exceptional job."

A little later we headed onto the water in a small launch. The wind was already beginning to fill in the unprotected areas. Sweeney directed the two varsity eight boats toward the dam, where there was less wind. This morning they were going to practice sprinting up and back—a drill he called "working the wall." Each boat would race approximately 750 meters six times with a brief recovery in between. Including the warm-up and cool-down, the rowers would cover the equivalent of 7.5 miles. Sweeney took out his stopwatch and instructed the number one varsity eight to get ready. A moment later the boat sprinted away with surprising speed and then just as quickly settled into a rhythm. The overall effect, I thought, was of a water spider gliding over the surface.

Hanna Wiltfong, a former Kansas State rower now serving as a graduate assistant, was sitting cross-legged on the hood of the launch studying the rowers. "Look at that," she said to Sweeney. "Haney is sitting all wrong. Look at the curve in her back. She is throwing herself back too much."

Madi Haney was a freshman who'd been rowing only a few months. She was enormously talented, which explained why she was rowing with the varsity team, but still raw technically. She was, Sweeney and Wiltfong agreed, having a rough morning. "You look like a sack of potatoes," Sweeney shouted at her through a megaphone. "Get your shoulders up, weight down. Keep your core strong, Haney. Do you understand me?"

Haney, sitting in the fifth seat, grimly nodded back. For a few moments her form was perfect, quiet and more or less erect, but then she started to bow again, forming an *S* shape as she pulled and released her blade.

"Haney, straighten up; clean up your blade!" There was more urgency now in Sweeney's voice. Although it was only April, he could already sense the season slipping away. "What you are seeing this morning is the lack of water time," he said.

"Rowing is a magical sport," Wiltfong said a moment later. Her words seemed to come out of thin air, so I asked her what she meant. She was tall, with a wave of blond hair, and incisively funny—the good cop to Sweeney's bad cop in this morning routine. "When it's beautiful out here, you can just go and go," she said. "You listen for the blade. When it hits the water perfectly, it makes a small booming sound." Here she imitated the sound: "Boom, boom, boom. If you hear that sound when you are racing, you think, *Shit, they're coming up on us, walking the boat.* But when it is working right, rowing is one body, one sound; eight people, one body. Boom, boom, boom. Skim. Rise. Pop."

It is Hanna Wiltfong who is magical, I thought.

There were fifty to sixty rowers in eights, fours, and even a few pairs. The boats crisscrossed the water, hugging the flint walls, out of the rising wind. The number of rowers was down by one third from the fall count that the school had reported for Title IX purposes, but that was to be expected, Sweeney said. As soon as the women came to realize the demands, they weeded themselves out. By spring, the racing season, only the truly committed remained.

Like other Division I programs, Kansas State is allowed the equivalent of twenty full scholarships, the most of any NCAA-sanctioned women's sport. Sweeney carves up the awards into shares so he can spread the money around. He rarely gives unproven freshmen more than books, and then increases their awards if they remain in the program.

This led to a conversation about Sweeney's recruiting philosophy. "I'd call what we do a homebred program," he laughed. "We can't recruit stars and we don't recruit internationals [Olympic-caliber rowers from foreign national teams], so we concentrate on the Kansas high schools. The team is almost entirely walk-ons: Kansas girls who played basketball and other sports. I would actually prefer to recruit someone like Haney, who never rowed in high school, and teach her. 'We'll walk you into it' is our approach. We'll teach you from the bottom up."

What he was more or less describing was the most democratic sport on campus—the one sport where anyone interested and willing to put in the work actually had a chance of becoming a member of a Division I varsity team. Football and basketball, as well as most college sports, didn't operate this way. They had more athletes to pick from than they could use. Women's rowing, on the other hand, had a surplus of positions and not nearly enough rowers to fill them—at least not accomplished rowers. It was a poorly kept secret that some coaches practically threw scholarships at mediocre high school rowers to make their numbers. Others filled their boats with foreigners. The only schools that didn't seem to have problems meeting their quotas were located on the coasts, where there was good water and warmer weather.

Being squirreled away in the middle of the country, however, inspired the coaches to devise creative and sometimes surprising solutions to recruiting. Sweeney and his assistants sent out questionnaires to each of the 368 high schools in Kansas inquiring about promising athletes—meaning long, strong women who probably played basketball or volleyball and thus were ideally suited to gain leverage in a narrow, two-foot-wide rowing shell. Most of these girls weren't good enough to play their high school sport at the Division I level, but they might be talented enough to continue at a smaller school or a junior college. It was Sweeney's job to persuade them to come row.

Many of these young women came from tiny farm towns with populations of one hundred or less. Unlike football players, they did not have the luxury of staying on campus during the summer and taking classes. "Mainly what they do is go home and work on the farm. That's how they make money," Sweeney said.

After practice, Sweeney and I talked in his cluttered basement office in one of the old athletic buildings. He was literally set up in the cellar in a cramped, airless space, surrounded by boxes of Nike gear—"swag" he awarded to varsity rowers. I asked him about the numbers again and he shrugged. "It's all about Title IX, staying in balance," he said.

The only sport that wasn't significantly affected by these maneuvers was football, which wasn't entirely surprising because it was the money sport. Assistant football coaches weren't assigned to shadow would-be players in orientation lines. Football set the ceiling, and all of the other sports, including women's rowing, followed along. Again, this wasn't necessarily a bad thing as much as it was an awkward fact of life. Rowing supplied the bodies, and football supplied the money. Kansas State, for example, was expanding its football stadium, adding luxury boxes and premium seating. The additional revenue was helping to pay for an indoor facility for the women's rowing team, with two tanks large enough to hold practice shells. Sweeney was thrilled. Finally they would be able to train on water in the harsh winter months, even if it wasn't real water.

NUMBERS GAME: FOOTBALL AND WOMEN'S ROWING

SCHOOL	FOOTBALL	WOMEN'S ROWING	PERCENT WOMEN ATHLETES
Wisconsin	120	205	44%
Washington	111	154	46%
Michigan	114	147	35%
UCLA	128	123	31%
Ohio State	103	103	25%
Iowa	121	108	32%
Kansas State	104	82	36%
Kansas	126	76	26%
Alabama	138	77	29%
West Virginia	128	80	30%

Source: NCAA reports; author's analysis.

•   •   •

Title IX is not a pure abstraction, though it is often treated that way by its critics, who seem to consider it more an annoyance than a reality. A short history of the law might be summed up this way: Before 1972 there was very little organized rowing for women at the college level. Today there are 145 teams and 7,300 athletes spread across large and small schools, scholarships covering roughly 2,000 athletes, and a national championship held each June. Multiply that by a dozen other women's sports—soccer, lacrosse, field hockey, et cetera—and you begin to see the impact of the legislation.

But the passage of Title IX was not the end of the story; it was merely the beginning. For instance, the most basic question of all had to be solved: How do you measure fairness in athletics? Is it the number of athletes, the amount of money you spend per athlete, the size of a coach's salary, or even the relative lavishness of locker rooms? All of this had to be sorted out—and even now, four decades later, continues to be negotiated. Many outsiders assume that Title IX requires schools to spend equally across men's and women's sports. But in fact there is nothing approaching financial equity in college sports, and once again the reason is football. Football is so big and expensive it overwhelms all comparisons.

I crunched a few more numbers and found that in 2012 the average Division I football team spent eleven times as much on each football player as women's rowing teams spent on each rower. The gaps included everything from recruiting to travel to salaries. My analysis found that head football coaches were paid the equivalent of thirty thousand dollars for each player—women's rowing coaches about one thousand. Overall, male coaches accounted for nearly three-quarters of all the money available for coaching salaries—a disparity so large that I didn't believe it at first. Part of the reason was that, like a lot of other people, I'd bought into the narrative that Title IX had changed everything, when really what it had changed was everything except the money.

Back in 1974, two years after Title IX was passed, the University of Texas football coach Darrell Royal was so worried that the new law would ruin his beloved sport that he started lobbying his Texas senators for help. Royal hoped to obtain a full-blown exemption from Title IX. He didn't get that, but college football did benefit from language subsequently inserted into an education bill by New York Republican senator Jacob Javits. The amendment acknowledged the unique nature (i.e., high cost) of some sports (namely, football) and effectively blocked federal regulators from comparing the cost of football to other sports as part of their Title IX investigations. Javits was merely trying to get a bill passed while accommodating fellow senators from football-mad states like Texas. Still, his amendment was a significant gift, for it allowed schools to spend lavishly on their football teams without fear and in the process inadvertently encouraged decades of runaway costs that haunt college presidents to this day.

Football coaches wanted to keep most, if not all, of the money that football generated for their teams. They "supported" Title IX and women's sports, they contended, but not if it limited opportunities for men. Officials at Penn State, for example, worried that providing women athletes with scholarships would take away from men's sports like tennis and golf, university archives show. At the time, in the mid-1970s, two hundred male athletes at Penn State received full athletic scholarships. Women athletes received eighteen.

Over time, women have generally caught up in scholarships, and Penn State is now among the leaders in women's sports. But the gyrations that athletic directors still go through to achieve a balance sometimes lead to surprising results. For example, some of the largest, richest football schools, especially in the SEC and Big 12, get there by sharply limiting the number of sports for men. The schools typically offer as few as five or six sports for men, with football accounting for half or more of all male athletes. Instead of spending a little less on football and adding a men's team or two, the athletic directors appear to have decided it is easier to punish the men.

"It's counterintuitive that some of the largest universities with the biggest athletic budgets offer fewer opportunities for both men and women than many smaller schools," said Nancy Hogshead-Makar, a former Olympic gold medalist in swimming, an attorney, and an advocate for women's sports. "You would think it would be the exact opposite. But football jacks everything up so much, the cost of everything, that it just allows these huge disparities."

•   •   •

The quickest and simplest way for schools to comply with Title IX is called the "proportionality prong." Say 50 percent of the undergraduates at the University of Wisconsin are female. In theory, then, 50 percent of the varsity athletes should be female, mirroring the demographics of the student body. As it happens, 51.6 percent of Wisconsin undergraduates are female, and 53 percent of the athletes are female, so the school easily meets its gender equity requirement.

As a matter of fact, Wisconsin is one of a small number of elite football schools with more female than male athletes—415 versus 372, according to its 2011 NCAA filing. One of the main reasons is its huge women's rowing squad. That year Wisconsin reported 171 women rowers and 107 football players. Four of every ten varsity female athletes on campus were members of the rowing squad. It was, in nearly every sense, an extraordinary number.

I was curious what criteria Wisconsin used to count its athletes. I also wanted to know a little about the economics of Wisconsin rowing and how it compared with football. So I called Terry Gawlik, an assistant athletic director who works with the rowing program. She explained that the rowing numbers reported to the NCAA (171 in 2011 and 205 in 2012) were taken during tryouts in September, when the number of rowers was at its peak. They did not reflect the number of actual rowers in the spring, after large numbers of athletes quit.

That sounded to me as if Wisconsin were fudging its count to increase the number of women athletes. But Gawlik explained that it was what the NCAA asked for; the NCAA instructed the schools to report the count during their fall tryouts, when it was highest. Gawlik insisted that it accurately reflected the interest in rowing. "Here's the deal," she said. "Are we giving those kids an opportunity to be in a boat? Yes, we are."

By spring, the number of rowers might be closer to 100 or 120, including the varsity open weight (no weight limits), novices (first-time rowers), and lightweights (rowers under 130 pounds). Wisconsin is one of only a handful of schools with a lightweight program. In the late 1990s it added the lightweights, ice hockey, and softball as part of a settlement of a twelve-year-old gender-equity investigation. Since then the lightweights have won several national championships. However, unlike the open weights, lightweight rowers don't get scholarships.

With its large number of women rowers, Wisconsin is even able to add a spot here and there for men in other sports and still be in compliance with Title IX. "It's part of what we call roster management," Gawlik said. "We figure out our target numbers and match them to our campus enrollment. We're always looking at our numbers. . . . We massage them as we can. It is a work in progress every year."

I asked Gawlik why football got eighty-five scholarships and women's rowing got only twenty. She said the NCAA set the numbers, not the schools. She suggested that it would be hard for smaller schools that field Division I football teams (known as midmajors) to afford more than twenty scholarships, adding, "But that's a guess." I noted that those smaller schools didn't seem to have trouble coming up with enough money to pay for eighty-five football scholarships. Here Gawlik paused. "We're still not in sync for scholarships," she acknowledged.

Wisconsin spends $2.3 million on women's rowing, which sounds like a lot but is actually a bargain. By comparison, football costs $24 million, including $2.7 million for scholarships alone. In 2013 the head football coach earned nearly twice as much in one month ($225,000) as Bebe Bryans earns in a year ($122,000). "We're our own worst enemies," Gawlik said, meaning, I suppose, that women should ask for more.

Bryans had an interesting take on the salary issue. "They got us for cheap in the beginning because we were really grateful for the opportunity," she said, "and we still are." Years ago, while at another school, Bryans calculated that with all of the hours she was putting in she was making the equivalent of the salary of a grocery bagger at Safeway. But she acknowledged, "The people who go into coaching women's rowing are different. We're supporting what college athletics are really supposed to be about, making the kid a better person, a better student, a better citizen. We're not in the entertainment business the way football is. We just aren't."

Bryans was speaking to me by phone from her second-story office in Porter Boathouse overlooking Lake Mendota, which frames the northernmost edge of the campus. It was the spring of 2013, and I was trying to arrange a visit. Normally Bryans's team would be practicing on open water, but it had been the coldest winter in decades, and there were still ten inches of ice covering the lake. "It's so thick you can land a plane on it," she sighed.

"So can I come out?" I asked.

"You *have* to come," Bryans said, "but you should wait until September, when we hold tryouts. Otherwise you'll miss it."

"Miss what?" I said.

"The absolute chaos," Bryans said, not missing a beat. "It's awesome."

·   ·   ·

One of the things you quickly realize about Bebe Bryans is that there is nothing ordinary about her. She is so totally invested in her sport that she doesn't just want her athletes to experience rowing; she wants them to give up their bodies and minds to it. "There is nothing harder physically than rowing," she told me, "and there's nothing as challenging mentally. There are so many points when it would just be easier to quit. You have to get up early in the morning. You row in the cold and rain. You lift weights. You run. And then you row between twelve thousand and eighteen thousand meters in practice, day after day. There is no way to fake that. You are either committed or you aren't. That's what makes the difference between really good rowers and all of the other rowers: their level of toughness and commitment."

The fifty-six-year-old Bryans scuba dives with whales and sharks in Mexico and has a tattoo. She left her last coaching job because she found the area boring and Madison struck her "as a really interesting place." She describes her coaching philosophy as old school. Rowers have to earn their place in her program, working their way up from novice to one of the varsity eights or fours. "That's one of the things I love about rowing," she says. "You can come in here knowing nothing and leave being an Olympian."

"So rowing really is one of the last truly democratic sports," I suggested.

"I never thought of it that way," Bryans said. "But I like it. It's all about looking at yourself in the mirror every day and asking whether what you did was enough."

Bryans herself came to rowing sideways. As a young girl in northern California she was a promising swimmer, but like many promising swimmers she flamed out at an early age. She took part in multiple sports at Los Altos High School, played the viola, and was in the marching band. "It was before the age of specialization," she observed.

Smart and curious but restless, Bryans left USC after one semester ("still my biggest regret") to be closer to a boy up north. She lingered a year at San Jose State before deciding she needed to take a year off to find herself. One year morphed into seven and an eclectic string of jobs, including managing a restaurant, until she decided that she needed to go back to school.

By this point Bryans was involved in a small rowing club across San Francisco Bay in Oakland. "I just sort of wandered over there one day and started rowing," she said. "This old guy was running the club. A bunch of high schools were rowing out of there. One day he didn't feel like coaching his team. He asked me to take them out. I didn't even know how to run a motorboat." Bryans wound up coaching two teams and discovering a secret: She loved coaching and was good at it.

While she was finishing her master's degree at San Francisco State, a small, private school for women in nearby Oakland asked her to coach its rowing team. Bryans also served as the sports information director and taught two phys ed classes. "And I had another job on the side. I was a full-time coach but I had to have a second job to pay the bills." She stayed four years at Mills College and even managed to beat a few Pac-10 (now Pac-12) teams.

In the mid-1990s Michigan State hired Bryans to be the first head coach of its women's program. The squad was "big and enthusiastic but not very fast." Nevertheless Bryans coached them up to the point that they made the NCAA championships five of the seven years she was in East Lansing. "My whole take on Title IX is it would be great if everybody did the right thing because it was the right thing, but I'll take what it is because, look, we have all of these women."

•   •   •

A week after Labor Day in 2013, more than two hundred women showed up at Porter Boathouse for practice. I watched as a group of tall, dispro-portionately blond athletes shouldered sixty-foot-long, two-hundred-pound shells back and forth to the launch, barely avoiding errant bicyclists hurtling by at breakneck speeds. Some of the boats had inspirational names. One was called *Crediamo*, which translates to "We Believe." The smaller pairs were named after dances. One was called *Salsa*. Another, *Merengue*.

"Two hundred girls is amazing," Bryans said, but in one respect it wasn't necessarily surprising. Women have been rowing on Lake Mendota since the late 1800s, and in the 1970s Wisconsin was one of the first schools to sponsor a varsity program. Even with its long, harsh winters,

Wisconsin is almost always competitive. Part of that is the tradition, and part is the spectacularly competitive nature of its head coach, who refuses to see ordinary and almost always sees potential greatness.

As at Kansas State, many of Wisconsin's recruits were high school basketball and volleyball players who had never rowed before. What they had—and what Bryans saw—was height, leverage, and heart. A few of them filtered through the summer camps that Wisconsin ran. Anne Rauschert, a powerful six-foot athlete with extraordinary discipline, came to Bryans that way. Rauschert participated in volleyball, basketball, and track at Wayland Academy in Beaver Dam, Wisconsin. The summer of her junior year she came to the rowing camp "on a whim." Three days in, Megan Cooke told Anne that she had Olympic potential. "I laughed so hard," Rauschert recalled, yet four years later she was closer to achieving that than she had ever imagined. In 2013 Rauschert had been selected to row in the United States eight boat that won a World Championship in Austria, and she is now ranked among the nation's elite young rowers. Rauschert neatly fit Bryans's definition of a type A personality. She trained and rowed with great discipline, was a strong student majoring in art, painted, and even took wedding photos on the side.

"Many of these girls haven't been bad at something in a long time," Bryans observed. "That's why rowing sometimes is such a shock to their system. They're achievers. They get good or great grades and major in real hard subjects like biochemistry or bacteriology. Many become teachers and nurses. They want to be great people. They just don't know what that means yet. That's part of what they learn being on this team."

We were standing outside the boathouse watching dozens of eager novices shouldering boats to the water. Bryans, who is five feet ten, with thick auburn hair she tucks under a baseball cap and bright hazel eyes, was responding so rapidly to my questions that I was having trouble keeping up. Apparently I wasn't the only one. Her intensity sometimes frightens younger rowers "who are scared of going so hard," Rauschert told me. "I love Bebe. The only complaint I have is sometimes she talks too much and she can only focus on one thing at a time."

· · ·

Bryans divides fall workouts to accommodate the big numbers and focus on teaching. The varsity rows in the morning, novices in the afternoon. "With over two hundred rowers, it's a little bit like herding cats," she said.

There were sixty-five novices at one of the practices I attended. They came in all shapes and sizes, and while some had rowed before, many more hadn't. "There are no rules; each school has a different take on novices," Bryans explained. "We generally have every freshman who comes in row freshman [novice] for at least two months. We do that for a couple of reasons. One is to give them time to adjust to college life; college is the biggest change in their lives. Another is to allow them to bond with their teammates. Then if someone picks it up quickly and stands out, we may move them up to practice with the varsity."

So much of rowing is muscle memory, Bryans later explained as she deftly steered a small motorboat away from several pairs rowing out and back on a route known as Picnic Point. "In the eights the rowers don't talk. They're not supposed to talk. It is supposed to be experience and grit." Conversely, the rowers in pairs are expected to communicate. "Pairs are much less stable," Bryans said. "The margin of error is much smaller. Every little mistake shows. That's why we use them for training—to get rowers to communicate. That's how they learn trust. They have to talk their way through."

"How do you motivate your team?" I asked at this point.

"It's not my job to motivate them," Bryans responded over the sound of the university marching band practicing in the distance. "It is my job to inspire them."

A little later she pointed to a rower struggling with her oars. "Use your oars as an extension of your arms," she shouted, "instead of as a stick coming out of your arms." Then, to another rower slouching on her seat: "It's the same posture before the catch as after the catch. Keep your weight centered on the seat. Keep your belly button tall. Focus on your core."

At the end of practice Bryans announced she was satisfied. There was a lot of power and potential speed on the water. It was raw but it was there. "We're going to be good next year," she said. "The question is, can we be good this year [2014]?"

•   •   •

The following morning I was up at 5:00 A.M. and on my way to varsity practice. It was carbon black outside, no wind. *Great*, I thought, *the lake should be glassy.* A moment later a surge of light splashed across the sky, followed by large drops of rain.

By the time I reached the boathouse, the rain was a downpour. Bryans waited on the steps holding a cup of coffee. "Time for plan B," she announced. "We're going to do a step test this morning."

I had no idea what a step test was but followed her as she sprinted up the steps to a room packed with erg machines. It was only 6:00 A.M., but the room was already overflowing with women in unis and various other pieces of athletic apparel that would be banned at Catholic schools. They stretched and flexed as lightning flashed outside the tall glass windows. The room was stifling hot, music booming. It was then that I saw Megan Cooke standing to the side, wearing the slightest trace of a grin.

"Okay," I asked, "what is a step test?"

Cooke explained that a step test was a drill to see how far and hard a rower could push herself before breaking. And each and every one of the fifty-odd rowers in the room would break, she told me, because the "machine is god. No one can beat the machine. The machine always wins."

"The step test is a test of failure," Bryans added. "Everyone will fail."

Some would fail sooner than others. They would anticipate the pain and quit as soon as it surfaced, afraid of what Bryans called "the dark room." Others would hang on a little longer but then give up. Still others, like Anne, would push herself to the edge before letting go. "Part of being an elite athlete is adapting to pain," Bryans said. "Once you have gone through it, you adapt to it the next time, and the time after that, so you know what to expect and can push yourself to the next level."

A few minutes later the first set of rowers settled onto their machines. They were starting at 140 watts, which wasn't considered particularly hard, and would work their way up at 30-watt intervals, with brief rests in between. Cooke likened the exercise to lifting weights: On each rep you add a little more weight until gravity eventually wins out.

A minute or two passed. The rowers glided easily forward and back on their seats. Occasionally they looked at a small screen that fed back their speed, time, distance, and heart rate. The idea was to stay as close to the wattage on the screen as possible: to not slip below the rate or spurt ahead of it. Other rowers stood behind the machines recording numbers and shouting encouragement.

I stood behind Anne to see if I could understand her magic. But her expression never changed, even as the watts inched higher and higher. She was completely fluid and efficient in her movements. One of the coxswains cranked up the music and the room began to thump. Megan Cooke laughed. "This is how Bebe and I keep up with the culture," she said.

One by one the rowers slipped inside the pain until finally Anne was the only one left. The other rowers crowded behind her, cheering. The Watts were now up to three hundred, or maybe it was four hundred? It was impossible to see through the knot of bodies. It occurred to me that she might keep going forever. Some girls were monsters on the erg but mediocre on the water. Anne was great on the machine and on the water. The light outside slowly shifted from black to gray as the storm moved away. I noticed a sign on the far wall. It read: BIG TEN CHAMPIONS 2010. And then, just like that, Anne was finished. There was no announcement. She simply had reached the end. No one, not even Anne Rauschert, beat the machine.

There were many other stories inside the erg room that morning. Some of them I understood and some I didn't. A rower named Steph unexpectedly came close to matching Anne's score. Another who should have done better gave up. "She should be so good, but she never will because she's not willing to hurt," Bryans said.

The morning of the step test was when I fell in love with women's rowing: with the toughness, the pain, the attention to detail, even the idea of a dark room. It was disturbing how easy it was to create a narrative that didn't respect women as athletes, that minimized their sports because they didn't attract huge crowds or make money or even blamed them for cutting into men's sports, the way critics did. The striking thing to me about women's rowing was how it accomplished so much with so little. In so many ways it seemed the model for how sports should be, not a form of entertainment but a personal journey, and at a fraction of the cost of football.

Seven

• • •

TO HAVE AND HAVE NOT: HOW COLLEGE PRESIDENTS FUMBLED REFORM

BY THE MID-2000S MANY OF the presidents of the largest and richest football schools knew they were selling an illusion. Their schools marketed themselves as elite educational institutions, and yet their best-known product, the product they relied on to prop up their brands, had nothing to do with education. In so many ways football had subsumed the higher purpose of their schools. If they weren't dealing with the latest football scandal—cheating, drugs, sexual assaults, robberies, barroom battles, gun-wielding players, et cetera—they were taking calls from reporters about the coach's multimillion-dollar salary or the dismal academic performance of the team. The games themselves now seemed to stretch over the course of an entire week—turn on cable, and there was your team playing at 11:00 P.M. on a Wednesday in Provo or Boise. And to what end? How did playing football in the middle of the week benefit anyone except the fabulously rich sports channels? More and more it seemed as if the athletic department were an extension of ESPN.

Even more damaging, the university itself felt like an entertainment channel, there to amuse the masses.

In 2006 the schools' leaders acknowledged all of this and more in a remarkable document prepared by the NCAA's Presidential Task Force on the future of college athletics. That the report was issued by the NCAA was confusing, as the organization had surprisingly little control over football and its riches. More to the point, the association was viewed by many as a hapless bureaucracy, not an agent of change. True, it did release reports; it had an entire library gathering dust at its Indianapolis headquarters. But most of the reforms the NCAA did introduce were at the margins, tinkering with this regulation or that regulation, and by no means the kind of bold, game-changing moves that were needed to restore integrity and fiscal sense to a multibillion-dollar, media-driven enterprise gone ballistic. There was simply too much money at stake, so it was easier for both the association and the schools' administrations to look the other way. College presidents had become very much like politicians who bitterly complain about the money-driven election system as they march out the door to collect their next campaign check.

Which was why, at least at first glance, the NCAA task force's 2006 report seemed so surprising, even radical, in its tone and direction. In a letter accompanying the report, the association's then-president, Myles Brand, detailed the unsustainable economic reality of college sports, with its inflationary spending, irrational arms race, and media-driven values. The report's authors, fifty university presidents and chancellors, then made an extraordinary admission, writing that it was time to abandon the prevailing financial model, which encouraged their athletic departments to operate as stand-alone businesses. That philosophy "has pushed the enterprise away from the university, created an unhealthy atmosphere of autonomy and in some cases activated a level of commercial collaboration outside of the values of higher education," they concluded.

Considering the source, the admission felt momentous. For the first time the presidents were publicly acknowledging that they were wrong; that the financial model they had relied on for decades had shape-shifted into a kind of monster that was now rampaging across their campuses, knocking down everything in its path. Moreover, the presidents wrote, universities' attempts to elevate their status through football were a fool's errand—"little more than a 'get rich quick' branding initiative."

But instead of calling for all-out reform—say, by asking the NCAA or Congress to draft an entirely new financial model limiting salaries and spending—the presidents called for more and better presidential control. Their exact words were "There must be presidential leadership that begins at the campus level, and there must be institutional accountability for the conduct of the enterprise [football and athletics]."

I could see where this was leading: The same presidents who had fostered this mess now expected that, by being slightly more vigilant, they would be able to fix it. And they were going to do so without making major changes—for example, by bringing their athletic departments back in-house and subjecting football and the other sports to the same budgetary limits as the history and English departments.

How is this going to work? I wondered. For example, when the president of ESPN showed up on their doorsteps with a bagful of money to play football in Spokane on a Thursday, were the presidents simply going to turn him away?

The 2006 task force wasn't the first time the presidents had complained about the tsunami that was now college athletics. In fact, they had been making essentially the same argument—with similar results—for three decades. In 1987, for instance, they'd gathered for two days at the Loews Anatole Hotel in Dallas, Texas, to talk about reforming their athletic empires.

It was the sixth time they'd met in a decade or so, and each time they'd retreated to what was now their default position: The presidents should exert more control over their athletic departments. It was what the presidents did whenever one scandal or another blew up to national proportions; they called for a task force or a special convention to study the issue. It was what they did, and they did it well.

The almost-two-hundred-page transcript from the 1987 Dallas gathering was revealing only in the sense that it wasn't revealing at all. Ira Michael Heyman, then chancellor of the University of California at Berkeley, laid out the issue at hand starkly. "We have overemphasized athletics to the point that athletics has become more important than education," he told his colleagues. "Somehow, we have committed ourselves to staging huge television extravaganzas. We can no longer just compete against each other. We have to put on a show for the nation." He continued: "Given these circumstances, we should not be surprised that many of us begin to act not as educators but as producers, promoters, impresarios and entrepreneurs."

Another president pointed out the fundamental contradiction in the presidents' thinking. If sports are truly educational, as the presidents claimed, why were they so reluctant to fund their teams with university dollars? Why would they instead turn their athletic departments into businesses and tell them to go find their own funding, which, inevitably, had led to the overcommercialization of sports and the problem of scale—ever-bigger budgets, salaries, stadiums, and scandals?

The problem couldn't have been stated any more clearly, yet when it came to actual reforms, most of the meaningful proposals that were put forward were ultimately defeated by the football coaches and athletic directors.

"Honestly, most college presidents are cheerleaders when it comes to football," Ronald Smith, a sports historian and former professor at Penn State, told me. "The presidents have been in complete control of the NCAA for almost two decades. My question is are NCAA schools better off with fewer violations than before the presidents were in control? I don't think so. I think presidential control has been a big failure."

In 2009 the Knight Commission on Intercollegiate Athletics, which was started in 1989 by the John S. and James L. Knight Foundation to study college athletics and propose reforms, issued a long report highlighting the unprecedented surge in spending on football and other sports. Again I was struck by several admissions in the report. The presidents told the commission they favored "serious change" but no longer saw themselves "as the force for the changes needed." Nor had they "identified an alternative force" they believed could be effective. In so many words, then, the presidents seemed to be saying: Somebody, anybody, please save us from ourselves. In a few years they had gone from "We'll take care of it" to "We don't have an answer."

Two years later, in August 2011, the NCAA sponsored a two-day retreat for the presidents of the biggest and richest football schools to debate the arms race in college athletics. The report from the meeting noted that spending on athletics had been growing at a rate two to three times faster than that of higher education itself for at least two decades. At the same time a significant gap had emerged between the richest football schools and the next tier of schools aspiring to join them. "The disparity in expense budgets leads to the question of competitive success and what will happen to competitive success in the future," the report's authors warned.

The presidents suggested several possible solutions, one of which called for a "redistribution of wealth" to close the income gap. This idea, of course, went nowhere. In fact, even as the presidents were going through the motions of reform, they were devising a new multibillion-dollar play-off scheme that would further enrich their schools at the expense of smaller, poorer football programs. The play-off would pump hundreds of millions annually into the five football superconferences while all of the other Division I conferences (think Sun Belt or Mountain West) watched from the sidelines.

None of which stopped the NCAA from issuing an ironic press release following its 2011 gathering: Division I leaders call for sweeping changes to college athletics. "The presidents all came together with a very clear, strong consensus that the status quo and continued order of the day is insufficient and that we need to have change in a number of key areas and we need to have it quickly," said the new NCAA president, Mark Emmert. Needless to say, significant change did not follow, and the gap between the five power football conferences and all of the others has only widened since. In fact, even as I write, the five superconferences have persuaded the NCAA to allow them to spend even more money on football scholarships, or what the football schools are calling "fully funding the cost of attending college."

At about this time two embarrassing episodes occurred that highlighted the futility of the reform efforts. The first involved Gordon Gee, a mercurial academic leader who, at least at one point, viewed himself as an agent of change. In the course of his career Gee had traveled among some of the most prestigious centers of learning and become famous for his bow ties and flamboyant speeches. In 2003 he had overhauled the athletic department at Vanderbilt and eliminated the title of athletic director. It was, in hindsight, largely a symbolic gesture, but it did get Vanderbilt and Gee a lot of good press. In the intervening years Vanderbilt had effectively lapsed back to standard operating procedure, jacked up its football program, and even restored the title of athletic director.

Gee, meanwhile, had returned to Ohio State, where he'd worked earlier in his career, but this time as president. In 2011 the head coach of the Buckeyes, Jim Tressel, was entangled in a bizarre scandal when some of his players traded Ohio State memorabilia for tats at a local tattoo parlor. It probably would have passed as a fairly minor scandal except that Tressel made the fatal mistake of trying to cover it up. Gee decided to suspend his coach and called a press conference. One of the reporters asked if Coach Tressel would lose his job, at which point Gee famously replied: "Are you kidding me? I'm just hopeful the coach doesn't dismiss me."

Later, Gee said he had been joking.

The second episode received far less attention. In June of 2013, in the wake of the Jerry Sandusky child-molestation scandal, Penn State announced it was giving then–head football coach Bill O'Brien a $1 million raise for guiding the team to a winning record during turbulent times. The raise was approved by the school's acting president, Rodney Erickson, who himself had earlier received an $85,000 raise. I didn't know which was more surprising: that Penn State would give any of its highest-ranking employees a raise so soon after the worst scandal in school history or that it thought the football coach's efforts were twelve times more valuable than the president's.

I asked to speak with President Erickson but was informed by his spokeswoman: "Dr. Erickson is respectfully declining. His travel and meeting schedule leaves little time for an interview—even one of short duration." This was pretty much word for word the same response I'd gotten from the presidents at Alabama and Oregon. I decided to look for a president who wasn't out of town, someone deep in the trenches who could help explain the gilded age of college football and what it all meant. The first stop in my journey ended at a wooded corporate retreat where the chancellor of the University System of Maryland holed up when he wasn't on the road.

•   •   •

Brit Kirwan struck me as ideally suited to talk about our national obsession with college football. For one thing, he had actually played football at a major university before becoming disillusioned with the sport.

Since then he had spent the entire half century of his professional career working at large public universities with extravagant football aspirations. He also happened to be one of the more outspoken members of the Knight Commission and was generally critical of college football's impact on the culture of schools.

His own flagship university, the University of Maryland, was a poster child for schools living beyond their means. For years its athletic department had been borrowing from a reserve fund to cover its annual losses—until 2011, when it couldn't borrow any more, and the department blew up. By "blew up" I mean it imploded: The athletic department was forced to cut eight teams and scale back spending. Now the university was fleeing the Atlantic Coast Conference for the Big Ten, where it would collect many more millions annually from the larger conference's lucrative football and basketball television deals.

The morning I visited Kirwan he was stuck in traffic near Baltimore and running forty minutes late. I knew this because he called every five or so minutes with an update. When he finally arrived, he immediately started talking, as if to make up for lost time. Kirwan had been a two-way end in high school in Lexington, Kentucky, in the 1950s, good enough to earn an athletic scholarship to the University of Kentucky. But after just one year of playing there he soured on the experience. "I was a mathematics major, but I found myself spending a disproportionate amount of time on football," he explained.

It doesn't make for much of a story when someone stops playing football—unless it's a football coach's son who quits. Kirwan's father, Albert, had been the head football coach at Kentucky from 1938 to 1944 and later served as the school's president. "There was a culture issue in that you were not expected to be a serious student. What you were supposed to focus on is football," Kirwan said. "I just felt like the right thing was to focus more on school."

Kirwan collected a doctorate at Rutgers, then started his academic career at the University of Maryland, working his way up to department chair and provost before serving as president for ten years. In 1998 he moved to Ohio State as president, before returning to Maryland in 2002 as chancellor of the entire system. He was now seventy-six and gray. But his back was straight, and when he stood to greet a visitor, I quickly noticed he was still split-end tall.

"Ultimately, I think the obsession with football is very corrupting to higher education," Kirwan said. At Ohio State the sport seemed to dominate the school. "It was such a football culture in Columbus; I found it very disturbing. The culture of football allegiance and reverence was disturbing. But nonetheless, because of it they can raise any amount of money they need to raise."

"Is money alone a problem?" I asked.

"No. But as the Knight Commission has shown, money becomes a problem when you are spending so much more on football and athletics than you are on academics. That is well documented not just for the big, rich schools but also for the schools that lose money. There are lots of schools that are using student fees and tuition to subsidize their money-losing athletic departments. A lot of them are losing $10 million a year. That money is being transferred from the university budget to prop up athletics."

According to Jeff Smith, a finance professor at the University of South Carolina Upstate, the smaller, poorer Division I schools spend $3.7 billion on athletic subsidies in an effort to catch up with the big guys. That is the failure of the football financial model: The rich schools get all of the money while the smaller, poorer schools have to resort to tapping student fees to subsidize their teams.

Kirwan encouraged me to look at one of his system's schools: Towson State University, outside Baltimore. Towson is a large school with twenty thousand students and a decent reputation academically. It also has aspirations to be great at football. The problem is that not many people share its enthusiasm for the game—attendance is dodgy, even when the team is good, and Towson doesn't come close to making money from football. Nearly 85 percent of the school's $21 million athletic budget comes from university subsidies: primarily student fees tacked onto tuition. The school also struggles to meet its Title IX requirements. In 2012 the administration tried to kill the men's baseball and soccer teams to achieve a better balance between men's and women's sports, but the state legislature kicked in hundreds of thousands of dollars to bail out the teams, though for how long it will do so is anyone's guess.

"Towson is an example of a school that wants to play big-time football but can't generate enough revenue from external forces," Kirwan said. "The sad part is there are probably a hundred and fifty other schools out there just like it."

I asked Kirwan directly why the presidents didn't put a stop to this foolishness. Here his answer surprised me. "The irony is it sounds like presidents are wimps," he replied. "But there is very little that presidents can do. Imagine the president of Alabama saying, 'We're going to deemphasize football.' How long would he [she] be president? The board wouldn't tolerate it. It has infected our culture such [that] the demand and expectation for big-time athletics becomes an irresistible force. And I do think it has a corrupting effect on education. Shame on us and shame on larger society. I am very critical of the media. They are the first to absolutely hammer universities when anything goes wrong. But then they venerate athletics every other day of the week."

It was a fair criticism, I thought, and not without its own irony. The newspapers, talk radio shows, and cable sports channels all feed off college football and make large amounts of money doing so but are quick to cluster-bomb every passing scandal—sexual abuse allegations at Florida State, cheating at North Carolina, football players arrested at Vanderbilt, et cetera. But blaming the media only got Kirwan so far. Did he actually think the presidents were powerless?

"No," he clarified. "It is part of their job to be involved. All I am saying is there are limits to how much they can do without losing their heads."

In December 2014 Ray L. Watts, the president of the University of Alabama at Birmingham, proposed eliminating his school's football team. UAB was a perfect example of what Kirwan was addressing: a school that didn't make money on football but nevertheless wanted to play with the big boys. Following the announcement, rallies and protests broke out on campus, and the Senate Faculty gave Watts a vote of "no confidence," later compelling him to abandon the idea. This even though UAB had won just one of every three football games it had played in the last decade (44 and 82) and was "taxing" its students to the tune of $18 million annually to play football and other sports. Indeed, student fees and university subsidies now accounted for two of every three dollars of revenue collected by UAB's athletic department, records showed.

I suppose Kirwan sensed my uneasiness at his response, because he quickly began to fill in some of the gaps. "I am not one of those people who think athletics doesn't have a role. Sure, it's part of the overall mission. Does that mean you have to believe in this grossly excessive enterprise we have created? Look at the money universities are spending on salaries for coaches. The salaries are so disproportionate to the compensation of the faculty it is inconsistent with the values and mission of the institutions.

"Here's where I think we went astray: the idea of making athletics self-supporting. If we had taken the revenue from intercollegiate athletics to support athletics but also to support the core of the institution, I

BILLIΟΝ-DΟLLAR BALL

would have no problem. The problem, in my view, is that an enormous amount of money the conferences get goes to support athletics. Compare that with intellectual property. Let's say a faculty member invents something. Some of the revenue goes back to the faculty member. The rest of the revenue goes to the institution."

"A lot of the big football schools do think of their teams as intellectual property," I pointed out.

"Except they don't get the revenue, or not very much of it," Kirwan replied.

This seemed to bring the conversation full circle. Maryland had imploded because it hadn't had enough money and had overreached, supporting as many as thirty teams before the cuts. "We had a big appetite but not the food to feed it," Kirwan said. "As painful as the cuts were, we had to right-size the athletic program relative to the revenue."

But now Maryland was joining a football-first conference, in large part for a fatter paycheck. It felt like a surrender to the inevitable, like Kirwan and his university were conceding that big football and big money ruled college athletics.

Apparently I wasn't the only one who felt this way. Jennifer Lee Hoffman, a researcher at the University of Washington who studies the role of college presidents in athletics, told me that Brit Kirwan was the only one not smiling in a 2012 photograph commemorating Maryland's decision to join the Big Ten.

"I don't know if he would admit he was uncomfortable," she said. "But it's hard to see how he wasn't. Dr. Kirwan has been involved in reform issues and outspoken on the role of money in college athletics since at least 2001. I saw that picture, and he just looked clearly uncomfortable."

When I asked about the photograph, Kirwan smiled ruefully but quickly added that he hadn't been uncomfortable. "I was very supportive of the decision, but not for the reason we were getting more money. There's no question it's a lot more revenue. But the president [of the University of Maryland [Wallace Loh] agreed that this just can't be about spending more on athletics. I asked that some of this revenue is spent on the university. Some of it has to go to the university. And he has agreed. Into the future we'll see how it all plays out."

In the meantime the Atlantic Coast Conference and the University of Maryland were suing each other over the question of how much Maryland should be charged for the privilege of exiting the conference. The ACC was asking for $52.2 million. The State of Maryland, representing its flagship university, was countersuing for $156.8 million. Among other charges, the state's attorney general alleged that the ACC had wildly inflated the exit fee.

Maryland had belonged to the ACC for sixty-one years, but college athletics were no longer about loyalty or tradition. If a larger, richer conference offered you a bigger paycheck, you were considered naive not to listen. In the last decade, dozens of schools had jumped from one conference to another, including many big football schools: Pittsburgh, Syracuse, Boston College, Missouri, and Texas A&M, among others. Still, there was something odd about Maryland (and Rutgers, another mediocre football school that had been invited to join the Big Ten) moving to a midwestern conference. But from the standpoint of the Big Ten, the additions made perfect sense. The schools would expand the conference's geographic reach, which is another way of saying they would help to secure more eyeballs to watch football and basketball games on the conference's popular Big Ten Network. And more eyeballs would translate into bigger fees the next time the Big Ten negotiated a television deal. It was all part of a land grab by the five power football conferences as they positioned themselves for a future in which they dominated the airwaves and the money.

In that context the fact that lawsuits would follow Maryland's decision to flee the ACC seemed almost normal, the result of a business
disagreement. And if you doubted that point, all you had to do was talk
with Bob Kustra, the indefatigable president of Boise State University,
and he would be more than happy to help you clarify your thinking.

•   •   •

It's not every day I take a phone call from a university president fulminating about how his football team is getting screwed. And I do mean
fulminating. Bob Kustra was practically feverish with indignation when
we spoke in late January 2014.

For more than a decade Boise State had fielded one of the best college
football teams in America, winning 145 games while losing only 23. No
one, not even mighty Alabama (101-47) could match its record. Given
that, you might assume that Boise State was making gobs of money playing football or that the five football superconferences would be fighting
one another to sign up the Broncos. That's certainly what the standard
financial model suggests should have happened, rewarding Boise State
generously for its winning ways.

And yet here was Bob Kustra arguing that Boise State not only was *not*
cashing in, but it was also being excluded from any reasonable chance of
doing so. Instead of rewarding an upstart like Boise State, the financial
model was penalizing it and in the process exacerbating the great divide
in college football between the haves and the have-nots.

"What's happening in Division I college football is all of the high-
resource conferences, the power conferences, are breaking off from
everyone else," Kustra explained during a long deconstruction of the
financial model. "The high-resource conferences have a very subtle but
powerful strategy—and I'm not going to sugarcoat this—to separate
themselves from the have-nots and the low-resource conferences." Boise

State belonged to one of the low-resource conferences—the Mountain West. Its budget for athletics, while not insignificant, was one third that of Oregon. "The end result is that the high-resource conferences are sucking up all of the [television and bowl game] money, and the low-resource conferences are getting left behind. That isn't fair, in my opinion, and it's not healthy for college football."

Recently Kustra had come into possession of a one-page summary of the superconferences' strategy. It was a copy of a copy of a copy of a copy, he said, lowering his voice to a conspiratorial whisper. It'd come from either the SEC or the Big Ten; he wasn't sure. "I suppose they probably wrote it for the commissioners. To me what it says is Division I football is being professionalized. All of the amateurism is being squeezed out of it. The high-resource conferences are the power conferences. What they're saying is if your budget isn't high enough, you would automatically be excluded from membership."

The average athletic budget of the sixty-five schools in the football power conferences was about $90 million. With a budget for athletics of roughly $40 million, Boise State wasn't going to make the cut.

Our conversation took place just three weeks after the 2014 Bowl Championship Series (BCS) National Championship. Each of the participants—Auburn and Florida State—had collected a check in the neighborhood of $20 million. Boise State wanted a crack at that football jackpot, but as a low-budget member of a low-resource conference it had little chance of doing so, Kustra said.

The superconferences had designed (critics might say "had rigged") the play-off system so that their teams were first in line for the national championship game. Even if Boise State finished with a perfect record, a one-loss team from the SEC or one of the other big football conferences would likely vault ahead of it. For Boise State to even have a chance at the new four-team play-off it would have to rank higher than every other team outside the five football superconferences, an unlikely scenario.

True, Boise State might get invited to play in one of the richer bowl games outside the new play-off system. But Kustra was still upset. "It serves the interests of the wealthy power conferences first, and I feel sort of powerless to do anything about it," he complained.

The presidents of the have-nots—the sixty-five or so schools playing Division I football that are not members of the football superconferences—are well aware that they are being screwed. The outsized television deals negotiated in the last few years by the largest and richest football schools have only exacerbated their sense of inequality. The commissioner of one small southern conference estimated that 90 percent of the new television dollars were going to the five power conferences. "We're happy if they just throw us a million or two," he said.

Part of the reason Kustra was irate was that he was using football to leverage his school's profile—or trying to, in any case. Despite a bump in applications following an iconic 2007 win over Oklahoma, Boise State still wasn't the school Kustra wanted it to be academically or financially. In 2013 *U.S. News & World Report* ranked Boise State as the sixty-fifth-best regional university in the West, down three spots from the previous year. The majority of students who applied to Boise State were accepted, hurting its image as a highly selective school. Only a fraction of the 23,000 undergraduates lived on campus, reinforcing the impression that it was a commuter school. The way Kustra spun this demographic was that the 2,800 students who lived in campus housing were "like a small liberal arts campus in the midst of a large university." Thanks to Kustra, the research budget had grown, but was still a relatively modest $50 million. Boise State did offer several unique majors. For example, it had the only degree program in raptor biology in the nation, according to its Web site.

Boise's location, hundreds of miles from the nearest major cities—Salt

Lake City, Portland, Seattle, and Denver—was both a blessing and a curse. The upside was that Boise State didn't have to compete with a professional football team for fans. It more or less was the pro team. At the same time there was no escaping that Boise was the most remote city of its size (about 700,000) in the nation, and not easy to get to.

All of this helped to explain why Kustra was trying to use the football team to grow Boise State's brand and attract more and better students and faculty. It was not necessarily a novel idea; scores of other universities were also trying to boost their brands by investing heavily in football, with varying degrees of success. But what made the Boise State story so interesting was that it already had a great football team, yet it was still struggling, or at least wasn't where Kustra had hoped it would be.

"Yes, it is about the football team," Kustra said when I inquired about his branding strategy. "But we sit by one of the cleanest rivers in the country. We look up at the foothills in the Rockies. It's warm in the winter term. We only get eleven inches of rain a year. The interest may start with football. But we have a lot of faculty and donors who come to us through football."

Kustra is seventy-one. He was an Illinois state legislator and lieutenant governor before working his way west. He is nothing if not enthusiastic. "I've had a great opportunity to sell the university and I've done that in unabashed fashion the last ten years," he told me.

The challenge now was to get out of football purgatory so that he could gain an even bigger platform from which to launch his university. In 2011 he had expected that Boise State would be invited to join the larger and richer Pac-10 Conference. The conference was looking to increase its own geographical reach and, at least in Kustra's mind, Boise State and its successful football team seemed like a good match. But the Pac-10 presidents wound up extending invitations to the University of Colorado and the University of Utah instead.

At first glance those choices seemed odd: Utah was a good but not outstanding football team and while Colorado had once briefly been great, it was now mostly disappointing and its athletic department was struggling financially. But when you looked more closely what you saw was that the decision hadn't been entirely about football. It had also been about television and eyeballs—and, at least on some level, even, education.

The Pac-10's decision effectively locked up the valuable Salt Lake City and Denver markets, which would help in its upcoming television negotiations. Colorado and Utah were also both large, established universities with substantial medical complexes and research capabilities, which was in keeping with the research-oriented profile of the conference's current members, schools like USC, UCLA, and Washington.

I asked the [now] Pac-12 commissioner Larry Scott about all of this when I visited him at his office in Walnut Creek, California. He deflected most of my questions about Boise State and then diplomatically added that the Pac-12 presidents had no immediate plans to get bigger. "Could we grow again at some point? Sure. But right now we're focusing on what is in front of us," he said.

The Pac-12 can afford to be patient. In the last three years the conference's revenues have doubled to $334 million. Much of that reflects its new $3 billion television deal with FOX and ESPN. The Pac-12 has also started its own regional television network, which is expected to kick in many millions more by selling subscriptions to games that aren't covered by the national networks. When it is all said and done, the shares the conference distributes to its members may double to an estimated $30 million per school, Scott explained.

All of which is to say that inequality is deeply entrenched in college football and is likely to remain that way. What passes for an equitable system is essentially a plutocracy ruled by the five power football conferences and their very smart and extremely rich commissioners. At least for now, they have no incentive to change or share their riches. Could that change at some point? Of course. But whether that happens in a year or five or ten years is anyone's guess.

What remains, then, is a left-behind story, with cavernous gaps between the haves and have-nots of college football. Clearly, the Mountain West Conference will never be confused with the Pac-12. According to its most recent tax filing, the Mountain West had revenue of about $11 million, compared with the Pac-12's $334 million. And even with its own new television deal, Boise State, the conference's best team, will make only $2 million to $3 million from television appearances, according to school officials, not $15 million or $30 million.

So to recap: The University of Colorado, which has won 64 games in the last decade while losing 87, will collect $30 million. Boise State, with its gaudy 145-23 record, will be rewarded with $3 million, give or take a few hundred thousand.

"I'm still upset," Kustra said at the end of a second lengthy interview. "We want fairness when it comes to the distribution of revenue. If we are going to call it Division I football and all be in it together . . . then we ought to distribute the revenue fairly across the board."

What Kustra seemed to be arguing for was a luxury tax on the rich, like they have in Major League Baseball to help boost the small-market teams. But that has as much chance of passing as a tax on big banks or hedge funds. Because big football schools aren't going to give up their riches to help the less privileged, it struck me that Kustra needed to find another way—assuming, at this point, that there still is another way.

•   •   •

In a sense the widening inequality in college football is a reflection of the hollowing-out of the larger economy. For his part Kustra might well be able to bullhorn his way to greater riches; only time will tell. But smaller, poorer schools like Akron, UAB, Massachusetts, Idaho, New Mexico State, Eastern Michigan, and scores of other football aspirants are unlikely to ever close the gap. That raises an interesting question: Why should they bother trying?

The answers I got from presidents of the have-nots were almost always baffling, and at times it even felt as if they were reading from a script: Football helps to unite the campus and energize the community. Football widens the brand and attracts donors. Football is necessary; without football, it doesn't feel like a real school.

"You can't buy that kind of exposure from a PR standpoint," Luis Proenza, the president of Akron, asserted during a visit, even as his football team was playing before a half-empty stadium and losing millions. But then Proenza said something I found even more interesting: "From a larger perspective, I can't get that large an audience focused on any other aspect of the university—period."

So it had come to this: It was football or nothing—the University of Football. That led me to ask Proenza, what was the opportunity cost of playing football?

"That's a very good question," he said. "If I look at it strictly from a business sense, it doesn't make sense. The question right now is we're betting on the future, recognizing it takes a number of years. I will remind you that a lot of teams don't make money. We're not alone in that."

One of those other teams was Eastern Michigan University, in Ypsilanti. Football there was largely an exercise in futility. Since 2000 the team had won 38 games while losing 119. In 2009 the Eagles went 0-12; the succeeding two years were only marginally better: 4-20. "We haven't had a winning season since 1995," an accounting professor, Howard J. Bunsis, told me. "You have to try hard to be that bad."

Not surprisingly, no one came to the games. According to the NCAA,

Eastern Michigan had the lowest attendance of any school playing Division I football. Roughly five thousand fans showed up for home games in the school's thirty-thousand-seat stadium. "They can't attract flies," said David Ridpath, an Ohio University business professor who studies the finances of college sports.

But even the five thousand figure was misleading. Eastern Michigan, like many other have-not schools, bought steeply discounted tickets from itself and then gave them away to local elementary schools. It also asked vendors like PepsiCo to buy tickets as part of their contracts. Such tactics were fairly commonplace. The NCAA required Division I football schools to average fifteen thousand fans per game over several years. But it largely left it up to the schools to determine how they got to that number.

Eastern Michigan faced another hurdle: It was just a short drive from Ann Arbor, where the mighty University of Michigan played in the largest stadium in the nation. Given the choice, where do you suppose football fans went? Richard Vedder, an economist at Ohio University and a colleague of Ridpath's, estimated that Eastern Michigan lost $20 million annually on football and other sports—or the equivalent of about $900 per student.

Nearly 85 percent of the athletic budget at Eastern Michigan came from general revenues and student fees—money that could otherwise be earmarked for academics, records show. "The board has this belief that football is the window to the university. If we just put the resources into football, we will really help enrollment," Bunsis said. "I think they are wrong. We are stuck. We really can't be successful at D-I. We need to get out."

I wanted to ask President Susan Martin why Eastern Michigan was still playing football, but I was advised by a spokesman: "Given the many demands on her time and schedule we will not be able to participate." *Not again*, I thought, though I did manage to find an interesting comment Martin had made in 2013. "The decision to be a Division I school was made many years ago," she told a local newspaper. "We have a 30,000-seat football stadium. We're not going to teach history 101 in it. We need to figure out how to be competitive. . . . It's not unreasonable to think if we were competitive that we could fill the stadium for some of the games or have a much larger crowd to help support football and some of the other sports."

The dilated optimism was impressive. But given its history, maybe Martin *would* be better off scheduling classes in its stadium. After all, Akron was using its stadium for fund-raisers and various administrative functions, according to Proenza. Why not a history class?

•   •   •

Another school I had been following was New Mexico State University. It too had a football problem. Since 2000 the team had won just 46 games while losing 123—a 0.272 winning percentage. The Aggies hadn't played in a bowl game since 1960, when Dwight D. Eisenhower was president, or recorded a winning record in over a decade.

The team's performance had taken a serious toll on the finances of the football program. Back in 2009 things got so bad the head football coach appealed to families and fans to donate snacks for the hungry players. Donors wasted no time, bringing the team trail mix and peanut-butter-and-jelly sandwiches. One fan even delivered a shipment of watermelons. In 2012 New Mexico State lost about $2 million on football. Most of the $4.4 million in football revenue that it reported came from two sources: university subsidies and payments that the team received to play bigger, richer football powers. Ticket sales were a paltry $801,000, which indicated that New Mexico State football was a hard, if not impossible, sell.

In 2013 New Mexico State's president, Garrey Carruthers, ordered a review of the struggling athletic department, with a special focus on boosting attendance at Aggie home games in Las Cruces. Among the strategies that the university came up with was offering cash prizes of up to two thousand dollars to one lucky student who stayed until the fourth quarter. "Student attendance is often disappointing," Carruthers, a former Republican governor of the state, explained to me. "We might get two thousand or three thousand students. The idea is to give them a reason to come."

Depending on your point of view, this was either an extremely clever idea or possibly one of the most desperate ideas ever. In any case, if the plan had been intended to attract publicity, it worked, though probably not in the way Carruthers anticipated. On September 28, 2013, New Mexico State revealed the first winner of its student lottery: Iraqi-war veteran and double amputee Matthew Zajac. It was a perfect outcome except for one small problem: Zajac hadn't attended the game, a requirement to collect his prize. He had purchased a ticket but had opted to help his grandmother with her cooking and cleaning, something he did often, according to newspaper accounts.

When the story went viral, New Mexico State officials scrambled to save face. "We are delighted this program gave us an opportunity to learn more about one of our students," the athletic director was quoted as saying, in a not particularly artful spin. The school said it would look for another way to honor Zajac. In the meantime fans from the Aggies' archrival, the University of New Mexico, in Albuquerque, took up a collection to cover the two-thousand-dollar prize. Zajac was so overwhelmed by the gesture that he announced he would donate half of the money to a charity that assists veterans with housing.

As for boosting student attendance, the lottery plan fell short. The game against San Diego State that Zajac missed attracted just 1,371 students—or 1,000 fewer than the prior two games. Maybe it was a mistake to try to compete at the highest levels of college football, I suggested to Carruthers. Maybe the Aggies should step down to a lower level or even give up football entirely.

Here Carruthers wavered. "I think football has many advantages," he said. "We just haven't been very good at it." When I asked about the advantages, he told me it wasn't up to him; the university's Board of Regents had to decide. "It is their policy. They are clearly in charge." A little later he said it would be hard politically to abandon football. "Let me tell you, the pressures brought to bear on a major university in a small rural state even though not successful [at football] are substantial and driven by stakeholders."

I took stakeholders to mean the small cadre of die-hard fans and boosters who enjoyed football, good or bad.

The Aggies finished the 2013 season with 2 wins and 10 losses, including a season-ending victory against an equally hapless 1-11 Idaho squad. The official attendance was reported as fourteen thousand or so, a figure that felt overly generous, given that overhead shots showed a mostly empty stadium.

Meanwhile, New Mexico State officials continue in their efforts to try to get football right. They have hired a new coach, and in 2014 the team joined a new conference—the Sun Belt, headquartered in New Orleans, 1,135 miles away—which Carruthers hoped would direct a little more money his school's way. "Let me put it this way," he said, leaving his best finishing touch on our conversation. "I'm just optimistic about our future."

·   ·   ·

There was one more person I wanted to speak with, but he was keeping a low profile and not giving interviews. That wasn't surprising, for really, when I thought about it, there was no good reason for Holden Thorp to talk with me. Our conversation would only bring back bad memories, and that's exactly what Thorp was trying to escape: a surplus of bad memories from his previous job as chancellor of the University of North Carolina at Chapel Hill.

For years North Carolina had been considered one of the good guys of college sports. It didn't cheat or cut corners, its athletes went to class and behaved themselves, and its budget, for a major athletic power, was relatively modest. The athletic department even had a catchy phrase to describe its philosophy, "the Carolina way," which was synonymous with doing things right. It was, at least for a time, even true.

But in 2010, Thorp's second year as chancellor, it all started to come undone, as allegations surfaced about football players getting improper payments, followed by claims of academic fraud, including so-called paper classes—classes that never met and required only a short term paper to collect a favorable grade. The scandal slowly metastasized; one year became two, then two became three. NCAA investigators arrived on campus, followed by local prosecutors. A professor and a tutor were indicted. Damaging stories appeared, each one more incredible than the last. And there was Holden Thorp, one of the golden boys of academia, left to sort it all out.

By his own admission, Thorp was possibly the least prepared college president in America to police a cascading athletic scandal. He knew almost nothing about sports and didn't care that he didn't know. What truly mattered to him was teaching, research, and ideas. He'd rolled through his undergraduate studies, collected a PhD in chemistry at Caltech, and then ascended the academic ranks at Carolina as a professor, department head, provost, and finally chancellor. Intellectually Thorp understood that athletics were important, but he cared only as much as the head of any major public university was obliged to care, which is to say he cared enough to make sure the finances were in order.

When disaster arrived in 2010 in the form of a relentless stream of ugly, embarrassing allegations, Thorp blinked, staggering through each revelation and badly mishandling press conferences. He was left wondering if this was truly what he was meant to do with his life. It was a good question with a surprisingly complicated answer. For while Holden Thorp might not care much about football, he did care passionately about the University of North Carolina, and he didn't want to be remembered as the chancellor who steered the university into an iceberg and watched it sink.

I wasn't terribly interested in the tick-tock of the scandals, which had already been covered in detail by Dan Kane and other reporters at the *Raleigh News & Observer*. What I was curious about was Holden Thorp's perception of them and what he had imagined he could and couldn't do in response to them. I was especially curious what it had been like at ground level as his world collapsed and he scrambled to put the pieces back together. In a larger sense I suppose what I wanted to find out was the nature of the role of college presidents and whether they could—or even wanted to—rein in their athletic empires, or if this idea was one more piece of the magical thinking that now dominated college sports.

And so in the waning months of 2013 I sent Thorp a detailed note explaining my request for an interview. I was right about one thing: He quickly wrote back saying that the last subject he wanted to discuss again was North Carolina. But then he added a surprising caveat: If I was willing to travel to St. Louis, where he was now provost of Washington University, he would meet with me. I immediately asked if he could find an hour in his busy schedule. At which point Thorp informed me that it was going to take a lot longer than that, at least two or three hours, and that he would set aside an entire morning to talk.

•   •   •

Holden Thorp is a boyishly handsome forty-nine-year-old with wire-rim glasses and a shag of fading blond hair that tends to flop across his forehead. He grew up in Fayetteville, a military town about an hour and a half—and several light-years—from Chapel Hill. His dad was a small-town lawyer. His mother, Bo, ran the regional theater. "It was sort of like our family farm," Thorp recalled. "The family schedule revolved around rehearsals. I went to the theater and did whatever job needed to be done. I did the lights, directed the orchestra, whatever else was needed to get ready." Thorp didn't see himself as an actor, but he learned the roles anyway. "So I have played big parts, but only because someone got sick that night," he chuckled.

"I famously was a nonparticipant," he says, regarding sports. He did keep the stats for his elementary school's basketball team and, like all good Carolina boys, he listened to Carolina basketball games on the radio. As chancellor Thorp attended basketball games with his wife, Patti, an avid fan, "who was always going crazy in the stands and still bleeds Carolina blue."

Most kids Thorp's age were unintentionally smart, if they were smart at all. Thorp was intentionally smart. He was curious and analytical, mastering algebra and geometry textbooks by sixth grade. His passion was music. He played guitar, jazz piano, and bass and was good enough that his parents sent him to a summer program at the prestigious Berklee College of Music in Boston to see if he wanted to pursue music as a career. One weekend Thorp saw an advertisement in the *Boston Phoenix* for a Rubik's Cube contest at a suburban Boston mall. The prize was five hundred dollars. The seventeen-year-old Thorp competed against adults and won. He said he used the money to buy a guitar. While we were talking, I noticed a small cube on Thorp's desk and asked how fast he could solve it now. "I could probably do it in a minute and a half," he replied, the closest thing to a boast I heard all morning.

When it came time to pick a college, there was never any question where Thorp would go: Five generations of Thorp men had matriculated at North Carolina, and his parents had also met there. To an eighteen-year-old from Fayetteville, Chapel Hill seemed exotic. What Thorp loved most about the university—and still does—was that it was large enough to accommodate many different interests. "There was a strong Greek life and sporting events. But you could also fit in with the music crowd, Dungeons & Dragons, activists."

Thorp recalled attending one football game his freshman year, but he couldn't remember the opponent. Basketball was different. He watched the games on a ten-inch black-and-white television in his dorm room with the window open so he could listen to the roar from the arena when Carolina scored. Thorp studied chemistry and music, planning to go to medical school, but at the last minute opted for a doctorate at Caltech, which he finished in three years instead of the usual five. He had three job offers, including one at Procter & Gamble to work on liquid Cascade. He chose teaching and research instead and joined the faculty at North Carolina in 1993.

Thorp rapidly worked his way through the ranks of academia, winning teaching awards and a full professorship in record time. He also collected nineteen patents and started two companies. In 2007 he was named dean of the College of Arts and Sciences and a year later was chosen as chancellor at the absurdly young age of forty-three.

I wondered, given his general indifference to sports, what Thorp knew about Carolina athletics when he was hired and, more to the point, what he was expected to know. "Did anyone ask you about athletics during your interviews?" I asked.

"That's an incredibly important point," Thorp said. "Athletics are an incredibly important part of the identity and experience at Carolina. There is real sentimentality people feel about all of this. But there was nothing about 'What are we going to do to rein in spending?' or 'Do you think we're doing all of this honestly?' It had been fifty years since Carolina had an NCAA violation. The whole narrative and what now seems like magical thinking was that we had some special way of winning all these games without doing anything wrong. We spent years telling our constituents they didn't have to worry about all of the hypocrisy of college sports because we were winning. So in the interview [for the chancellor position] I talked sentimentally about my feelings about Carolina basketball and how I really loved the nonrevenue (Olympic) sports . . . and that was the end of it, on to the next question."

After he became chancellor, Thorp said, he was expected to attend football and basketball games. "There is a lot of pressure for presidents to be enthusiastic about sports," he said. "So naturally that leads the president to want the teams to win, because it makes everybody feel good."

It also fosters what Thorp sees as a fundamental conflict in the role of presidents: Are they there to lead the cheers or to keep a close watch on spending and academics? For years the Knight Commission and other reform-minded groups have called for presidents to take back control of their athletic departments, but Thorpe isn't sure it's that simple. "It is very hard to see how the president is the person who leverages athletics to build support of the university and at the same time is supposed to be responsible for compliance and keeping athletics reined in financially," he said.

"If not the presidents," I asked, "who should be in charge?"

"I have suggested it should be placed back in the hands of the athletic directors, who report to the presidents and chancellors. If you look at the recent scandals in big-time college sports, the problems have always overwhelmed the presidents. The irony is that presidential control was supposed to fix the problems in big-time athletics, which is sort of laughable, because it hasn't worked."

This was an arresting idea. In so many words Thorp was suggesting that the presidents cede control over athletics to the parties with the most financial interest in seeing athletics prosper and grow. It was precisely the opposite of the Knight Commission's recommendations that presidents assert stronger control over their athletic financial empires.

•   •   •

The North Carolina scandals started in the football program and involved players who allegedly accepted cash and other benefits from agents. In the course of their investigation NCAA representatives also uncovered evidence of academic fraud, including at least one tutor in the athletic department who was allegedly rewriting players' term papers. The *Raleigh News & Observer* and other media subsequently discovered an array of academic abuses, including no-show classes for football players in the Afro-American Studies Department, altered grades, and phony signatures on grade rolls.

Thorp told me that he was surprised by the extent of the cheating. But other than graduation rates, he said he received little information about the academic performance of the football team. "When things were going well, I wouldn't hear a lot. Again, it was part of the narrative we told ourselves for so long that all of this was done well and we didn't have massive problems. In retrospect I'd like to have seen a whole lot more, what their progress was."

North Carolina—like many other football schools—admitted players unprepared to handle the academic load. Then it spent millions on tutors and other services to help the players stay eligible. A former reading specialist in the academic support program, Mary Willingham, told me that some football and basketball players arrived in her office unable to read.

"How are you going to get by?" she asked them.

"You're going to read to me," they told her.

"They actually said that?" I asked.

"I remember one did," she said.

North Carolina is one of the more competitive public universities in the nation. "We got forty thousand applications for four thousand slots," Willingham said. "From an admissions standpoint, the kids were amazing. They all had 4.0s and were looking at double majors. Then you would see the worksheets [transcripts] of our [football and basketball] athletes, and they would look completely different."

Thorp said he met with Willingham, who left the university in 2014, and also spoke with her on the telephone. "The narrative of what she is saying has a lot of truth to it," he told me. "A lot of guys at Carolina and every other selective university have a huge challenge to succeed academically. Whether that means they can't read is probably something that depends on your perspective."

In 2011 the UNC scandals reached new, disturbing proportions. When Thorp fired the football coach, Butch Davis, just a few weeks before the season opener that year, Tar Heels fans erupted, blaming Thorp for wrecking the team and unfairly jettisoning a popular coach. Thorp's in-box was filled with hundreds of ugly, threatening e-mails. The campus police were dispatched to protect his family and remained posted outside his house for two weeks.

"It was like being in an episode of *24*, only it doesn't end in one day," Thorp said, referring to the popular television show. "Something like this happening is just so far from anybody's mind. You don't think about it until it happens, and then it just explodes."

By late 2012 Thorp had had enough and announced that he planned to step down at the end of the school year. At this point a remarkable thing happened: Hundreds of students, faculty members, office staff, and maintenance workers rallied outside South Building, the main administration center, begging Thorp to reconsider. Students wore buttons reading Heels for Holden. Others held posters proclaiming: We trust you Holden Thorp. An a cappella group sang Tom Petty's "Won't Back Down." "It was wonderful," Thorp recalled.

"People who analyze this and say I should have done better . . . I'll take that criticism," Thorp said. "If I've got the students and housekeepers and the English professors, those are the constituencies I want."

There was only one more piece left to complete the story. At the time of his announcement that he would step down, Thorp wasn't considering leaving Chapel Hill. But then the job of provost opened up at Washington University, which annually ranks among the top schools in the country, and his thinking shifted. "The scandal had consumed more and more of my time," he said. "I really felt I was running out of energy. If I could be provost at a great school like Washington University, it was a chance to focus all of my time on academics."

The average SAT score of incoming freshmen at Washington University is about 1490. "There are no special admissions for athletes," Thorp said. "A lot of our athletes are engineering and premed." The football team plays in a stadium that is smaller than those of many high schools. In 2013 the Washington University Bears went 8-3 and made the Division III play-offs. More impressive, seven of the players were named to the 2014 College Hall of Fame Honor Society for maintaining 3.2 or better GPAs throughout their careers.

Thorp has not completely severed his ties with Chapel Hill. His oldest son, John, is an undergraduate there, extending the Thorp streak to seven generations. "It's a world-class school that changed my life," he said. "Yes, it broke my heart to leave and it breaks my heart to think there were all of these problems for all of these years. But it is still a great place to get a great education."

I looked at my watch. It was almost exactly three hours since we'd started talking. Holden Thorp had called it down to the minute.

• • •

Several months after I visited Thorp, the NCAA announced that it was reopening its investigation into academic fraud, bogus classes, and inflated grades in the North Carolina athletics program. Then, in October 2014, the university released an extensive report on the scandal that had been prepared by a former general counsel for the FBI.

Among other findings the report noted that cheating and fake classes at North Carolina weren't new phenomena, but dated back at least eighteen years. Remarkably, in 2009 some of the counselors assigned to help the football players had met with the coaches to warn them that the bogus classes that they depended on to keep players eligible were being eliminated. The counselors even used a PowerPoint presentation to drive home the issue.

"We put them in classes that met degree requirements in which . . . they didn't go to class . . . they didn't have to take notes . . . have to stay awake . . ." according to the report. "THESE NO LONGER EXIST!"

The report concluded that no high-level administration officials knew about the sham classes.

Epilogue

. . .

THE DEATH STAR

NEAR THE END OF 2013 I flew back to Eugene to tour the Football Performance Center at the University of Oregon. Like most of the other football facilities at Oregon, it was underwritten by Phil Knight, at a cost of nearly $70 million, and is far and away the most lavish building in America devoted solely to college football players.

During my prior visit to the campus, construction crews had still been adding finishing touches—"finishing touches," in this case, meaning biometric key codes for the players to come and go, climate-controlled lockers, and Brazilian ipe hardwood flooring in the weight room. I didn't know what Brazilian ipe hardwood was, or why it mattered, until Craig Pintens brought me up to speed during our walk-through.

"Brazilian ipe is the densest wood in the world," the senior associate athletic director for marketing and public relations explained. "And it won't catch on fire. As you know, there is a problem with weight rooms catching on fire."

"Actually, I didn't know that," I said.

"It happens a lot, apparently."

At the time, we were standing on a fifth-floor alcove overlooking the 25,000-square-foot weight-lifting area. I made the mistake of mentioning that I had recently visited the University of Alabama's new weight room, which Alabama claimed was the biggest in the land.

Pintens's expression soured. "It isn't just about having the *biggest* weight room," he said. "We don't know if we have the biggest weight room. We don't care if we have the biggest. It's all about offering the best student-athlete experience and taking the best care of you."

Of course, it didn't hurt that offering the best experience, as Pintens put it, was essential to luring the best recruits. "Absolutely," Pintens quickly agreed. "Pretty much everything we do is about recruits."

In this Oregon was hardly alone. The entertainment model of college football had elevated recruits to celebrity status. They traveled around the country from school to school, flexing their muscles and demonstrating their skills at summer camps. In return it was expected that the football powers would go to embarrassing lengths to demonstrate how much they wanted any given athlete.

In 2013 Alabama sent star running back Alvin Kamara 105 letters in a single day. Not to be outdone, Notre Dame sent six-foot-six, 350-pound defensive tackle Matt Elam 270 letters—a number that cleverly matched Elam's area code. Apparently Elam wasn't sufficiently impressed, as he committed to the University of Kentucky instead.

For the most part Oregon's Football Performance Center reminded me of an upscale shopping mall. Each time we turned a corner we came upon another expensive bauble or design to consider: a players' lounge with PlayStations and two custom-made foosball games imported from Portugal; a barbershop for quick prepractice trims; a ring room to display all of the rings Oregon players received for playing in bowl games; meeting rooms with seats made out of Ferrari leather; locker rooms with floor-to-ceiling glass walls and marble flooring imported from Italy; a separate room for NFL scouts to download practice video; and so on and so forth. This was the athletic arms race on steroids.

Pintens insisted that the Football Performance Center wasn't entirely about opulence. He kept using the words "function" and "purpose," as in, the players had their own biometric thumbprints so they could get in and out of the center quickly and with purpose. "We even used a stopwatch to time how long it would take them to walk across to Autzen [Stadium] to practice," he said. The trip took something like one minute and thirty seconds.

Of course, form also played a role. The 145,000-square-foot building was arranged in obsidian black stacks surrounded by black basalt walls. This was done in keeping with the Nike-inspired idea that black was the new cool, as well as to encourage a sense of mystery and foreboding. Some of the locals had taken to calling the building the Death Star, after the battle station in the Star Wars movies, but that only raised the question of whether Knight was playing the role of Darth Vader.

•   •   •

The notional idea that college football is still a game, as opposed to an elaborately rich entertainment, is rapidly receding from the American landscape of sports. Oregon, with its extraordinary facilities, is only the most risible example. Recently the University of Central Florida, a rising football power, announced that it was adding a "Florida-themed social area," including an open-air sun deck and covered lounge, at its Bright House Networks Stadium. School officials described the expansion as part of a "new premium seating experience," which was another way of saying they were adding more high-priced seats to pump up their revenue. "The [new sand park] will provide a window into the UCF/Central Florida culture and personality to potential students, recruits, fans, friends and supporters," UCF athletic director Todd Stansbury told the local newspaper.

Whether it matters that the fiction of college football as education is finally being accepted is a more complicated question. At its core college football is an extension of a series of concepts that give it structure: players are student athletes, not professionals; mandatory payments to secure premium seats are charitable gifts, not fees; the market for lavishly paid coaches is in fact a market. But what happens if that structure collapses, if, say, some ambitious member of Congress actually questions the football-as-charity paradigm?

In July 2014 Senator Jay Rockefeller held a hearing that was largely an opportunity for senators to lob verbal grenades at the NCAA and its president, Mark Emmert. In that respect it was like most congressional hearings: carefully staged Kabuki theater. Nevertheless, Rockefeller did say one interesting thing: "Playing college sports is supposed to be an avocation. There's a growing perception that college athletics, particularly Division I football and basketball, are not avocations at all. What they really are is highly profitable enterprises."

He continued: "This country is now so soaked in the culture of ESPN, plus I guess a couple of other stations . . . it's undermining our values. I'll tell you one thing for sure: I think it's undermining our commitment to education."

A day later two members of Congress introduced a bill to make financial information about college athletics public. They apparently didn't realize that the NCAA already had all of that data, and all they had to do was order the NCAA to put it up on its Web site. In any case, given Congress's record on college football, I wasn't optimistic.

Still, even I had to acknowledge that the narrative was shifting. The most recent plot twist involved the players, some of whom were trying to form a union to better represent their interests. Others were filing lawsuits challenging the antitrust status of college football and the NCAA's profiting off their images in video games and broadcasts. The underlying assumptions in all of these cases were that football players were employees first and students second and that they were underpaid and deserved a larger share of the riches. Whether that meant a few thousand dollars or many thousands remained to be seen.

To my own surprise I wasn't buying the players-as-victims narrative— or, to put it another way, I wasn't as sympathetic as I expected I would be. It wasn't that I undervalued the players; I fully appreciated that it was they who generated the fortunes enjoyed by the football powers. But the argument that they were underpaid was less persuasive and made sense only if you accepted that the sprawling financial model of college football was not broken or absurd. In that context a $40,000 or $50,000 athletic scholarship did seem like a pittance when the head coach was being paid $5 million or $6 million. But the players weren't arguing that the scale and commercialism of college football undercut the arc of being a true student athlete. They were simply arguing that they wanted a bigger slice of the pie.

If you approached the matter from a different angle—namely, that college football was tarnishing education—you inevitably arrived at a different conclusion: Maybe the players weren't victims, or at least not in the way they were portraying themselves. After all, they were graduating (the ones who went to classes, anyway) debt free while their fellow students were exiting school with tens of thousands of dollars of debt and facing years, even decades, before they would be free of that yoke.

And then there were all of the other perks: the tutors, academic advisers, and class checkers to make sure players remained eligible; free books, meals, and snacks; a separate NCAA clothing allowance and fund to pay for emergencies, such as a death in the family. Add to this list the personal trainers, sports psychologists, and faculty mentors who orbited around the team. Finally there was my favorite: the swag that players picked up when their teams appeared in postseason bowl games.

It works like this: Imagine a red-carpet event for college football players.

Only instead of the Academy of Motion Picture Arts and Sciences handing out goodie bags, it is one of the now forty postseason bowl-game sponsors. The NCAA allows these sponsors to give up to $550 worth of gifts to 125 participants per school—or $137,500 total to two teams. Schools and conferences are permitted to supplement that with another $400 each in swag. So, when all is said and done, players can walk away with up to $1,350 worth of goods, which is not bad considering that nearly half of all Division I football teams play in a bowl game. And the number of bowl games is growing. Only the other day, ESPN announced that BitPay, which it described as the world's leader in business solutions for bitcoin digital currency, would sponsor one of the dozen bowl games it owns. Yes, ESPN *owns* bowl games. Think of it as vertical integration, or one more way to gin up live content.

Bowl sponsors spend about $5 million on gifts. Some run their player handouts like *Supermarket Sweep*, setting up "gift suites" in the players' hotels. Others allow players to pick and choose from an online suite. According to the *SportsBusiness Journal*, some of the more popular items in 2014 included Fossil watches, Ogio bags, Oakley sunglasses, Sony PlayStations, Microsoft Xbox One consoles, 4, Beats by Dre headphones, iPad Minis, GoPro HERO4 Silver cameras, and Best Buy gift cards. My personal favorite was the Southern Motion Viva home theater recliner with two USB ports for mobile phones and a frame large enough to accommodate a three-hundred-pound offensive lineman.

My point here being the players-as-victims argument gets you only so far.

Nevertheless, that is the narrative du jour being scripted by the media and lawyers, with the NCAA performing the role of bureaucratic dunce. Most of the elite football schools appear more than willing to play along. In fact, after they threatened to break away and set up their own conferences, the NCAA agreed to loosen its rules on amateurism and allow the five football superconferences to pay their players.

The plan calls for giving football players four or five thousand dollars, which the schools would call a stipend, as opposed to pay, thus avoiding the messy complications of paying taxes and the players-as-employees conundrum. But once you start to remunerate players or set up your football team as a semiprofessional affiliate, can you still claim it is part of an educational charity? And will fans still feel the same emotional attachment? Finally, how long will the relatively modest stipends keep the players at bay before they want more?

The largest and richest schools in the SEC and other power football conferences can easily afford such payments. Where it gets problematic is with all the other teams—the Florida Atlantics, New Mexico States, and scores of other have-nots of college football. I doubt that the wealthy schools will be inclined to help them out as part of some grand gesture to save college football. More likely it will mark the final break between the five power conferences and the have-nots, as Boise State's president, Robert Kustra, has suggested.

Then there are the many other implications. For example, what of the athletes in the poor sports: the women rowers, runners, and soccer players, for example? Will they get stipends as well? If they do, then what was a relatively minor cost suddenly becomes real money for athletic departments, numbering in the millions of dollars, putting even more stress on the football financial model. Alternatively, can the elite schools limit the stipends to a few sports—say, football and men's and women's basketball—without being sued by Title IX proponents? I can't imagine how. The further down the bench you move, the more complicated the issues become.

All of this is still a few years out from becoming real. For now, the college football elites don't appear especially concerned. And why should they be? They are extraordinarily rich and expect to stay that way. When I asked the commissioners of the Big Ten and Pac-12 if they worried about a bubble, they only laughed in response. How could there be a bubble when schools were building larger, more expensive stadiums and cable companies were throwing comical sums of money their way to lock up live content? The payouts from the Big Ten had jumped from $4 million to $24 million. "And no one shows any sign of slowing down or wanting to spend less," commissioner Jim Delany told me.

It was hard to argue the point. It truly was the gilded age of college football. But the thing about gilded ages is they eventually collapse on themselves, and even the smartest people in the room occasionally miss the warning signs of impending trouble. If I were Jim Delany at the Big Ten or Larry Scott at the Pac-12, I would be concerned about the disruptive implications of tablets, cell phones, and other gadgets not yet imagined. More to the point, I would be worried about the younger generations of fans who aren't nearly as committed to the live-game experience as their parents and grandparents were. There is a reason why student attendance is down at many schools and why even students at mighty Alabama are leaving games at halftime and not coming back. It is that little portable screen they keep fiddling with to distract themselves. In my opinion the biggest threat to college football isn't concussions or paying players but the short attention spans of eighteen- and nineteen-year-olds raised on PlayStation, Facebook, and Twitter. After all, why spend three hours sitting on a hard bench when you can drop in on a game online at your convenience or stream some fabulous play and then quickly move on to the next new thing?

In the fall of 2014 I experienced my own version of this phenomenon. There were now so many college football games on television I couldn't decide which game to watch. Instead of picking one and settling in, I found myself furiously clicking from game to game to see what the scores were and what I had missed. Some might see this as progress: Look at all of the choices you now have! But I was restless and increasingly bored—unable to enjoy any single game because of the spectacle of the many. Finally I stopped clicking and switched to a movie. The way I figured, I could always watch one of the sports shows later and catch up on the scores.

A Note on Sources

• • •

THIS BOOK IS BASED ON hundreds of interviews with athletic directors, university presidents, coaches, economists, and others who shared information and insights with me over the course of two years. As with any book, there was far more information than space, and I had to make difficult choices about who got in and who didn't. Jim Delany and Larry Scott, the commissioners of the Big Ten and Pac-12, provided valuable insights about the impact of television on their conferences, but make only limited appearances. Ed Ray, the president of Oregon State, sat with me for several hours and helped me to frame several of the book's themes. Mark Coyle, the smart young athletic director at Boise State, schooled me on the challenges of programs outside of the five superconferences. In cases where individuals declined to be interviewed, I relied on secondary sources, including newspapers, magazines, books, university archives, and press releases to help draw biographical sketches.

The data on football revenues and profits, coaches' salaries, buyouts, numbers of athletes in each sport, spending per sport, and academic performance come from a variety of sources. Universities file detailed financial statements annually with the NCAA. For some reason, the non-profit considers the information secret. However, I was able to obtain dozens of reports by filing Freedom of Information requests with the schools. I already had a baseline of data on football revenues and profits from a project I wrote in 2000 with my former *Philadelphia Inquirer* colleague Frank Fitzpatrick. That allowed me to analyze the growth in revenue and spending, by school, over fifteen years. Data on buyouts were contained in coaches' contracts, university tax filings, financial records, and newspaper accounts. Conference distributions and data on television payouts were also contained in the tax returns and financial records. All of the calculations and interpretations are my own; any mistakes are also my own.

Until a few years ago, universities also were required to file Self Studies with the NCAA in which they reported on their admissions policies for athletes, academic performance, and academic support programs (tutoring, study halls, writing labs, class checkers, et cetera). I used Open Records requests to obtain several dozen of these voluminous reports from public universities; occasionally, schools posted the reports on their Web sites. Data on academic support programs were obtained directly from the schools, during visits, or by telephone interviews. Data on women's rowing programs were also obtained directly from schools or from the reports they filed with the NCAA. Press releases and school histories helped to fill in the gaps. Special thanks to the coaches at Kansas State and Wisconsin for allowing me to visit their programs.

The history on the tax treatment of college football (and college sports generally) is contained in an array of law journals and other scholarly texts. There are far too many to list here. But some of the more seminal studies were written by Richard Kaplan and John Colombo, professors at the University of Illinois Law School. The full saga of the 80 percent deduction for seat donations was pieced together from journal articles, newspaper stories, interviews, and university archives, especially those at Carnegie Mellon and the State University of New York at Stony Brook. I was able to find Peggy Pickle, the daughter of former U.S. representative Jake Pickle, after she wrote a letter to the editor of the Austin newspaper decrying the growth of college athletics. Thanks to Peggy for filling in her father's story.

The long, tortured history of college presidents and football is outlined in a series of musty NCAA reports and congressional hearings dating back decades. Sports historians and legal scholars have also helped to flesh out the role of the presidents, especially Ronald A. Smith, a professor emeritus at Penn State. In recent years, the Knight Commission of Intercollegiate Athletics, funded by the John S. and James L. Knight Foundation, has acted as a de facto sounding board for presidents interested in reforming the financial model for college sports. Several of the commission's studies and reports were sources of valuable information.

Acknowledgments

• • •

EVERY AUTHOR NEEDS A MENTOR or two to see his way through; in my case, dozens helped to shape the heart of this book.

For assistance in understanding the financial and cultural impact of college football on modern universities, I thank Bill Battle, Ian McCaw, Rob Mullens, Jim Bartko, Patrick Chun, Gary Walters, Larry Kehres, DeLoss Dodds, Sandy Barbour, Fred Glass, Charlie Cobb, David Ridpath, Howard Bunsis, Drew Roberts, Steve Ross, Scott Roussel, Phil Savage, Ronald Smith, Rodney Smith, Jeff Smith, Murray Sperber, David Williams, Jim Delany, Larry Scott, Karl Benson, and dozens of others. I am especially grateful to Ken Baldwin, Paul Buskirk, Steve Stolp, Andrew McNall, and Renée Dorjahn for allowing me to visit their academic support centers and honors colleges. Nathan Tublitz, Thomas Palaima, and Max Page provided valuable insights about the conflicts between education and athletics. Thanks also to Griffin Hamstead, Daniel Moore, and Mary Cesar for sharing their stories.

I didn't know a thing about women's rowing before I began this book.

Special thanks to Bebe Bryans, Megan Cooke Carcagno, Nancy LaRocque, Anne Rauschert, Carrie Graves, Terry Gawlik, Pat Sweeney, Hanna Wiltfong, and Grace Ure for introducing me to an extraordinary sport. I am also grateful for the presidents who spoke with me about the role of football, including but not limited to Ed Ray, Robert Kustra, Brit Kirwan, William Bowen, Daniel Weiss, Garrey Carruthers, Anthony Catanese, Mark Becker, Holden Thorp, and Louis Proenza. Also, thanks to Terry Hartle and Jennifer Lee Hoffman. No doubt several earlier books on college sports helped to influence my thinking, including Murray Sperber's *Beer and Circus*, *Unpaid Professionals* by Andrew Zimbalist, *The 50 Year Seduction* by Keith Dunnavant, and *Reclaiming the Game* by William Bowen and Sarah Levin.

Friends and family members provided encouragement and insights, including Cathy Gaul, Greg Gaul, Kristy Cole Gaul, and Jane Dinger Candy. Special thanks to Frank Corrado for reading an earlier draft and offering numerous helpful suggestions. My agent, Barney Karpfinger, gave me both confidence and encouragement. Finally, endless thanks to Rick Kot at Viking, for allowing me the freedom to shape this book as I saw fit and then gently taking that shape and molding it into something real and good.

Index

• • •

Note: Page numbers in *italics* indicate tables and charts.